Japanese business success

Comparative and International Business Series:
Modern Histories
Edited by Geoffrey Jones and Mira Wilkins

Banks as Multinationals
Edited by Geoffrey Jones

Industrial Training and Technological Innovation
Edited by Howard F. Gospel

The Rise and Fall of Mass Marketing
Edited by Richard Tedlow and Geoffrey Jones

The Growth of Global Business
Edited by Howard Cox, Jeremy Clegg and Grazia Ietto-Gillies

Adding Value: Marketing and Brands in Food and Drink
Edited by Geoffrey Jones and Nicholas J. Morgan

The Precision Makers
Mari E.W. Williams

Information Acumen
Edited by Lisa Bud-Frierman

Japanese business success

The evolution of a strategy

Edited by Takeshi Yuzawa

London and New York

First published 1994
by Routledge
11 New Fetter Lane, London EC4P 4EE

Simultaneously published in the USA and Canada
by Routledge
29 West 35th Street, New York, NY 10001

© 1994 Takeshi Yuzawa

Typeset in Times by
Ponting–Green Publishing Services, Chesham, Bucks

Printed and bound in Great Britain by
Mackays of Chatham PLC, Chatham, Kent

British Library Cataloguing in Publication Data
A catalogue record for this book is available from the
British Library.

Library of Congress Cataloging in Publication Data
Japanese business success: the evolution of a strategy/edited by
   Takeshi Yuzawa.
      p. cm. – (Comparative and international business. Modern
   histories series)
      Includes bibliographical references.
      ISBN 0–415–05561–X
      1. Industrial management–Japan Case studies.
      2. Strategic planning–Japan–Case studies.
      I. Yuzawa, Takeshi, 1940–   II. Series.
   HD70.J3J3934   1994   658.4'012'0952–dc20
                                                            93–48301
                                                                 CIP

ISBN 0–415–05561–X (hbk)

To Shin'ichi Yonekawa

Contents

Figures and tables

FIGURES

TABLES

Contributors

Etsuo Abe is Professor of Business History at Meiji University. He has recently published *Daiei teikoku no sangyo haken* (*Industrial Supremacy of the British Empire – The Case of the Steel Industry*), 1993.

Hans-Jürgan Clahsen is a Visiting Fellow of Hitotsubashi University and is now studying at Waseda University.

Shin Goto is Professor of Business History at Kanagawa University, and has written mainly on shipbuilding and transport.

Toshikatsu Nakajima is an Associate Professor at Kyoto Sangyo University. He has written on French manufacturing industry.

Tamotsu Nishizawa is an Associate Professor at the Institute of Economic Research, Hitotsubashi University. He has written on the relationship between the educational system and economic development.

Noboru Nisikawa is Professor of Accounting at Kanagawa University. His recent publication is *Mitsui-ke kanjo kanken* (*A Study of the Accounting History of the Mitsui Family*).

Tomoaki Saito is Professor of Business History at the Science University of Tokyo. He has written chiefly on the petroleum industry in its worldwide context.

Tsuneo Suzuki is Professor of Industrial Economics at Gakushuin University. He has written on the chemical and synthetic fibre industry, and also on industrial policy in Japan.

Kazuo Wada is an Associate Professor of Business History at Tokyo University. He gained his doctorate from the London School of Economics for his work on the history of the British electric power industry.

Seiichiro Yonekura is an Associate Professor at the Institute of

Business Research, Hitotsubashi University. He is the author of *The Japanese Iron and Steel Industry, 1850–1990: Continuity and Discontinuity.*

Takau Yoneyama is an Associate Professor of Insurance at Kyoto Sangyo University. He has mainly written on the business history of the insurance industry in the United Kingdom and Japan.

Takeshi Yuzawa is Professor of Business History at Gakushuin University. He is the author or editor of several books in Japanese and English, including *Igirisu tetsudo keieishi* (*A Business History of British Railways*), 1988, and *Foreign Business in Japan before World War II*, edited with M. Udagawa, 1990.

Series editor's preface

This volume is an important addition to the literature on business in modern Japan. Over the last decade, knowledge about Japanese business, both in the contemporary period and historically, has grown substantially. *Zaibatsu* and *keiretsu*, *ringi* decision-making and the *kanban* system have become familiar words and concepts worldwide. Neverthless there remains a tendency towards excessive generalization and oversimplification about the nature of Japanese management. This volume, with its focus on the historical development of individual firms and industries, performs a valuable role in highlighting the diversity to be found in Japanese business. Additionally, it provides an opportunity to see how the Japanese themselves explain and understand their business and management system. Much of the West's knowledge about Japanese business has come from Western scholars or from highly 'Westernized' Japanese. This work has often been outstanding, but it has inevitably been influenced by its Western preoccupations and outlook. Japanese academics have sometimes approached their subjects in different ways. This book enables English speakers to glimpse into this other world.

This book has been written in honour of Professor Shin'ichi Yonekawa. Yonekawa has played a seminal role in Japanese business history over the last three decades. As a researcher, he has made major contributions to the history of cotton textiles, of trading companies, and of business history in general. A particular hallmark of Yonekawa's work has been his stress on the need for internationally comparative research, and for research to be based on archival sources. As a professor at Hitotsubashi University, Yonekawa inspired a generation of graduate students to study business history, and especially the history of foreign countries. Yonekawa's influence has been far from being confined to Japan, however. I first met him in the late 1970s when he was a visiting professor of the London School of Economics, and I was a young researcher. Although already immensely distinguished, Shin'ichi was noteworthy for his warm-hearted humility and his willingness to treat all scholars, young or old, as his equal. His commitment to high standards of scholarship, to the study of business in an internationally comparative context, and to the importance of teaching the next generation inspired me then, and has continued to do so over the years. Like so many others, Japanese and non-Japanese, I owe a debt of gratitude to this outstanding scholar and wonderful man.

Geoffrey Jones

Acknowledgements

This book was originally planned in honour of Professor Shin'ichi Yonekawa, to celebrate his sixtieth birthday. The contributors are all scholars who are obliged to him for his guidance in their studies. The project was delayed for a number of reasons, but I am now pleased that the work is completed. We hope that it will provide a fitting tribute to Professor Yonekawa, in recognition of the importance of his contribution to the study of business history in Japan.

We would like to thank Rosemary Nixon at Routledge for her generous support of this project and Frances Bostock for her considerable editing of the English text.

Takeshi Yuzawa
Gakushuin University, Tokyo

1 Japanese business strategies in perspective

Takeshi Yuzawa

This book offers new perspectives on the evolution of modern Japanese management and corporate strategies. There is now an enormous English language literature on both the historical evolution and the contemporary strategy and structure of Japanese business.[1] As a result, the main features of Japanese corporate organization, and the management practices that brought competitive success to Japanese enterprises in sectors such as motor vehicles and electronics, have become well-known both to Western academics and to Western companies, which have tried to emulate parts of the Japanese 'success formula', such as just-in-time and quality circles.

The aim of this volume is not to duplicate this extensive literature, but to supplement it. It focuses on individual Japanese enterprises – rather than on the system as a whole – and traces their growth over a span of several decades, often reaching back to long before the Second World War. This approach reveals the diversity of the Japanese business experience, which is sometimes overlooked in the more superficial Western studies of the subject. Failures as well as successes are noted and explained by the team of Japanese business historians represented here, each of whom is a leading authority in his industry or field.

The study is organized in three parts. Part I deals with cases of high-tech innovative industries, which represent the modern and progressive aspects of the Japanese economy and which display the secrets of their competitiveness in the world market. Part II discusses the restructuring industries, in which traditional Japanese companies are struggling against challenges from the newly industrialized economies (NIEs) and promoting dynamic policies in order to succeed in the arena of international rivalry. These industries may well be crucial in predicting the future of the Japanese economy. Part III looks at an important service sector activity, life insurance, and at aspects of the evolution of the accounting and business education systems, which can be considered to be of considerable importance in understanding modern Japanese business development.

The remainder of this brief introductory chapter puts the subsequent case studies in a wider context by sketching the long-term evolution of Japanese industrial and business structures.

JAPANESE INDUSTRIAL GROWTH IN ITS LONG-TERM PERSPECTIVE

Japan's modernization started in 1868 with the Meiji Restoration, when various efforts started to be made to catch up with the industrialized countries of the West. A typical slogan under successive Meiji governments (from 1868 to 1912) was 'a wealthy nation and strong forces'. During this period the governments themselves transplanted and promoted major modern industries, while at the same time the private sector grew with the emergence of the *zaibatsu*.[2] Although Japan's economic growth was the result of a successful partnership between government and business, basically ambitious entrepreneurs in the private sector led the industrialization process, concentrating on the export of goods such as textiles and supported by abundant cheap labour.[3]

Japan's own 'industrial revolution' started in the last years of the 1880s and ended in the latter 1900s, though there are various arguments on this point.[4] There was high economic growth during the First World War, as shown in Figure 1.1 and Table 1.1. However, the overall size and importance of the Japanese economy remained modest before the Second World War, compared with Western nations. As can be seen in Tables 1.2 and 1.3, Japan's relative share of world manufacturing output was 3.3 per cent in 1928, and of world exports of manufactures only 3.9 per cent in 1929. Rapid economic growth began after the Second World War, especially from the late 1950s. Tables 1.2 and 1.3 also indicate that Japan's economic power in the world can really only be recognized as becoming competitive with the United States, the world's strongest economic power, after the effects of the first oil shock in 1973 were overcome.

Behind the economic growth of the post-war period, there were considerable structural changes in the Japanese economy. As shown in Figure 1.2, in terms of share of employment the primary sector fell off sharply after the Second World War, while the tertiary sector increased. The number employed in manufacturing rose, though this trend peaked around 1973, manufacturing's share of total employment subsequently falling and stagnating at around one-third. There has been, therefore, a significant shift of labour from the primary to the tertiary sectors. The primary sector's share of national output also fell very sharply, as seen

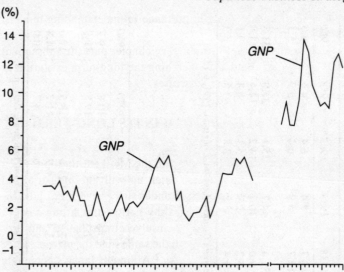

Figure 1.1 The growth rate of GNP (%)

Source: Kazushi Ohokawa, Miyohei Shinohara and Mataji Umemura (eds), *Estimates of Long-term Economic Statistics of Japan since 1868*, Tokyo, Toyokeizaishinposha, 1976, vol. 1, p. 12.

Table 1.1 Relative growth of GDP per man-year, 1873–1973

	Annual percentage growth rates					
	UK	*USA*	*France*	*Germany*	*Italy*	*Japan*
1873–1899	1.2	1.9	1.3	1.5	0.3	1.1
1899–1913	0.5	1.3	1.6	1.5	2.5	1.8
1913–1924	0.3	1.7	0.8	-0.9	-0.1	3.2
1924–1937	1.0	1.4	1.4	3.0	1.8	2.7
1937–1951	1.0	2.3	1.7	1.0	1.4	-1.3
1951–1964	2.3	2.5	4.3	5.1	5.6	7.6
1964–1973	2.6	1.6	4.6	4.4	5.0	8.4
1873–1973	1.2	1.8	2.0	2.0	2.4	2.6

Source: David Reynolds, *Britannia Overruled: British Policy and World Power in the Twentieth Century*, London, Longman, 1991, p. 12.

Table 1.2 Relative percentage shares of total world manufacturing output, 1860–1980

	1860	1880	1900	1913	1928	1938	1953	1963	1973	1980
UK	19.9	22.9	18.5	13.6	9.9	10.7	8.4	6.4	4.9	4.0
Germany/W Germany	4.9	8.5	13.2	14.8	11.6	12.7	5.9	6.4	5.9	5.3
USA	7.2	14.7	23.6	32.0	39.3	31.4	44.7	35.1	33.0	31.5
Russia/USSR	7.0	7.6	8.8	8.2	5.3	9.0	10.7	14.2	14.4	14.8
Japan	2.6	2.4	2.4	2.7	3.3	5.2	2.9	5.1	8.8	9.1
France	7.9	7.8	6.8	6.1	6.0	4.4	3.2	3.8	3.5	3.3

Source: David Reynolds, *Britannia Overruled: British Policy and World Power in the Twentieth Century*, London, Longman, 1991, p.18.

Table 1.3 Percentage of world exports of manufactures, 1899–1980

	1899	1913	1929	1937	1950	1960	1970	1980
UK	33.2	30.2	22.4	20.9	25.5	16.5	10.8	9.7
Germany/W Germany	22.4	26.6	20.5	16.5	7.3	19.3	19.8	19.9
USA	11.7	13.0	20.4	19.2	27.3	21.6	18.5	17.0
Japan	1.5	2.3	3.9	6.9	3.4	6.9	11.7	14.8
France	14.4	12.1	10.9	5.8	9.9	9.6	8.7	10.0

Source: David Reynolds, *Britannia Overruled: British Policy and World Power in the Twentieth Century*, London, Longman, 1991, p.18.

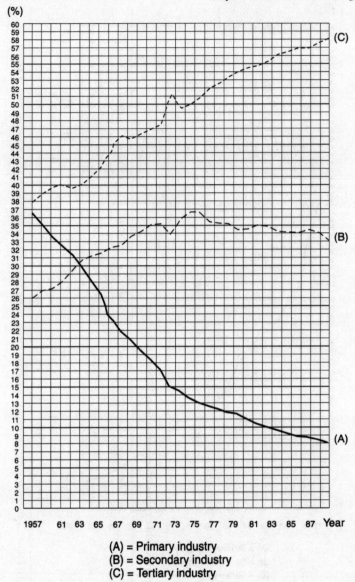

(A) = Primary industry
(B) = Secondary industry
(C) = Tertiary industry

Figure 1.2 Structural change of economy by employment (%)
Source: Yuzawa, 'Changing Industrial Structure in Japan'. See note 5.

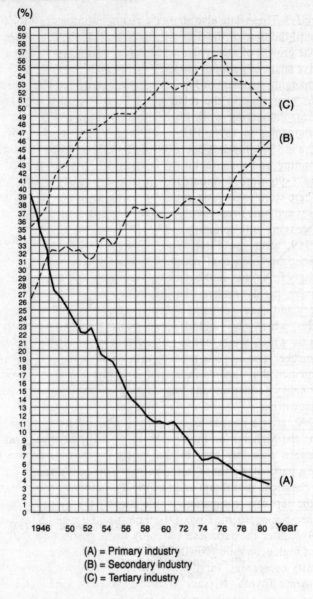

Figure 1.3 Structural change of economy by share of national output
by sector (%)

Source: As for Figure 1.2.

in Figure 1.3. These data also show the rising importance of the tertiary sector until the time of the first oil shock. During the remainder of the 1970s, the growth of the dynamic secondary sector resulted in a rise in its relative share of national output.[5]

The changing structure of Japanese manufacturing can be observed in the shifts over time in the relative size and importance of Japanese companies. Pioneering work on changes in the ranking order of the major companies in 1896, 1919, 1940 and 1972 was done by Aoshi Nakamura in 1974, his data being based on the total assets of companies in the mining and manufacturing industries.[6] The top-ranking companies in 1896 were dominated by textile firms, especially spinning firms. There were twenty-six cotton spinning firms among the top fifty companies and nine firms involved in other areas of the textile business such as weaving, silk spinning and hemp.

By 1919, after the First World War, when Japan had already experienced her industrial revolution, heavy industries had become increasingly important in the national economy, and companies in this sector were highly ranked. Shipbuilding, steel, mining, industrial machinery and chemical firms accounted for over half of the top fifty companies, which now included only eight spinning firms and four other firms which were textile-related. There were also eight sugar firms, one beer firm and one tobacco firm amongst the fifty companies. This indicated that Japan's industrial structure had become oriented towards heavy industries and, to a lesser extent, towards consumer supply industries.

By 1940, after a decade as a quasi-wartime economy in the period following the Manchurian Incident of 1931, the industrial structure of the Japanese economy was biased much more towards the heavy industries, particularly those in the defence sector. Shipbuilding, steel, mining, chemical, petroleum and electrical enterprises were prominent among the top fifty companies, while there were only five spinning companies: Kanegafuchi, Toyo, Dainihon, Katakura and Kureha.

By 1972, after the Japanese economy had experienced well over a decade of high economic growth, there had been major changes among the top fifty companies. Firstly, five car manufacturing firms appeared among them: Toyota, Nissan, Matsuda (Mazda), Isuzu and Honda. Secondly, seven general construction firms were included, demonstrating the large demand for new houses and factories and the provision of infrastructure. Thirdly, the number of spinning companies had fallen to only two, Kanegafuchi and Toyobo, while synthetic fibres companies like Toray, Asahikasei and Teijin appeared for the first time. The Japanese economy was changing to an industrial structure based on modern technologies, though steel and shipbuilding companies still remained in the upper ranks of the top fifty companies. After the 1973 oil shock, the Japanese economy entered a new stage, supported by high-tech industries such as cars and electronics.[7]

Recent research, undertaken by Hiroaki Yamazaki, has examined the changing structure of industries based on the number of products and the turnover in the benchmark years of 1929, 1943, 1955, 1973 and 1987. His study indicates the industries that entered the top ranking for the first time, and those that exited. Two conclusions emerged. On the one hand, Yamazaki stresses that banking and electricity have constantly been the two major industries in the Japanese economy, which is most unusual when compared with other industrialized countries. On the other hand, he shows that there have been frequent changes over time in the identities of the industries and companies in the manufacturing and commercial sectors. This implies that the Japanese economy has been quite flexible and, at the same time, quick to adapt itself to new economic conditions, and that dynamic competition, even among companies in the same industry, has promoted rapid economic growth.[8]

It should be added here that W. Mark Fruin's new book has deepened even further our understanding of the evolving Japanese industrial structure, by providing a ranking of the 200 largest Japanese industrial firms in 1918, 1930, 1954, 1973 and 1987. This unique dataset includes information on corporate assets, capitalization, sales/revenue, number of employees, and product lines.[9]

THE REBIRTH OF THE JAPANESE ECONOMY AFTER THE SECOND WORLD WAR

After the war, the regime of the American Army of Occupation, known as General Headquarters (GHQ), had a major influence on Japanese political and economic policies. GHQ ordered the dissolution of the *zaibatsu*, which were considered to have promoted and supported the sources of Japanese military power, and an agricultural reform designed to change the relationship between landowners and tenant farming. GHQ also reformed the educational system, basing it upon the American one, in order to promote democracy in Japan.[10]

American management methods were introduced into Japan from 1949 to 1951 through the American Occupation Army, which was exploiting various kinds of training methods for top and middle-ranking officers in the forces. The Civil Communication Section (CCS) in GHQ had already started, in 1949, what was called the 'CCS Course' for Japanese managers of big firms to teach them how to control the quality

Table 1.4 The changing industrial structure in Japan as shown by the industry distribution of the top fifty companies

Industry	1896	1919	1940	1972
Cotton spinning	27	9	6	2
Weaving	4	–	–	–
Wool	1	2	1	–
Other textiles	3	1	–	–
Leather	1	–	–	–
Paper	3	3	1	–
Cement	2	1	1	–
Glass	–	–	1	–
Chemical	2	3	7	6
Pharmaceutical	–	–	–	1
Brewing	2	1	1	–
Sugar	1	8	4	–
Tobacco	–	1	–	–
Fisheries	–	–	1	–
Synthetic fibre	–	–	–	3
Petroleum	–	2	1	5
Shipbuilding	1	6	2	5
Industry machinery	–	–	–	3
Electrical appliance	–	3	6	6
Automobile	–	–	1	5
Steel	–	6	10	6
Non-ferrous metals	1	–	–	–
Mining	2	4	7	1
Construction	–	–	–	7
Totals	50	50	50	50

Source: Aoshi Nakamura's tables; see note 6, op. cit.

of products. Then, in 1950 the Far East Air Force opened their 'MTP [Management Training Programme] Course' to Japanese managers.[11]

To understand post-war Japanese manufacturing and engineering development, the importance of the quality control (QC) and production systems, which were also introduced from the United States, has to be appreciated. Many businessmen were eager to learn, and to transfer QC and production systems into Japanese companies under the aegis of such organizations as *Nikka Giren* – the Union of Japanese Scientists and Engineers (UJSE), a society formed to promote the spread of the scientific management movement in Japan. The statistician, Dr William Edwards Deming, came to Japan in 1950 as a consultant to GHQ, to advise the Japanese government on the way to formulate statistics. He was to exercise a considerable influence on the strategies used by

Japanese firms to control the quality of their products. In 1951, supported by *Nihon Keizai Shinbunsha* (Nikkei Newspaper), the UJSE instituted the Deming Prize as a reward for those firms which were best at quality control, and this came to symbolize high product quality. Many excellent companies competed for the prize so as to raise the quality of their manufacturing process and of their products.[12]

Over time, the QC movement in Japanese firms developed a new style. Firstly, the QC movement was organized and came to be practised in the work-place by small groups of fewer than ten employees, after their work hours. Basically, the movement was promoted through the voluntary service of employees, who committed themselves to it with a kind of collectivism and strong feeling of mutual burden-sharing, which was promoted by the lifetime employment system. Secondly, although it was originally thought that the QC movement would encourage the improvement of manufacturing methods and processes in factories, it gradually developed in such a way as to concern other sections, such as the sales and administrative departments. The new-style QC movement was called the Total Quality Control (TQC) movement. In other words, not only factory workers but also office workers were to be involved. To qualify for the Deming Prize, all these various aspects were assessed along with the performance and results of the firm.[13]

The establishment of the Japan Productivity Centre (JPC) in 1955 was epoch-making for the modernization of Japanese firms and management. It emulated the Anglo-American Council on Productivity (AACP), which had been established in 1948.[14] At first, Kohei Goshi, the first managing director of JPC, researched the AACP in detail, and he was very impressed by Graham Hutton's *We Too Can Prosper*.[15] Goshi learned that American production methods were introduced into European countries with a 'European mind' (in other words, they were adapted to suit European ways), and that the methods should be revised when applied to Japanese firms so that they were introduced with a 'Japanese mind'. Over the following years, the productivity movement in Japan acquired an idiosyncratic Japanese dimension.[16]

In 1955, fifteen groups (174 members in all) were despatched to the United States; the next year, twenty-seven delegations (307 members, including representatives of trade unions) were sent to investigate every aspect of American business and companies. When they returned, they had many meetings to disseminate what they had seen and learned of American business and manufacturing. The meetings were held in various cities nationwide, and thousands of people went to them.

In four years, 186 groups, comprising 1,785 delegates, were sent overseas, mainly to the United States but to certain European countries as well, under the auspices of the JPC. In ten years, the numbers had increased to 660 groups and 6,600 delegates, and in 1978, the total number sent by the JPC reached 18,500, around 10,000 of whom went to the United States. The JPC also laid stress on the modernization of smaller firms, whose representatives sent to the United States learned from the strength and creativity of smaller firms there. It is important to note, too, that prominent American businessmen and scholars came to Japan to lecture to the senior management of firms and to the leaders of unions about modern American business and labour relations.

In the first five years of the productivity movement, two quite conspicuous tendencies became apparent. Firstly, the JPC began to steer the movement away from merely learning from American practice and towards a more original Japanese emphasis. Increasingly, it came to recognize that the productivity movement should be transformed to suit Japanese conditions, and to create the original ideas and methods of the movement. Secondly, the trade unions gradually came to accept what the productivity movement meant, and to participate positively in it. Millions of workers joined the movement annually. It may be difficult to assess to exactly what extent the productivity movement contributed to Japan's rapid economic growth, which only began in the late 1950s. However, it is surely right to think that, directly or indirectly, American management methods, manufacturing techniques and labour relations profoundly influenced the development of the Japanese economy in its recovery from the chaotic conditions of the post-war period.[17]

THE REASSESSMENT OF JAPANESE MANAGEMENT

In 1958 James C. Abegglen published *The Japanese Factory*, a book which was translated into Japanese by K. Urabe, a leading professor of management. The book profoundly shocked Japanese scholars, because Abegglen valued Japanese management greatly while they were accustomed to consider it as backward and pre-modern. Abegglen insisted that Japanese management should be regarded as a positive factor in Japan's economic growth, which was in fact well under way by the time his study was published.[18]

Abegglen used a cultural anthropology approach to analyse the characteristics of Japanese management. He was impressed by the 'wage system of nenko', which was the traditional wage system based on lifetime employment and seniority. Abegglen and Urabe stressed that lifetime employment had arisen as a result of the peculiar aspects of the Japanese relationship between employer and employee, supported by the narrow labour market in Japan.[19] This argument has not found universal acceptance. Kazuo Koike, for example, has argued that the Japanese management system is not especially unique when compared with the European and American versions, particularly in the field of employment and promotion; rather, he emphasized the company training system, the job-rotation system, and the long-term perspective taken in assessing labour skills formed within the company.[20]

On the subject of groupism in Japanese management, Hiroshi Hazama has analysed this as stemming from managerial familism. This is a kind of paternalistic management style, originating in the pre-modern merchant houses and established during the First World War when there was a shortage of labour as a result of the economic boom.[21] Masumi Tsuda also emphasized the collective aspect of Japanese management. In particular, he considered the Japanese company as a kind of community for labour.[22] Ryushi Iwata saw a characteristic of Japanese management to be its tendency towards being group-orientated, but stressed Japanese psychological traits, originating from medieval rural life. He argued that the principle of community had gradually developed in Japanese agricultural society, which, given the national psychological mentality, sought above all communal stability, co-operation among its members, and the joint liability of its members.[23]

In his *Theory Z*, Ouchi found the clan, a Japanese-type group, to be quite common in some excellent American companies. He referred to companies organized on a clan-basis as Z-type company groups. Z-type companies have some special characteristics, such as long-time employment, a promotion system by rotation, and assessment of employees from a long- rather than a short-range perspective. They can provide a haven for people who have a nostalgic feeling that the rise of modern society has led to a collapse of the community and a loss of psychological unity among people.[24]

Pascale and Athos pointed out that the excellence of Japanese management appeared dependent on informal management, like corporate ideas, management skill and style, and personnel management, rather than on formal management, like strategy and structure, corporate organization and system. They also stressed that American firms which performed well had much in common with those excellently managed Japanese firms.[25]

Imai and Itami analysed the relationship between the market and firms, and pointed out that one of the characteristics of Japanese firms was their use of an intermediate organization between the firm and the market. They argued that the presence of these intermediate networks in the organized market mechanism made the Japanese economy and Japanese business more effective and competitive.[26] Itami, with others, gave consideration to the advantages to the Japanese automobile industries of this network system.[27]

In the mid-1980s, Abegglen and Stalk tried to explain the secret of the competitiveness of Japanese firms by pointing to a management system that was dependent on co-operation between employers and employees to attain a common purpose. Characteristically, Japanese firms looked first of all for company growth, by concentrating on the expansion of market share, rather than stable growth and solid profit.[28] From this it could be construed that Japanese companies were in fact owned not by shareholders but by employers and employees. In contrast, European and American companies were owned, both formally and in reality, by their shareholders; therefore all employees, even directors, were obliged to work for the shareholders' interest. The theme of Japanese firms as a 'coalition of stakeholders' has been taken up by several recent writers.[29]

Economists who study industrial organizations are fond of distinguishing the Japanese economic system from the American economic system by representing the former as operating by internal organization instead of by the market mechanism. In other words, the Japanese economy, as characterized by internal organization, performs better – in terms of stable labour relations, long-range perspectives and transaction costs – in a *keiretsu* (a kind of fixed and stable relation between parent firms and subsidiaries) than in a system based on the market mechanism.

There are four reasons why internal organization has advantages for Japanese firms.[30] The first is that employers and employees in Japanese companies using the internal organization paradigm can have a common information system, what is known as 'organizational rent', in addition to information about cost and price. The second is that the companies can achieve high productivity and maintain highly skilled labourers in a long-term labour relationship. The third is that a stable relationship between employer and employee established over time can mutualize risk-sharing in a time of price fluctuations and economic changes. Finally, Japanese companies making use of the advantages of internal organization can plan a strategy from a long-term perspective and accomplish it in the long run.

However, while economists analyse the economy from the viewpoint of market mechanism, management scholars analyse the management system from the viewpoint of seeking the best combination of four managerial resources: human, facilities and materials, capital and information. It may be correct to say that the competitiveness of Japanese companies is the result of Japanese management, but there are many arguments about why this is so. At the present time, there is no single conclusion, but recent trends stress the management system as a whole rather than such individual functions of Japanese management as management strategy, career and wage systems, and so forth.

Itami used three concepts to compare the American and Japanese economic systems – the concept of corporation, the concept of burden-sharing, and the concept of the market. In a classic capitalist system like the American economy, shareholders have important rights over company policy; decision-making and information are usually concentrated in top management; and, needless to say, the American market is comparatively free from various sorts of regulation.[31]

In the case of Japanese firms, shareholders are not as strong or active as in American ones; decision-making and information are decentralized and held in common by both employers and employees; and markets are internalized and networked to make the behaviour of a company more effective and competitive. In this sense, according to Itami, the Japanese corporate economy is quite reasonable and successful in terms of economic effectiveness and organizational unity.[32]

Itami also suggests that the Japanese company system is not based on what is called capitalism, but on 'humanism'. Japan's corporate system lays emphasis on the human networks in the company, and considers, first and foremost, the human being as the basis of the market mechanism and the company organization. In America's corporate economy, on the other hand, money or capital is the basis of the market and the organization. The American economy, therefore, can rightly be termed capitalist.[33]

From these various arguments, it is possible to suggest some crude contrasts between the corporate economies in Japan and the United States, though the dangers of such over-simplified generalizations have to be recognized (See Table 1.5).

SOME SECRETS OF JAPANESE ECONOMIC GROWTH: THE IMPORTANCE OF RECIPROCAL INFORMATION IN JAPANESE MANAGEMENT

Long and continuous service

Long-term and continuous transactions are found in many aspects of the Japanese management system. In addition to the lifetime employment, wage and promotion practices, relations between assemblers and parts producers are also stable and long-term, as they are (usually) between the firms and banks. Banks and firms hold each others' shares, which

Table 1.5 Comparisons between the Japanese and US corporate economies

	Japan	*United States*
Aim of the company	Long-term marginal value	Short-term profit
Capital	Mainly loan	Mainly reserved
Company ownership	Employers and employees	Shareholders
Shareholding pattern	Stable (reciprocal)	Fluctuating (seeking high return)
Strategy	Growth-orientated	Profit-orientated
Division of profit	For reserves initially	For dividends initially
President	Representative of all employees	Representative of shareholders
Trade union	Single union	Functionally organized plural unions
Decision-making	Bottom-up	Top-down
Education	On-the-job training	Off-the-job training
Worker	Plural jobs, general	Single job, specific
Employment	Lifetime	Contract
Wage, promotion	By years of service	By ability

tends to guarantee the long-term business relationship between them. Even employees may be encouraged to work harder and maintain stable labour relations because, through company shareholding societies, they may own a certain number of their company's shares.[34]

The practice of lifetime employment ensures that employees receive on-the-job training (OJT), and also that they have opportunities to improve their professional abilities through job rotation. They are trained inside the company, and undertake a long-term educational programme prepared by the company. By these means, employees can gain a knowledge of the company's affairs and business which they hold in common with their co-workers in other sections. Moreover, internal job rotation and the promotion system gives them a high and comprehensive level of information in common with their employers.

Needless to say, under the Japanese wage and promotion system, based on length of service to the company, employees are not necessarily assessed in terms of their ability but rather by their number of years of service with the company. There are many companies which are currently introducing sophisticated wage systems like job classification plans and payment schemes, based on the ability to carry out the job; but length of service to the company remains the usual standard for assessing jobs and work done. Managers have a tendency to consider that the ability of employees to do their job will increase in proportion to their length of service, and that employees with a longer service record should be compensated for the comparatively low wage they earned in their earlier days. It may be that, eventually, the total wage earned by employees is duly paid in terms of lifetime employment.[35]

Assembly firms and parts suppliers have good relationships through long-standing contracts by means of which they can accumulate both relevant information and skills. This kind of appropriate knowledge cannot necessarily be found in manuals, and can be hard to grasp in any short-term dealings. For instance, Toyota's *kanban* system is introduced to its subsidiaries, and also to related companies, in order to get parts from suppliers 'just-in-time'. It takes a long time for suppliers to understand the essence of the assembler's production system, and it is both reasonable and inevitable to establish long-range contracts between the assembler and suppliers in order to have a continuous and substantial exchange of information.[36]

As for relationships between banks and firms, these are also stable and long-standing, because continuous transactions effectively reduce the cost of providing an interchange of new information and trading skills between them. Sometimes banks send members of their staff to client companies to collect inside information and to observe the condition of their finances. This practice may be reasonable in order to reduce the uncertainties that accompany dealings, by way of long-standing and stable transactions.[37]

Genba-shugi

In Japanese '*Genba*' means shopfloor, or the actual place of work or business; '*shugi*' just means 'ism'. The meaning of *Genba-shugi*, therefore, is essentially that Japanese management values the production line and sales field, and these are where the information vital for a company's decision-making process should be amassed. The bottom-up system of decision-making is supported by the positive participation of workers, who are in a position to know the actual business, the problems that arise, and details of the solutions found; they produce the original proposals on the basis of accurate information. Thus proposals made at the level of the lower ranks are sent to the upper ranks of management, and thence to top management, where the decision is finally made. In other words, in the Japanese management system, the right to participate in the decision-making process is decentralized; even workers at the lower levels of a company can participate in the decision-making process. All information relating to the company can, therefore, be commonly held, from bottom to top, though the scope and quality of this information may be restricted in the case of lower-level employees.[38]

Genba-shugi can be realized through the OJT popular among Japanese companies. Indeed, OJT is an educational system based on a combination of daily work and practical training in the field; and the job rotation aspect of it is an important opportunity for employees to experience various types of job and to build a wide range of human networks within the company. At first, employees are asked to accomplish simple and easy tasks, then to execute more difficult tasks or be transferred to related jobs, and gradually to form their own career paths. Through these OJT methods, white-collar workers will develop, it is hoped, into all-rounders with various skills and business knowhow, and blue-collar workers into multifunctional-type workers with a knowledge of factory production skills and methods.[39]

The overriding rights of employees

In Japanese companies, it is considered that the basic plans and policies originate from the employees, and that they therefore have a prior claim on the results of their company's performance. The reason why Japanese employees were able to assume such overriding rights, after the Second World War is usually explained as follows.

The dissolution of the *zaibatsu* after the war was conducted by the Holding Company Liquidation Commission, under the guidance of the Allied Supreme Commander. The headquarters of the *zaibatsu* were abolished and the members of the *zaibatsu* families were forbidden to take any top-management post in the related companies. However, when groups of associated enterprises began to be formed again at the beginning of the 1950s, some of the most powerful were descendants of the pre-war *zaibatsu*. Others, with no direct linkage to the pre-war *zaibatsu*, also appeared, by acquiring new business opportunities after the war.

In the course of this new phase of economic development, the groups of enterprises were re-combined, in most cases, by the principal banks, not by the pre-war *zaibatsu* families. The new enterprise groups were owned by banks, other financial institutions, and industrial firms, and largely by other members of their own group. The shares of the component companies of a group are owned mutually amongst themselves. In these circumstances, it is not the dominant shareholders or capitalists, but the professional managers who assume the sovereignty of the company. The company's finances are largely dependent on loan capital, and the capital market does not play a major role in raising such capital. As a result, the shareholders cannot influence company policy to any extent; they look therefore not for high dividends, but rather for high premiums from booming share prices. In this sense, shareholders support the policies of the professional managers, in expectation of the high premiums that might be realized by able professional managers using internally reserved resources. Companies are thus able to follow competitive and growth-orientated policies, sometimes at the expense of high dividends.

THE BEGINNING OF THE END?

The early 1990s was a period of upheaval for the Japanese political system, and of considerable pessimism about Japan's continued economic vitality. The bursting of the 'bubble economy' of the late 1980s badly damaged the Japanese financial system and helped to produce a recession, during which some of the essentials of Japanese management, such as lifetime employment, have been called into question. The question arises whether this is the beginning of the end for Japanese competitive success.

The available evidence suggests that such a conclusion would be premature. Japan's economic performance in the early 1990s was unsatisfactory, but hardly comparable to the severe problems experienced by the United States or, even more, by the United Kingdom. Japanese real GDP *rose* 14 per cent between the end of 1988 and the middle of 1993: British real GDP actually fell over the same period, and remained lower at the end than at the beginning. Moreover, and more significantly, the problems of the 'bubble economy' in Japan were caused mainly by over-borrowing for investment in land and housing, and the recession started in the financial sector and then spread to the industrial sectors. So far as Japanese manufacturing methods are concerned, these may well be able to maintain Japanese competitive advantage over Europe and the United States, provided factories continue to be operated under the assumption that their workforces are as or more important than the stakes of their shareholders or the income of their directors. The fundamental structures which have been driving the Japanese economy over the last three decades appear to be unchanged, although the rapid and dramatic appreciation of the yen in 1993 made the business environment much worse.

It is possible that Japanese business has reached a turning point, and that it will fail to overcome the competitive challenges posed by the NIEs of Asia, now including China. But from the perspective of 1994, the case is far from proven.

NOTES

1 The two most important recent studies are W. Mark Fruin, *The Japanese Enterprise System*, Oxford, Clarendon Press, 1992; and Hidemasa Morikawa, *Zaibatsu, the rise and fall of family enterprise groups in Japan*, Tokyo, University of Tokyo Press, 1992. See also Keiichiro Nakagawa, 'Business Management in Japan – A Comparative Historical Study', *Industrial and Corporate Change*, vol. 2, no. 1, 1993.

2 Although there are several definitions of a *zaibatsu*, according to Morikawa a *zaibatsu* is 'a group of diversified businesses owned exclusively by a single family or an extended family': Morikawa, *Zaibatsu*, p. xvii; for a comprehensive bibliography, in English, on the *zaibatsu*, see William D. Wray, *Japan's Economy: A Bibliography of its Past and Present*, New York, Markus Wiener Publishing, 1989, pp. 62–70.

3 There are many arguments over the relationship between government and business. Johnson and certain other American scholars stress the role of government over business (see, for instance, Chalmers Johnson, *MITI and the Japanese Miracle: The Growth of Industrial Policy,1925–75*, Stanford, Cal., Stanford University Press, 1982). More recently American scholars have tended to be sceptical of Johnson's argument. For examples of recent conflicting approaches, see David Friedman, *The Misunderstood Miracle: Industrial Development and Political Change in Japan*, Ithaca, N.Y., Cornell University Press, 1988; Daniel I. Okimoto, *Between MITI and the Market: Japanese Industrial Policy and High Technology*, Stanford, Cal., Stanford University Press, 1989; and Patricia A. O'Brien, 'Industry Structure as a Competitive Advantage: The History of Japan's Post-war Steel Industry', *Business History*, 1992, vol. 34, no. 1. The general view among Japanese scholars has been that the co-relationship between government and business should be emphasized, and, if anything, the role of the private sector, which had grown up since the Meiji restoration and was partly based upon traditional business methods, should be given greater weight. For example, see K. Nakagawa, *Government and Business*, Tokyo, University of Tokyo Press, 1980; *idem*, 'The "Learning Industrial Revolution" and Business Management', in T. Yui and K. Nakagawa (eds), *Japanese Management in Historical Perspective*, Tokyo, University of Tokyo Press, 1989; T. Yuzawa and M. Udagawa (eds), *Foreign Business in Japan before World War II*, Tokyo, University of Tokyo Press, 1990.

4 Kanji Ishii, *Nihon keizaishi (Japanese Economic History)*, Tokyo, University of Tokyo Press, 2nd edn, 1991, pp. 180–2.

5 Takeshi Yuzawa, 'The changing industrial structure in Japan since World War II', in Waltraud Falk (ed.), *Sectoral Changes in Industry after World*

War II, Prague, Institute of History of the CSAS, 1991, pp. 67–71.

6 Aoshi Nakamura's Tables in the Appendix, Keiichiro Nakagawa *et al.* (eds), *Kindai Nihon Keieishi no Kisochishiki* (*Fundamentals of Modern Japanese Business History*), Tokyo, Yuhikaku, 1974.

7 Ibid.

8 Hiroaki Yamazaki, 'Senzen Sengo no Nihon no Daikigyo' ('The Fifty Largest Japanese Companies in the Pre- and Post-War Periods'), in S. Yonekawa *et al.* (eds), *Sengo Nihan Keieishi* (*Japanese Business History after World War Two*), Tokyo, Toyokeizaishinposha, 1991. See also Yoshitaka Suzuki, *Japanese Management Structures, 1920–1980*, London, Macmillan, 1991, Appendix: The Largest 100 Industries of 1935.

9 Fruin, *Japanese Enterprise System*.

10 Eleanor M. Hadley, *Antitrust in Japan*, Princeton, N.J., Princeton University Press, 1970; Takafusa Nakamura, *The Postwar Japanese Economy: its development and structure*, Tokyo, University of Tokyo Press, 1981.

11 Akitoshi Iki, *Shogen Sengo Nihon no Keieikakushin* (*A Witness of Management Innovation in Japan*), Tokyo, Nikkei shinsho, 1981, p. 25.

12 There are several categories of Deming Prize, but the most important one is the prize given to firms or factories. According to Izumi Nonaka, from 1951 to 1960 the Deming Prize was presented mainly to firms in the steel, pharmaceutical, chemical and electrical appliances industries; in the 1960s and 1970s to mechanical engineering, automobile and automobile-related companies; and in the 1980s to service, construction and electricity companies. S. Sasaki and I. Nonaka, 'Nihon ni okeru kagakuteki kanri no donyu to tenkai' ('Introduction and Development of Scientific Management in Japan'), in T. Hara (ed.), *Kagakuteki kanriho no donyu to tenkai: sono rekishiteki kokusaihikaku* (*Introduction and Development of Scientific Management: its international comparison in historical perspective*), Kyoto, Showado, 1990.

13 Ibid., pp. 273–80; Arthur M. Whitehill, *Japanese Management: Tradition and Transition*, London, Routledge, 1991, pp. 238–40.

14 Jim Tomlinson, 'The Failure of the Anglo-American Council on Productivity', *Business History*, 1991, vol. 33, no. 1, pp. 82–92.

15 Graham Hutton, *We Too Can Prosper: The Promise of Productivity*, London, George Allen and Unwin, 1953.

16 *Nihon Seisansei Honbu* (Japan Productivity Centre), *Seisansei Undo 30 Nenshi* (*Thirty Years of the Productivity Movement*), Tokyo, 1985, ch. 1.

17 Ibid., ch. 2.

18 James C. Abegglen, *The Japanese Factory: aspects of its social organization*, Glencoe, Ill., Free Press, 1958.

19 Kuniyoshi Urabe, *Keiei no Inobeishon* (*Managerial Innovation*), Tokyo, Nihon Seisansei Honbu, 1961.

20 Kazuo Koike, *Understanding Industrial Relations in Modern Japan*, Basingstoke, Macmillan, 1988.

21 Hiroshi Hazama, *Nihon romukanri shi kenkyu: Keiei kazokushugi no keisei to tenkai* (*Study of the history of Japanese labour management: formation and development of managerial familism*), Tokyo, Ochanomizu Shobo (repr.), 1978.

22 Masumi Tsuda, *Nihonteki keiei no ronri* (*Principles of Japanese Management*), Tokyo, Chuokeizai, 1977.

23 Ryushi Iwata, *Nihonteki keiei no hensei genri* (*The principles and process of Japanese management*), Tokyo, Bunshindo, 1977.

24 William G. Ouchi, *Theory Z: how American business can meet the Japanese challenge*, Reading, Mass., Addison-Wesley, 1981.

25 Richard T. Pascale and Anthony G. Athos, *The Art of Japanese Management: Applications for American Executives*, New York, Simon and Schuster, 1981.

26 Kenichi Imai and Ikuyo Kaneko (eds), *Nettowaaku Soshiki Ron* (*Network Organization Theory*), Tokyo, Iwanami, 1988. However, it may be that from an American point of view, such intermediate organizations create various impediments for exports to, and direct investment in Japan.

27 H. Itami, T. Kagono, T. Kobayashi, K. Sakakibara and M. Ito, *Kyoso to Kakushin: Jido-sha sangyo no Kigyoseicho* (*Competition and Innovation – Growth of Companies in the Automobile Industries*), Tokyo, Toyokeizai-shinposha, 1988.

28 James C. Abegglen and George Stalk, *Kaisha, the Japanese Corporation*, New York, Basic Books, 1985.

29 W. Carl Kester, *Japanese Takeovers. The Global Contest for Corporate Control*, Boston, Mass., Harvard Business School Press, 1991.

30 There is an enormous literature on *keiretsu*. See, for example, 'Keiretsu and Subcontracting in Japan's Automobile Industry', in *Japanese Economic Studies*, 1985, vol. 13, no. 4 (Special Issue); Michael L. Gerlach, *Alliance Capitalism: The Social Organisation of Japanese Business*, Berkeley, Cal., University of California Press, 1992; Kenichi Miyashita and D. Ruseel, *Keiretsu, Inside the Hidden Japanese Conglomerates*, New York, McGraw-Hill, 1993. There is now a large American literature on the economic consequences of *keiretsu*. For one recent discussion, concerned with their impact on trade patterns, see Robert Z. Lawrence, 'Japan's Difficult Trade Regime: An Analysis with Particular Reference to Keiretsu', *Journal of Economic Perspectives*, 1993, vol. 7, no. 3.

31 T. Kagono, I. Nonaka, K. Sakakibara, and S. Okumura, *Strategic versus evolutionary management: a US–Japan comparison of strategy and organization*, Amsterdam, North-Holland, 1985.

32 Alfred D. Chandler Jr, *Scale and Scope: The Dynamics of Industrial Capitalism*, Cambridge, Mass., Harvard University Press, 1990, p. 627.

33 H. Itami, *Jinpon shugi kigyo: kawaru keiei kawaranu genri* (*Human Capitalism: changing management and unchanging principles*), Tokyo, Chikumashobo, 1987.

34 See Hirosho Mito, *Nihon daikigyo no shoyu kozo* (*The structure of shareholding in Japanese big business*), Tokyo, Bunshindo, 1983.

35 However, recent trends in the wage system appear to be shifting the emphasis away from employees' length of service and towards their ability to do the job. For instance, while in 1981 56.6 per cent of an employee's wage used to represent length of service and 43.2 per cent ability by 1991 the ratio changed to 46.9 per cent and 53.1 per cent respectively. Rosei Jiho, in *Shunto bessatsu* (*Journal of Labour Relations*), Tokyo, 1991, no.1, p. 19.

36 Banri Asanuma, 'The Contractual Framework for Parts Supply in the Japanese Automotive Industry', *Japanese Economic Studies*, 1985, vol. 13, no. 4.

37 On problems peculiar to the aggressive financial policies of companies, and

to the relationship between banks and industry, see Abegglen and Stalk, *Kaisha*, pp. 161 ff.

38 The decision-making process in Japanese companies is usually called *Ringi Seido*. For an early analysis of the now famous phenomenon, see Ronald Dore, *British Factory – Japanese Factory*, Berkeley, Cal., University of California Press, 1973, pp. 227–8. See also Abegglen and Stalk, *Kaisha*, p. 208.

39 See, Toshiaki Cyokki, *Nihon no kigyo keiei: sono rekishiteki kosatu (Japanese management: its historical study)*, Tokyo, Hoseidaigaku Shuppankyoku, 1992, ch. 4.

Part I

High-tech and innovative industries

2 Inter-firm relationships between Toyota and its suppliers, in a historical perspective*

Kazuo Wada

INTRODUCTION

Toyota Motor Corporation is the largest of eleven car manufacturers in Japan, being responsible for about 40 per cent of car sales in the Japanese market. It is also now undoubtedly one of the biggest automobile manufacturers in the world.

When the company celebrated its fiftieth anniversary in 1987, it had produced 3.6 million cars. This represented almost 9 per cent of the world's total car production. When Toyota was founded in 1937,[1] the annual production of American automobile manufacturers had already reached a level of about four million cars. That year, the total production of the three biggest manufacturers, General Motors, Ford and Chrysler, came to about three and a half million cars, while Toyota produced about 4,000 cars. Even after the Second World War, it was evident that 'a clear gap existed in production scale between Japanese and American automakers, overwhelmingly in favour of the latter'.[2] In the late 1940s, Toyota's annual production still remained at quite a low level: 6,703 vehicles in 1948 and 10,824 in 1949.[3]

To make matters worse, in 1950 massive labour problems arose in Toyota, and the company was on the brink of bankruptcy. This resulted in the resignation of Kiichiro Toyoda, the founder of the Toyota Motor Company, Ltd. The financial crisis also led to the separation of the Toyota Motor Sales Company Ltd from the Toyota Motor Company Ltd.[4] After Kiichiro Toyoda's resignation, Taizo Ishida was appointed president in July 1950. At the end of the same month, Toyota received the first special procurement order for 1,000 vehicles from the US military, with several repeat orders

* The Pache Foundation of Nanzan University financed this study in 1990.

over the next few months.[5] The contribution of these orders to the establishment of Toyota's business on a solid basis was great, and the revenue derived from them helped to rebuild and modernize Toyota's production facilities.

In 1950, after the Japanese government permitted the import of passenger cars for use as taxis, lifting the restriction on the import of cars in general, foreign-made cars flooded in. Even after customs charges, foreign-made cars were cheaper than Japanese cars.[6] Since the quality of Japanese cars was generally lower, the importers argued that Japan's domestic automobile manufacturers should concentrate on producing trucks and buses, not passenger cars.

The government advised the Japanese automobile manufacturers to tie up with foreign manufacturers in order to catch up with foreign technology. In line with this policy, Nissan linked up with Austin, Isuzu with Rootes, Hino with Renault, and Shin-Mitsubishi with Willys-Overland.[7] Toyota began negotiations with Ford, but the outbreak of the Korean War interrupted this process.[8] Toyota thus had to establish itself as an automobile manufacturer without close connections with any established foreign manufacturer. In the early 1950s, the company seemed to have little hope of competing successfully with foreign manufacturers.

The production of an automobile requires the assembly of over twenty thousand parts. Automobile manufacturers do not produce large numbers of parts themselves but, to varying extents, purchase parts from suppliers. As a result, purchasing policies and relationships with suppliers have a considerable effect on the quality and cost of final products. While scholars have paid increasing attention to the Japanese automobile industry in general, as well as to particular manufacturers,[9] inter-firm relationships between an automobile manufacturer and its suppliers have not been fully investigated.[10] This chapter explains how the inter-firm relationships between Toyota and its suppliers evolved.

TOYOTA AND ITS SUPPLIERS: OVERVIEW

Before examining the historical development of Toyota's relationships with its suppliers, an overview of the situation as it stood recently is presented.

A survey conducted by the Small and Medium Enterprises Agency found that in 1977 a Japanese automobile manufacturer (apparently Toyota) dealt with 168 first-tier suppliers.[11] There were 4,000 second-tier suppliers, and 31,600 in the third-tier group. Japanese automobile manufacturers organize suppliers in a hierarchical order: first-tier suppliers form a *kyoryoku-kai* (co-operative association [of suppliers]), and they in turn organize second-tier supplier groups. Toyota's first-tier supplier group is a co-operative association made up of two parts, the *Kyoho-kai* (Parts Makers' Association) and *Eiho-kai* (Jig Makers' and Construction Companies' Association). As the intention here is to clarify the historical development of Toyota and its parts suppliers, the *Kyoho-kai* will be examined in 1984, when its affiliates outnumbered those of the *Eiho-kai* by 171 to 61.[12]

Usually, Toyota transacts business directly only with the first-tier suppliers, and not with those in the second and third tiers. Most of the 'Toyota group' companies can be found within the first-tier of suppliers and are closely connected with Toyota historically as well as through shareholdings.[13] Although ten Toyota group companies were affiliated in the *Kyoho-kai* in 1984, there were 161 other *Kyoho-kai* affiliates in the first-tier supplier group.[14] One might expect Toyota to have a large stake in these companies, and to be manning them with ex-company officials, but Shiomi's study revealed that Toyota has such bonds with only 25 of the 161 companies, and concluded that relationships between Toyota and the other suppliers are mainly determined by business transactions.[15]

If, then, Toyota does not have a large stake in most of its suppliers, how does it contrive to co-operate with them smoothly, and how does it prevent them from acting 'opportunistically' in pursuit of self-interest?[16] Toyota has a reputation for establishing close co-operation with its suppliers. It has developed this 'close co-operation' through management efforts. Let us now trace these efforts historically.

FIRST ATTEMPT AT MONITORING SUPPLIERS: 'KEIRETSU DIAGNOSIS' IN 1952–3

The *Kyoho-kai* originated in 1939, under the name *Kyoryoku-kai*, when it was merely a convivial annual meeting of Toyota and its suppliers.[17] In 1943, it was renamed *Kyoho-kai*. Through this organization, Toyota distributed materials to individual affiliates when, as a result of the war, they were finding it increasingly difficult to obtain materials. The end of the war and the period of post-war upheaval disrupted the *Kyoho-kai*'s activities. In 1946, however, at the suppliers' meeting, Kiichiro Toyoda expressed his keen desire to establish an automobile industry in Japan. He stressed the fact that the setting up of an automobile industry surely required the establishment of a parts industry, and that Toyota and its suppliers had a common destiny. Soon after the meeting, Toyota reorganized the *Kyoho-kai* into three regional divisions: Tokyo, Osaka and the Tokai district.[18] Suppliers in the Tokyo and Osaka areas tend to be the larger-scale enterprises that are fairly independent of Toyota, while suppliers in the Tokai district are rather small-scale and sell their output almost exclusively to Toyota.[19] For Toyota, the establishment of a parts industry essentially meant ensuring the stability and growth of these latter suppliers. In order to improve the quality of parts, therefore, and to build up the industry, Toyota's first managerial efforts had to be directed towards the Tokai suppliers. This reorganization of the *Kyoho-kai* symbolized a new era in relationships between Toyota and its suppliers.

In 1951, Toyota formulated its first long-term, five-year scheme for modernizing production facilities. However, the company could not afford to give technical instructions to its suppliers. Nor did it appear to have sufficient resources to improve suppliers' managerial abilities. Its purchasing department, with only forty staff, was engaged solely in ordering and receiving parts; it was not able to respond to requests for technical support from suppliers.[20]

The first attempt to modernize the management of the suppliers came not from Toyota but from the Small and Medium Enterprises Agency. From the time of its establishment in 1948, the Agency tried to modernize small and medium-sized enterprises and undertook a variety of consultations for their benefit.[21] The Agency also extended its consultations to groups affiliated with larger firms, and to their suppliers. This was called the '*keiretsu* diagnosis'. Toyota and its twenty-one suppliers in the Tokai district were beneficiaries of this diagnosis in 1952 and 1953. The *keiretsu* diagnosis had a significant effect on relationships between Toyota and its suppliers.[22]

A few officials from the Aichi Prefecture carried out this *keiretsu* diagnosis, visiting each plant and making recommendations on how to improve management abilities. They looked over the plant, collected data on management, and interviewed employees as well as employers. It took some days to observe and advise each supplier. Most suppliers were small-scale, employing under 100 people. Their management was haphazard rather than systematic: some suppliers, for example, did not keep proper accounting records and were unable to tell (with any degree of certainty) whether their businesses were making a profit or loss until the annual visit of the accountants to produce the balance sheet. The *keiretsu* diagnosis was a good opportunity for suppliers to acquire basic management skills and knowledge. One official recalled that suppliers were very doubtful about the diagnosis at first, and sometimes fearful, but that they changed their opinion when they recognized its value in improving productivity.[23] In the end, the suppliers greatly appreciated the diagnosis, expressing their gratitude by presenting the Aichi Prefecture with a bus.[24]

The officials produced a report based on their observations, which they circulated among the suppliers concerned. It described the strengths and weaknesses of management, and even suggested ways of improving plant productivity. The report also graded each supplier on the following points: management, production, labour, marketing and purchasing, finance, accounting and research. Although this grading system was rather simple, apparently Toyota had not undertaken any such an exercise before the consultations began.

After visiting all the suppliers, the officials produced a final report on the relationships between Toyota and its suppliers. This was presented at a meeting held at Toyota headquarters in the spring of 1953, to which senior government officials, as well as suppliers, were invited. At this ceremonial meeting, the officials disclosed their findings and recommended a number of ways to improve relationships between Toyota and its suppliers. They also tabulated the grading points given to all suppliers.[25] Although suppliers' names were not mentioned, each supplier received a report on its own plant and knew its own grading points. It was easy, therefore, for individual suppliers to find out their own rankings among the group. Suppliers with lower gradings forced themselves into improving their management skills for fear that they might receive fewer orders from Toyota.

The *keiretsu* consultations also taught Toyota how to advise, monitor and grade its suppliers.[26] Before them, Toyota seemed not to have any monitoring system at all. After the consultations, however, Toyota's staff began to visit the suppliers frequently and to check their manufacturing processes closely. In October 1953, Toyota decided to introduce quality control into every manufacturing process, establishing a special committee to monitor progress. Moreover, at the annual meeting of the *Kyoho-kai*, Toyota asked suppliers to introduce quality controls at their plants also. In responding to this request, the *Kyoho-kai* organized seminars on quality control. Toyota sent its own personnel to these seminars as instructors. After the seminars, Toyota's staff visited suppliers' plants, observing implementation of quality control and giving advice if needed.[27] Since it appears that Toyota had neither advised nor monitored its suppliers before the *keiretsu* consultations began, this demonstrated a remarkable change of attitude.

After the *keiretsu* consultations, the *Kyoho-kai*'s character also changed greatly. Up until that time, the *Kyoho-kai* had remained little more than a convivial gathering. After the consultations, however, the suppliers themselves visited each factory and together studied how to rationalize it. They established several study groups within the *Kyoho-kai*. As one observer remarked, 'The activity of Kyoho-kai really began at this time'; suppliers strove seriously to rationalize and improve their management.[28] The grading of the suppliers in the final report drove them, especially the lower-rated ones, to work harder. They now competed against one another. They also realized that Toyota would evaluate their efforts to rationalize their management, and this boosted their emerging sense of competition with one another.

In 1955, Toyota marketed Crown cars, 'Japan's first completely domestically-produced passenger cars'.[29] The following year, it introduced into its plants the 'supermarket system', a forerunner of the 'just-in-time method' of supply,[30] whereby suppliers brought some of their parts direct to the assembly line. Toyota could not have introduced such practices had it not been for the efforts made by suppliers to rationalize after the *keiretsu* consultations.

DIFFICULTIES OF A LARGE-SCALE OPERATION

From craft production to mass production

The Crown sold well. This enabled Toyota to enter the passenger-car market successfully, although most of its sales still consisted of trucks. After 1955, its total production volume also increased strikingly: in the region of 22,000 vehicles in that year, it more than doubled to 46,000 vehicles in 1957, and doubled again in 1958. In 1961, Toyota's annual production amounted to 210,000 vehicles.[31] In the space of six years, Toyota's annual production had grown about tenfold. This trend reduced production costs per unit, enabling Toyota to reduce prices, which in turn led to increased sales.[32] Nevertheless, considerable cost differences still existed between Japanese and overseas automobile manufacturers. Restrictions on automobile imports were scheduled to be lifted in the spring of 1963. Toyota therefore strove to build up its mass-production base in order to reduce production costs further. The construction of its Motomachi plant, which began operation in 1959, served as an example of its efforts.

The establishment of a mass-production base did not proceed. Toyota's technical expertise was far behind that of Western manufacturers. The company's first passenger car, the Crown, enjoyed a high reputation in Japan, as a good quality car, but an attempt to export the car to the United States failed because it performed poorly on the American freeways. Mr Seisei Kato of the Toyota Motor Sales Company described the event vividly:

> When the Crown was tried out on US freeways at 80 mph, loud noises soon erupted and power dropped sharply. More trouble occurred before we had logged even 2,000 miles. Although many people had praised the Crown as a 'baby Cadillac', for example, our engines, designed for the narrow-road, low-speed driving [conditions] of Japan in those days, could not even begin to handle the performance and endurance demands placed upon them. As our dreams [of exporting Japanese passenger cars to America, the 'home' of the passenger car] sank out of sight like a ship with a giant hole in its bottom, we wrote to Tokyo that it was advisable to simply throw in the towel.[33]

This incident showed quite clearly that the quality of Toyota's cars had not yet caught up with international standards.

Toyota also faced fierce competition from Nissan, the second largest automobile manufacturer in Japan. When Nissan's Bluebird model appeared on the market in 1959, the popularity of Toyota's Corona faded. Toyota introduced a new Corona model rather hastily in 1960, but the new model frequently broke down. The Corona developed a poor reputation in the market, and it was not long before it was referred to disparagingly as a 'lemon'.[34] Nissan, on the other hand, won the Deming Application Prize in 1960, and was boasting of its technical superiority. As a result of all this, Nissan's passenger-car sales in the domestic market outnumbered Toyota's for the three years from 1960 to 1962. The troubles experienced with the Corona suggested to Toyota's management that something had gone wrong. Whereas production had grown rapidly and employee numbers had increased, middle and lower management felt that co-operation between departments was getting worse.[35]

In addition to its internal management troubles, Toyota's monitoring of suppliers had become lax with the rapid increase in production. Internal documents mention that defects in suppliers' parts often disrupted production.[36] When, in 1958, Toyota received orders from the US Army Procurement Agency in Japan, the problems with the suppliers became more evident. The requirement of the US Army that Toyota guarantee the quality of its suppliers' parts led the company, in 1959, to survey its suppliers and evaluate their quality control systems. The survey was soon discontinued, however, because suppliers' efforts in quality control were so disparate. In addition, the level of quality control asked for by the US Army was much higher than Toyota managers expected.[37] It brought home to them the scale of the disparity between the production capabilities of Japanese and American automobile manufacturers.

Toyota had hastened to build up mass-production facilities in order to meet the rapidly increasing demand for cars in Japan, as well as to prepare for the lifting of restrictions on car imports into Japan. The transition from small-scale to large-scale operations tended to make both Toyota and its suppliers stress volume rather than quality. The troubles with the Corona model were closely connected with this attitude on both sides. Toyota also had to accept the fact that its technical and production capabilities still lagged far behind those of American manufacturers.

Introducing 'Total Quality Control'

Toyota's senior management was fully aware of the situation. To revitalize the spirit of its employees and re-establish a solid monitoring system over suppliers, Toyota's top managers chose to mount a 'Total Quality Control' campaign as their key policy. In 1961, Vice-President Saito announced the campaign to employees.[38] Toyota regarded Total Quality Control as a matter of concern for all of management, not merely for the production side. Although it was clearly essential to implement some statistical methods of quality control over production, the most important thing was to change the attitude of employees, from 'quantity first' to 'quality first'. The campaign extended to suppliers also, resulting in a remodelling of their relationship with Toyota.

Before Saito's announcement even, Toyota launched a new scheme for its suppliers. Since its abortive survey of 1959 had shown the quality-control standards of its suppliers to vary widely, Toyota first set out to learn each supplier's conditions in detail.[39] In 1960 and 1961 Toyota personnel visited sixty-eight suppliers and checked their management systems carefully, giving marks to each supplier in several categories. Based on this survey, Toyota classified suppliers into several groups. Then the company set a clear target for each group.

In addition, seminars were held for each group. The *Kyoho-kai* also established several new committees. One of these, the Rationalization Committee, went on a conducted tour of suppliers' plants with Toyota personnel. The purpose of the tour was actually to advise suppliers, just as the *keiretsu* diagnosis had done. The Committee visited fifty-seven suppliers in the Tokai district, and instructed them in basic management analysis.

As Toyota moved to larger-scale operations, the integration and implementation of its system for monitoring suppliers had virtually broken down. By means of the above-mentioned tour, Toyota began to re-establish a monitoring system on a larger scale. The idea of lagging behind US manufacturers in terms of quality, as well as the débâcle over the Corona, engendered in senior managers an obsession with quality. Their efforts bore fruit: Toyota was awarded the Deming Application Prize in 1965. The Deming Prize Committee, however, recommended that Toyota should improve even further its management of its suppliers. In order to accomplish this task, Toyota established a new department in 1966 – a Department of Purchasing Control, whose principal goal was to spread the campaign for Total Quality Control among suppliers. Masao Nemoto was appointed as head of the department.[40]

With great energy, Nemoto taught the suppliers how to implement the Total Quality Control campaign in their companies. He stressed that the campaign benefited suppliers. He visited suppliers and showed them how to reduce production costs and the number of steps in production processes. Toyota introduced an incentive system to encourage suppliers to reduce costs: if a supplier made a suggestion as to how the cost of some parts might be reduced, and followed this up by actually reducing such costs, the supplier was allowed to keep half of the amount saved. With this incentive, suppliers saw that they would be better off if they could reduce production costs. Suppliers thus welcomed Nemoto's guidance and accepted Total Quality Control as beneficial for their management. The incentive method worked so well that Toyota paid almost 20 per cent less for its parts in 1966 than it had in 1965 – an indication of the enthusiasm suppliers had shown in trying to reduce production costs. According to one calculation, within a six-month period in 1966, *Kyoho-kai* suppliers in the Tokai district actually eliminated 1.62 million production processes.[41]

Progress in Total Quality Control made possible the adoption of the *kanban* system at Toyota, which synchronized the production processes.[42] The *kanban* system gradually spread to all the suppliers.[43] But the success of such synchronization required a high standard of quality control over products, for if too many faulty parts were supplied to

Toyota's assembly lines, the lines would have to stop too frequently. The spread of the *kanban* system to the suppliers can be seen, therefore, as evidence of the extent to which suppliers improved quality control at their plants.

TRANSFERRING MONITORING KNOW-HOW TO FIRST-TIER SUPPLIERS

While Toyota expanded its volume of production, it did not expand significantly the number of its suppliers. As a result, existing suppliers rapidly increased in size. They, too, were able to enjoy economies of scale by increasing production rapidly, although they remained cautious about sales fluctuations at Toyota. In the late 1960s, however, the passenger-car market in Japan expanded rapidly.[44] Total Toyota production jumped from 477,643 cars in 1965 to 832,130 in 1967. Such a rapid increase in the demand for cars forced first-tier suppliers to rely on second-tier suppliers, and an internal survey showed that in 1966 and 1967 Toyota's first-tier suppliers were becoming heavily reliant on those in the second tier to get their orders filled.[45]

Toyota's main concern in this process was that the rise of second-tier suppliers might lead to production problems, and by careful observation it traced many faulty parts back to such second-tier suppliers. While reasonably satisfied with the management abilities of its first-tier suppliers, Toyota now encountered difficulties with those in the second tier. To prevent any possibility of a débâcle similar to that of the Corona in 1956, the company realized that something had to be done for the second-tier suppliers. It therefore decided to transfer its monitoring and controlling know-how to its first-tier suppliers, through a series of seminars. By so doing, Toyota expected its first-tier suppliers to control those in the second-tier. The result was the development of a hierarchical inter-firm structure between Toyota and its suppliers. The transfer of know-how was facilitated by the fact that Toyota refused to increase the number of personnel in its purchasing department.[46] While the growing demand for cars meant that orders to suppliers also increased rapidly, its relatively small staff prevented the purchasing department from instructing and monitoring second-tier suppliers directly; it had no choice but to transfer such know-how.

In 1969, Toyota established the 'Toyota Quality Control Prize'.[47] Awarded to a supplier if the standard of its management was above the level set by Toyota, the prize provided suppliers with an opportunity to check their level of Total Quality Control. Toyota evaluates each first-tier supplier candidate through discussions with its top executives, investigations of its production process, and appraisal of its management in general.[48] The prize therefore also provides an opportunity for Toyota to check its suppliers' capabilities. In addition, the prize serves to stimulate competition among suppliers, since the winning supplier demonstrates that it has been serious about implementing the lessons taught by Toyota.

CONCLUSION

Inter-firm relationships between Toyota and its suppliers are in great contrast to those of American automobile manufacturers. Direct managerial efforts have shaped these inter-firm relationships. Following *keiretsu* consultations, Toyota developed and refined its own monitoring system over suppliers. Later, it went so far as to transfer its monitoring know-how to its first-tier suppliers, so that they in turn would be able to monitor the second-tier supplier group. Toyota and its suppliers have co-operated closely. Nevertheless, Toyota always monitored suppliers' performance carefully in terms of cost, delivery, quality, and other factors. By means of such a monitoring system, Toyota has been able to stimulate keen competition among its suppliers.

NOTES

1 Toyota was originally founded as the Automobile Department of the Toyoda Automatic Loom Works Ltd in 1926, and established as an independent company in 1937.
2 Toyota Motor Corporation, *Toyota: A History of the First 50 Years*, privately published, 1988, p. 113.
3 For the annual production of Toyota, see Appendices of *Toyota: A History*, op. cit.
4 Both the Toyota Motor Company and the Toyota Motor Sales Company remained independent until they merged again as the Toyota Motor Corporation in 1982.
5 *Toyota: A History*, pp. 104–11. The special procurement orders ended in March 1951.
6 Japan Motor Industrial Federation, *Nihon jidosha sangyo-shi* (*History of the Japanese Automobile Industry*), privately published, 1988, pp. 106–7.
7 See Michael A. Cusumano, *The Japanese Automobile Industry: Technology and Management at Nissan and Toyota*, Cambridge, Mass., Harvard University Press, 1985, ch. 2.
8 The US government restricted overseas investment after the outbreak of the Korean War. As a result, Ford could not continue negotiations with Toyota, for a tie-up would have required investment in Japan and the sending of engineers to Japan.

9 See Cusumano, *The Japanese Automobile Industry*, op. cit.; Michael L. Dertouzos *et al.*, *Made in America*, Cambridge, Mass., MIT Press, 1989; James P. Womack, Daniel T. Jones, Daniel Roos, *The Machine That Changed the World*, London, Macmillan, 1990; Kim B. Clark and Takahiro Fujimoto, *Product Development Performance: Strategy, Organization, and Management in the World Auto Industry*, Boston, Mass., Harvard Business School Press, 1991.

10 The following article is an attempt to deal with the relations between an automobile manufacturer and its suppliers, but does not trace the historical development of those relations: Banri Asanuma, 'Jido-sha sangyo ni okeru buhin torihiki no kozo: chosei to kakushin-teki tekio no mekanizumu' (The Structure of Parts Transactions in the Automobile Industry: A Mechanism of Adjustment and Innovative Adaptation), *Gendai keizai* (*Modern Economy*), Summer 1984.

11 The survey does not reveal the name of the company, but, given the nature of the findings, it is obvious that the company is Toyota. See Haruhito Shiomi, 'Seisan rojisutikkusu no kozo: Toyota jidosha no kesu' ('The Structure of Production Logistics: A Case Study of Toyota'), in Kazuichi Sakamoto (ed.), *Gijutsu kakushin to kigyo-kozo* (*Technological Innovation and Enterprise Structure*), Tokyo, Mineruba Shobo, 1985, p. 81.

12 Ibid., pp. 84–5.

13 The 'Toyota group' consists of the following fourteen companies: Toyoda Automatic Loom Works, Ltd; Aichi Steel Works, Ltd; Toyoda Machine Works, Ltd; Toyota Auto Body Company, Ltd; Toyoda Tsusho Kaisha, Ltd; Aishin Seiki Company, Ltd; Toyoda Spinning & Weaving Company, Ltd; Kanto Auto Works, Ltd; Towa Real Estate Company, Ltd; Toyota Central Research & Development Laboratories, Inc; Toyoda Gosei Company, Ltd; Hino Motors, Ltd; Nihon Denso, Ltd; and Daihatsu Motor Company, Ltd.

14 Shiomi, 'Seisan rojisutikkusu no kozo', p. 85.

15 Ibid., p. 86.

16 For an interesting view on how supplier 'opportunism' affects vertical integration in automobile manufacturing, see Kirk Monteverde and J. David Teece, 'Supplier Switching Costs and Vertical Integration in the Automobile Industry', *Bell Journal of Economics*, Spring 1982, vol. 13, no. 1, p. 212.

17 The historical outline of the *Kyoho-kai* is based on the following document: Kyoho-kai History Editorial Committee, *Kyoho-kai no ayumi* (*The History of Kyoho-kai*), privately published, 1967.

18 Toyota Motor Company History Editorial Committee, *Toyota Jidosha 30 nenshi* (*The First 30 Years of Toyota Motor Company*), privately published, 1967, pp. 253–4.

19 *Idem*, *Toyota no ayumi* (*The History of Toyota*), privately published, 1978, pp. 150–1.

20 The Industry and Commerce Department of Aichi Prefecture, 'Keiretsu shindan-sho sokatsu: Toyota Jidosha Kogyo Kabushiki-kaisha' ('A Summary of Keiretsu Diagnosis: Toyota Motor Company'), privately circulated manuscript, 1953, p. 3.

21 See Ministry of International Trade and Industry, *Shoko seisaku-shi* (*The History of Policies for Commerce and Industry*), 1963, vol. 12, p. 646.

22 See, Kazuo Wada, 'Jun suichoku togo gata soshiki no keisei: Toyota no

jirei' ('The Formation of Quasi-Vertically Integrated Organizations: A Case Study of Toyota'), *Akademia* (Nanzan University), 1984, no. 83.

23 Kyoho-kai History, *Kyoho-kai no ayumi*, p. 24.

24 Ibid., p. 25.

25 The grading points given to individual suppliers are reproduced in Kazuo Wada, 'Jidosha sangyo ni okeru kaiso-teki kigyo-kan kankei no keisei: Toyota jidosha no jirei' ('The development of inter-firm relationships in the Japanese automobile industry: a case study of Toyota and its suppliers'), *Keiei-shi-gaku (Japan Business History Review)*, 1991, vol. 26, no. 2.

26 See Kanto Kyoho-kai History Editorial Committee, *30 nen no ayumi (The History of the First 30 Years)*, privately published, 1976, p. 32.

27 Wada, 'Jun suichoku togo gata soshiki no keisei'.

28 *Kyoho News*, 5 January 1967.

29 Seisei Kato, *My Years with Toyota*, privately published, 1981, p. 62.

30 See Taiichi Ono, 'Toyota seisan hoshiki' ('Toyota Production System'), *Daiyamondo*, 1978, pp. 49–51; Shigeo Shingo, *Study of 'Toyota' Production System from Industrial Engineering Viewpoint*, Tokyo, Japan Management Association, 1981, pp. 136–7, 256–7.

31 See the Appendices of *Toyota: A History*.

32 In 1956, for example, Toyota twice reduced the price of the Model SKB truck: ibid., p. 136.

33 Kato, *My Years with Toyota*, p. 69.

34 *Toyota: A History*, p. 138; Kato, *My Years with Toyota*, p.77.

35 Nihon Jinbun Kagaku-kai (ed.), *Gijutsu kakushin no shakai-teki eikyo (Social Effects of Technical Innovation)*, Tokyo, University of Tokyo Press, 1963, p. 58. Also see *Toyota Jidosha 30 nenshi*, p. 506.

36 *Toyota Management*, November 1961, p. 39.

37 Ibid., August 1959, p. 28; *Toyota Jidosha 30 nenshi*, p. 464.

38 *Toyota shinbun (Toyota News)*, 2 December 1961.

39 On this survey, and Toyota's policy towards its suppliers, see Wada, 'Jidosha sangyo ni okeru kaiso-teki kigyo-kan kankei no keisei', pp. 15–17.

40 Masao Nemoto, *TQC to toppu bu-kacho no yakuwari (TQC and the Role of Middle Management)*, Tokyo, Nikkagiren, 1983, pp. 151–2.

41 *Toyota Management*, December 1969, p. 35.

42 The *kanban* system is a scheme for controlling the amount of production at each step of the production process, using *kanban* (plates or slips) with clear operating instructions (such as the time, place, and amount of delivery). The *kanban* are circulated between steps. All steps in the production process follow the instructions of the *kanban*. For details of the *kanban* system, see Ono, *Toyota seisan hoshiki*.

43 For details of how the *kanban* system spread throughout suppliers, see Haruhito Shiomi, 'Kigyo gurupu no kanri-teki togo' ('Administrative Integration of a Company Group'), *Oikonomika*, Nagoya City University, vol. 22, no. 1.

44 In 1966, Toyota introduced its best-selling model, the Corolla. Targeted specifically at white-collar workers, it was Toyota's response to market trends which indicated that increasingly buyers wanted medium-size and small cars.

45 *Toyota Management*, December 1969, p. 35.

46 Ibid., May 1970, p. 26. Even in the late 1980s the personnel in Toyota's

purchasing department numbered only about 300. This was in sharp contrast with the 6,000 in GM's purchasing department. Cf. Dertouzos *et al.*, *Made in America*.

47 *Toyota no ayumi*, pp. 358–60.
48 This includes management policy, the assurance of product quality, cost management, and so on.

3 Innovation by externalization: a new organizational strategy for the high-tech industries – Fuji Denki, Fujitsu and Fanuc

Seiichiro Yonekura and Hans-Jürgen Clahsen

INTRODUCTION

The age of industrial capitalism has been closely associated with the rise of huge, diversified, multi-divisional companies which are involved in many different activities and which operate in several, often unrelated, market fields. As Alfred Chandler has pointed out, this pattern of growth through the creation of a multi-divisional structure had its origin in the United States. In the late nineteenth and early twentieth centuries, companies in capital-intensive industries consolidated to form single large enterprises, through mergers or takeovers. These companies moved on to pursue economies of scale by vertically integrating their organizational functions, thus optimizing the flow of raw materials, semi-finished goods and final products. Thus the multi-functional organization emerged, along with the rise of the first generation of big business.

After the First World War, these large integrated companies began to exploit their accumulated resources by diversifying into related or sometimes unrelated business fields. Diversification was started so that they could pursue economies of scope by maximizing their internal managerial resources. Because of the great difficulties of managing unrelated businesses, some pioneering companies created a multidivisional organization as early as the 1920s. But because diversification was not widespread in the 1930s and 1940s, the multidivisional structure did not expand. By the 1950s, however, as they increasingly encountered maturing core markets, companies were forced to move into new markets, especially those related to newly developed technologies in the fields, for example, of electrical engineering and chemicals. Many companies achieved diversification by adding new divisions to existing ones, thus adopting a multi-divisional organization. Over time, these companies grew larger and larger and came to represent what are now widely regarded as modern economic enterprises.[1] In addition, some economists came to regard the multi-divisional structure as a cost-saving form of organization, since internal distribution and transaction of managerial resources, capital, human resources, actual goods and information, was far cheaper and more rational than external distribution and transaction through the market mechanism.[2]

As their organizational structures grew to become even more complex hierarchies, however, multi-divisional firms began to lose their earlier dynamism. Increasingly, many of them came to be governed through intricate bureaucratic procedures which hampered entrepreneurial impetus and led to a slowdown of economic activity. Moreover, these complex, hierarchically organized companies also became afflicted by conflicts and struggles between the corporate centre and the divisions, or between divisions – another phenomenon which had a negative effect on their ability to exploit available economic resources as fully as management would have liked.[3]

Thus, while giant multi-divisional firms had once been regarded as the powerful driving force behind the rise of industrial capitalism in the United States and Europe, they came more and more to be associated in many industries with sluggish bureaucracy and the loss of entrepreneurial dynamism. Rather than being at the forefront of economic and technological development, they were characterized by the waste of economic resources within their own organizations due to inter-divisional friction and tiresome administrative procedures. As a result, in the 1970s and 1980s, the small business venture and internal corporate venture came to be recognized in the United States as useful alternative organizational forms.[4]

While the paradigm of big business came to represent the mainstream of industrial capitalism, there were exceptions. These were enterprises which, rather than integrating into giant multi-divisional units, took a different approach to growth by way of spinning off divisions as independent companies. The spinning-off pattern of corporate growth appears to occur more frequently in Japan than in any other industrialized country.

Looking at the history of the companies which have become closely associated with the image of Japan as arguably one of the most dynamic economies of the late twentieth century, it is apparent that many of these companies were members of the pre-war *zaibatsu*, or the postwar industrial groups which have engaged in very different kinds of activities. Many of them, too, originated as the offspring of former parent companies. One example is Toyota Motor Company, which was created by Toyoda Shokki, a manufacturer of weaving looms. Another example from the same sector is Nissan, which was founded by Yoshisuke Aikawa as the car manufacturing division of the Nissan Zaibatsu. Hitachi, now Japan's leading electrical machinery and appliances company, was also established as an independent company by the Nissan Zaibatsu.[5]

There are many more examples and, without mentioning them individually, attention can be drawn to the common pattern shared by the vast majority of these – companies which were founded as offspring, to deal with a newly developed technology, and which later surpassed their parents in terms of organizational dynamism and economic performance, and often in scale as well. This led to the emergence of large enterprises which, in many cases, spun off in turn yet other new companies, thus institutionalizing the successful development and exploitation of a new technology.

This chapter will focus on a company lineage which, during the course of its history, has twice spun off new enterprises that, using state-of-the-art technologies, developed into world leaders in their markets. What follows is a case study of Fuji Denki, Fujitsu and Fanuc. Fuji Denki, a Furukawa and Siemens joint venture, spun off its telecommunications department as an independent company in 1935. This company became known as Fujitsu, which developed into a leading telecommunications technology manufacturer before the Second World War and subsequently moved into computers in the early 1960s. Initially challenging IBM in its home market, it grew over time to constitute a serious challenge to IBM's predominance worldwide. Fujitsu in turn spun off one of its own departments, dealing with computer numeric control and automation technology, to form a new company, Fanuc, which rapidly developed into one of the world's leading manufacturers of factory automation technology and robotics. It achieved market shares in its field of 50 per cent worldwide, and 70 per cent in Japan.

In order to elucidate further the developments outlined briefly above, firstly the history of the companies involved will be summarized, and then an explanation of the motives and other factors underlying this type of corporate growth pattern will be attempted.

To begin with, the case of Fuji Denki, which constitutes the point of origin for the subsequent emergence of Fujitsu and then Fanuc, must be considered.

FUJI DENKI: A JAPANESE–GERMAN JOINT VENTURE

Fuji Denki (in full, Fuji Denki Seizo Kabushiki Kaisha, which can be translated as the Fuji Electric Manufacturing Corporation Limited) was established in August 1923 as a joint venture between Furukawa Denki Kogyo, a company belonging to the Furukawa Zaibatsu, and Siemens of Germany. The newly founded company had its headquarters in Kojimachi, Tokyo, and a capital stock amounting to ¥10 million, a quarter of which was paid-up capital at the time of its establishment.

Siemens, which provided the technological knowledge regarding products and production for the new company, was at that time already able to look back on a long history of business activity in Japan. In fact, Siemens had been the first foreign manufacturing company to make direct contact with Japan. It had considered the prospect of doing business there as early as 1870, and after consulting with Japanese officials in Berlin, a young engineer, Herman Kessler, was sent to Tokyo in 1877 to establish an office there.[6]

Kessler soon succeeded in making contact with the Furukawa Zaibatsu, the largest mining concern in Japan at that time. He contracted to supply machinery for the electrification of the Ashio Copper Mine in what is now the Tochigi Prefecture. After 1896 the Tokyo Bureau of Siemens and Halske A.G. was appointed as the sole agent of Furukawa. In 1905 it changed its name to Siemens Schuckert Denki, and by 1907 employed sixteen engineers, nine of whom were Japanese and the rest German. The company engaged in marketing the full line of Siemens' products in Japan.

The outbreak of the First World War, and the joining of Japan on the side of the Alliance against Germany, forced the company to close its office and suspend business. At the same time, however, the demand for heavy machinery and chemicals relating to the war brought an economic boom to Japan, which had been suffering from a chronic trade depression ever since the end of the Russo-Japanese War.

Since imports from Europe and America of those technology-related products in high demand were interrupted by wartime activity, Japan was forced to rely on her own technological resources. In consequence, the technological foundations of the Japanese economy were enhanced to a considerable extent. But despite this, the eagerness to import foreign technology, especially in the fields of electrical machinery and chemicals (where, Japanese efforts notwithstanding, the gap was still wide), remained unabated, and contacts with foreign companies were quickly resumed after the end of the war. German companies, on the other hand, faced economic restrictions imposed by the Peace Treaty of

Versailles, which prohibited the production of and trade in goods that could potentially be used for military purposes. Furthermore, the German economy as a whole was undergoing a period of severe inflation. Thus, given the unfavourable conditions for the export of finished products to Japan, Siemens shifted its export policy from its pre-war stance of direct exports to the export of technology, which meant the provision of licences for production in Japan.

In November 1919, Siemens approached its earlier business partner Furukawa Gomei Kaisha, the holding company of the Furukawa Zaibatsu, with a proposal to set up a jointly owned and operated manufacturing company, which would produce electrical equipment based on Siemens' technologies. Given its long-standing business relationship with Siemens, Furukawa responded positively and sent an executive, Hideo Kajiyama, to Berlin. He was to support the company's Europe representative, Heitaro Inagaki, who was already engaged in talks with the Germans.[7]

Negotiations were interrupted by a severe crisis, however, brought about by a speculative venture that ended in failure, which led to the bankruptcy of Furukawa Trading Company and threatened the very foundations of the Furukawa Zaibatsu. Furukawa managed to overcome this crisis, and talks with Siemens resumed in late 1921, being brought to a successful conclusion in 1923.

The new company, Fuji Denki Seizo Kabushiki Kaisha (hereafter, Fuji Denki), was established on 22 August 1923, its capital base of ¥10 million being divided into 200,000 shares, 60,000 (30 per cent) of which were held by Siemens. The field of business of the newly established company was to be the assembly, production and marketing of heavy and light electric equipment. However, telecommunications technology, which would later develop into a crucially important business, leading to the establishment of Fujitsu, was excluded from the scope of Fuji Denki's activities. This was because both parent companies had vested interests in the field. Furukawa Denko, therefore, which had been manufacturing cables and equipment in its Yokohama factory since June 1920, continued its own telephone and telegraph activities. Siemens, on the other hand, went ahead with importing equipment from Germany.

This situation, however, was at odds with the original intention of also granting Fuji Denki the right to market Siemens-made telephone and telegraph equipment, and the above-mentioned temporary solution notwithstanding, both sides persisted in their desire to execute the original plan. After long and complicated negotiations between the German and Japanese representatives, agreement was finally reached in

June 1925. It was decided that Siemens would hand over its own telephone and telegraph division to Fuji Denki, including the entire staff, which would take over from Siemens the import and marketing of telephone switchboard equipment. In turn, Furukawa Denko would abandon its own manufacture of such equipment (its production facilities having anyway been completely destroyed by the devastating Kanto earthquake). Thus, Fuji Denki became the sole importer and distributor of Siemens-made telephone and telegraph equipment.

The newly established company, and the telephone and telegraph business in particular, enjoyed a period of brisk expansion at first. In the late 1920s, Fuji Denki won several tenders for the supply of switching systems, especially in the Kansai area around Osaka and Kobe. From 1924 to 1934, Fuji Denki imported and installed twelve switching stations, with an overall number of 46,300 circuits.[8]

The economic environment of the late 1920s and early 1930s was unstable, however. The financial crisis of 1929, which triggered a sharp decline of the yen, and the worldwide depression, which led to a worsening trade balance and rapidly declining foreign currency reserves, called for a policy of reducing imports and fostering exports in order to improve the balance of payments and prevent the outflow of reserves. Successive governments were intent on promoting the national interest; accordingly, Japanese industry came under increasing political pressure to reduce dependence on foreign products and technology and to substitute domestically manufactured products for imported ones.

Fuji Denki, which was particularly reliant on Siemens' imports in its telephone and telegraph business, was no exception to this general trend. In the field of heavy electrical equipment, the company already had a production base in Japan, and continued to reduce its dependence on Siemens' technology. As far as telecommunications technology was concerned, however, Fuji Denki's efforts to 'nationalize' production had to start almost from scratch, and the company lagged behind other manufacturers, like Oki and Hitachi, which had started producing switching systems as early as 1929.

Pressure on the company to manufacture automatic switching equipment, which was a crucial component of Japan's nationwide telephone network, increased almost daily. Moreover, the Ministry of Communications (the *Teishinsho*) introduced a new procurement policy which required a written oath from the manufacturer certifying that the equipment delivered had been produced in Japan. Given this situation, the chances of winning a public order with imported products were diminishing. Hence, when Fuji Denki received an order to equip the Osaka-Minami switching station with an automatic switching system

imported from Germany, it was able to do so only because of considerations of technological compatibility, since the stations already
existing in the Osaka region used Siemens' equipment. The Ministry,
however, made it very clear that it would not tolerate the company's
policy of installing imported systems and demanded strongly that the
equipment be made in Japan.

Concerned about the company's future, Fuji Denki's executives
entered into negotiations with Siemens on the 'nationalization' of the
production of switching systems and other telephone and telegraph
equipment. Despite apprehensions on the German side about potential
rivalry in the telecommunications field, agreement was reached and, in
May 1932, the building of a factory for the manufacture of automatic
switching systems based on Siemens' technology began within Fuji
Denki's Kawasaki complex. Construction, including the installation of
machinery imported from Germany, was completed by March 1933, and
production at the newly established telephone division began in the
same year. Thus Fuji Denki ended an era of merely importing finished
products from Siemens and entered a new phase of development.[9]

The first two automatic switching systems manufactured at the new
factory were installed in Yokohama and Osaka, and both stations
successfully commenced operations. Consequently, in June 1934, Fuji
Denki received official recognition as a supplier of switching system
equipment to the Ministry of Communications.

By this time, the overall economic climate had greatly improved
and, fostered by a new economic policy, and the demand arising from
the Manchurian Incident and its economic consequences, Fuji Denki
enjoyed (albeit briefly) a period of brisk demand from both the public
and private sectors.

Fuji Denki's two main businesses, heavy electrical machinery and
telephone equipment, expanded rapidly. In pursuing these activities,
however, an important fact regarding the company's future development became increasingly clear: its two principal fields of business bore
little relation to each other. In other words, the manufacturing and
marketing of turbines for electric power generation and the production
of switching system equipment for the national telephone network were
very different matters. Furthermore, operating two different businesses
within a single organizational structure was likely to cause friction
which would impede the company's development. In the first place,
given that turbines for power generation, and other heavy electrical
equipment, and switching system equipment were unrelated products,
Fuji Denki was forced to maintain two different production facilities,
separate research and development facilities, two sales departments,

and so on. Thus, *de facto*, the company was split into two camps, unable to reap economies of scale or enjoy the benefits of technological synergy. Secondly, given that these two camps were managed by the same organizational hierarchy, there was a fight for resources between the two sides. By the mid-1930s, therefore, voices calling for the separation of the telephone business as an independent company were discernible; the problems of having two unrelated businesses operating within the same organizational structure were becoming increasingly apparent. The difficulties encountered by Fuji Denki at this point in time were no different to those that many multi-functional business enterprises experience in the early stage of their diversification. In the United States, for instance, the Du Pont Company had encountered similar dilemmas within its diversified businesses.[10] In order to overcome these problems, Du Pont had pioneered the multi-divisional organization to co-ordinate its different business activities.

Fuji Denki, however, spun off its communications department as a separate company – Fuji Tsushinki Kabushiki Kaisha (Fuji Communications Corporation) – on 20 June 1935. There were two reasons for adopting this course. The first reason was external. In February 1935, Fuji Denki signed a territorial business agreement with Tokyo Denki (later to become Toshiba) whereby both companies would co-operate in the field of communications technology. This meant that Tokyo Denki would focus on the production and marketing of wireless communications technology, a field in which the company has been a strong performer ever since, and that Fuji Denki would focus on its expanding telephone business, with neither company invading the other's territory. The co-operation agreement included a passage which stipulated that both companies should separate off their wireless and telephone businesses respectively as independent companies and exchange 20 per cent of the shares of the newly founded companies.[11]

The second reason was a historical one. As Fuji Denki was one of the member companies of the Furukawa Zaibatsu, it was accustomed to the practice of controlling subsidiaries as independent companies. The prewar *zaibatsu* system consisted of a parent holding company and several direct and indirect subsidiaries, and it was historically quite natural for Fuji Denki to spin off its telephone manufacturing department as an independent company. Moreover, because of the absence of an antitrust law at that time, there was nothing to prevent Fuji Denki from being the largest stockholder of its subsidiaries. In fact, Fuji Denki owned 94.7 per cent of Fujitsu's stock, before it exchanged 20 per cent of the shares with Tokyo Denki.[12]

Due to the intensifying problems arising from two different business activities, the agreement with Tokyo Denki, and its historical background as a member of the Furukawa Zaibatsu, therefore, Fuji Denki's decision to separate off its telephone department and found Fuji Tsushinki Kabushiki Kaisha was a logical one. The new company later changed its name to Fujitsu, by which it will be referred to hereafter.

FUJITSU: FROM TELEPHONE MANUFACTURER TO COMPUTERS

In retrospect, Fujitsu can arguably be characterized as one of the most successful companies in post-war Japan. Today, Fujitsu is by far Japan's largest computer maker and, unlike its domestic rivals such as NEC or Hitachi, computers are its dominant field of activity, accounting for 71 per cent of total sales in the fiscal year 1990.[13] Moreover, Fujitsu appears to be one of the very few computer manufacturers, if not the only one, capable of challenging the long undisputed position of the industry's giant, IBM, which is now encountering increased competition from Fujitsu not only in Japan but also in all major international markets. Fujitsu's ability to compete stems from its efforts in research and development which have enabled it to supply computers that are highly competitive in terms of both performance and price. In addition, Fujitsu's strong performance, not only in computers but also in the field of telecommunications and semiconductors, makes it possible for the company to offer an integrated approach to the transmitting, processing and storing of data, something which IBM, for example, has yet to achieve.

When Fujitsu was established in 1935, however, it did not look as if it was set to become a forerunner in high technology. As will become apparent, Fujitsu's metamorphosis from a manufacturer of switching and carrier transmission systems for the Ministry of Communications into a high-technology enterprise was a long and winding road. To understand the nature of this transformation, and to return to the question of whether spinning off divisions as independent companies provides conditions favourable to innovation and growth which would not exist in a huge multi-divisional concern, it is necessary to examine the internal conditions prevailing in Fujitsu from the time of its foundation and to reflect on its history and the activities of its leading engineers and managers.

Founded at a time of mounting international tension, Fujitsu's development up to the end of the Second World War was strongly shaped by the stringent conditions of Japan's wartime economy. As pointed out earlier, the company's major customer was the Ministry of

Communications. Thus Fujitsu's business activities largely depended on and fluctuated according to the Ministry's demand for communication equipment. Given this dependence, and the fact that, following Japan's invasion of Manchuria, resources were increasingly drawn away from the *Teishinsho* and other ministries to the military, Fujitsu encountered the problem of its principal customer being unable to pursue its policy of expanding Japan's domestic telephone network. As a result, Fujitsu suffered a direct drop in demand, which was only partially compensated for by increased military demand for communications equipment stemming from Japan's territorial expansion in China. Moreover, along with other private industrial companies, the management of Fujitsu became increasingly subject to government control. Its factories were designated as 'Army-controlled' (*gunju kaisha*), and the purchase of raw materials and sale of finished products were subject to the imperatives of a controlled economy.

The period from the company's foundation to the end of the Second World War was thus characterized by scarce resources, labour shortages, increasing government interference, and, finally, the destruction of production facilities by Allied air raids. It may seem as if the war had a wholly negative influence on the company's development, but this was not entirely the case. During this period, the company also learned how to overcome its dependence on foreign (i.e. Siemens') technology. Furthermore, a handful of young engineers, who would later become the driving force behind the development of the company's computer business, gained useful experience which made them realize the crucial importance of computer technology and its significance for Fujitsu's future.

During the final years of the war, Fujitsu was involved in the development and production of a technologically complex air defence system designed to protect Tokyo from Allied air raids. It was planned that this system would first detect the position of enemy aircraft and then transmit the information to the anti-aircraft defences in and around Tokyo; anti-aircraft artillery would then be directed according to the data supplied. Fujitsu's development team – which included a young engineer named Taiyu Kobayashi, who would later become one of the leading men behind Fujitsu's venture into the computer business and the first Fujitsu president and chairman to have risen from within the company – was in charge of the data transmission system. But although this system was brought into operation, it did not produce the intended results. While the individual parts of the system worked faultlessly, there was a fatal flaw – the absence of an adequate calculating device for the processing of data concerning the position of enemy aircraft. This meant that calculations of flight path and future position had to rely on a mechanical computing device which was far too slow to cope with the task. As a result, the system as a whole was a failure. This left a very strong impression on Kobayashi and the other members of the team. They realized the urgent need for such a facility, and felt an over-powering desire to develop and produce what they referred to as an 'electric computing device'. By the end of the war, therefore, there had emerged a small group of engineers who understood the value of speedy computers and who had sufficient curiosity and courage to pursue the goal of developing them. The main business activity of Fujitsu, however, remained focused entirely on switching and transmission systems. At the time, the company did not see any business opportunity in automatic computing.

After the war, Fujitsu poured its scarce resources into the restoration of the telephone system that had been destroyed by the bombing: the interest in computers remained alive only in the minds of some of the young engineers. The impetus behind Fujitsu's transformation from a pure telecommunications equipment manufacturer to its present status as a computer giant was provided by this handful of young engineers, who formed a group within the company. At best, this group was not taken seriously, and, at worst, it was despised by those who were then the mainstay of the firm, the 'communications people'.

The most senior member of the group was Taiyu Kobayashi, who had joined Fujitsu in the year of its foundation. The other leaders of the group joined Fujitsu and the computer enthusiasts after the war. Toshio Ikeda can, with good reason, be considered the intellectual leader of the 'computer group' and the brain behind Fujitsu's computer develop-ment, until his sudden death in 1964 at the age of fifty-one. Gene Amdahl, founder of the Amdahl Corporation and a personal friend of Ikeda, described Ikeda's contribution to the company as follows:

> Dr. Ikeda was the driving force in computers within Fujitsu Limited, and under his persuasive leadership Fujitsu had advanced its com-puter activities to where they were contributing approximately half the revenues of Fujitsu.[14]

Ikeda joined Fujitsu in 1946 and worked in the telephone develop-ment section. For the young Ikeda, who had developed an interest in automatic computing technology in his student days at the Tokyo Institute of Technology, this was a rather boring assignment and he soon managed to make his way into the research laboratory and thus into the group which shared his interest in computers. He found personal support from the then head of research and development, Hanzo Omi, who became a kind of protective father-figure for the computer enthusiasts.

Then there was Shinsuke Shiokawa who belonged to the research laboratory for electric power distribution technology at Fuji Denki. In 1938, he published the results of his research on a binary digit calculation system, which would become a relay-based computing device. When he presented his research at the annual meeting of the Academy for Electric Sciences in 1938, few people understood his work, which was several years ahead of the mainstream of technological development.[15] He was supported, however, by a professor at Tokyo University, Hideo Yamashita, who became a promoter of computer development and a mediator between the industry and potential customers after the war. Fuji Denki paid little attention to Shiokawa's research activities. His research was not considered relevant to the development of military technology, and the increasingly serious shortage of parts and raw materials brought an end to his wartime research activities.

Soon after the war, Shiokawa left Fuji Denki, disappointed that he had not been given enough attention and support to realize his dream of developing a computing device based on his relay technology. He then worked for a couple of years as an instructor at a technical training centre for Japan's national railway. One day, by chance, he read an article about IBM having developed an electric relay computer based on the same concept as his own research. Greatly encouraged by the fact that there was indeed the possibility of a practical application for his research, he contacted Fujitsu, where he was warmly welcomed by Fujitsu's 'computer group'. The group's position, in turn, was reinforced by now having an expert in computer logic as a member.

The group surrounding Kobayashi, Ikeda and Shiokawa represented the core and origin of Fujitsu's metamorphosis into a computer company. Since the members of the group were relatively young and inexperienced, and were considered in a sense to be outsiders within Fujitsu, they needed a high-ranking promoter in order to be able to pursue their activities within the existing organizational framework. This role was played by Hanzo Omi, chief of Fujitsu's research and development section. Omi supported the group as much as he was able to. He himself had realized the need for the development of computing systems and the prospects offered by a future market for data processing technology.[16] Furthermore, he had been interested in the latent relationship between communications technology amd data processing technology. In particular, after reading a book by Dr Kelly, director of the telephone research centre at the Bell Laboratories, he concluded that there was a mutual relationship between these two sectors and that it would be beneficial for the company's development as a whole to pursue business in both fields.[17]

Ikeda described the situation at the beginning of the group's efforts to develop computers as follows:

> For some strange reason, just the very same time I was getting interested in computers, Shiokawa joined the company. He had been working on relay technology based on the binary system since before the war and really did have some fantastic ideas. At that time, when Shiokawa came to Fujitsu, our group had by chance got a blueprint of the circuit diagram of the ENIAC computer. Only one single page though. We found it interesting and, using about 90 vacuum tubes, constructed a counting circuit. Before long, everybody had developed a profound interest in automatic calculating devices, and the idea of gradually developing a computer had emerged from amongst the young engineers. Thus, after Shiokawa had joined us, the idea to develop a computer quickly became the main topic within our group.[18]

At about the same time, the Tokyo Stock Exchange was considering installing a computer for the automatic processing of transactions in order to cope with the increased activity resulting from the economic boom which followed the outbreak of the Korean War. This involved Hideo Yamashita, the Tokyo University professor mentioned earlier, who then functioned as a kind of adviser to the Stock Exchange and as a mediator within the industry. Yamashita remembered Shiokawa and his research activities and contacted Ikeda's computer group. He asked them if they were interested in developing a data processing system for the Stock Exchange. Taiyu Kobayashi, then head of the research and development section, jumped at the idea, and Ikeda's computer group, with Takuma Yamamoto, the current chairman, Akinori Yamaguchi, Shiokawa as the adviser, and Hanzo Omi in the background, embarked on developing what was eventually to be Japan's first relay computer.[19]

To cut a long story short, the group managed to develop a data processing system which followed the specifications laid down by the Stock Exchange Committee. This system was not selected, however, because its calculating speed was inferior to that of a system offered by the Univac Corporation of America. But this defeat seems not to have discouraged those involved in the Fujitsu system. On the contrary, Ikeda and his team became even more motivated and went ahead with the development of a general purpose computer based on the knowledge and experienced gained from the Stock Exchange project.

Ikeda even managed to get the go-ahead for their computer project from the then chairman of Fujitsu. He described the rather curious circumstances in which he persuaded Junichi Ko to give his approval to the group's plan to develop a general purpose computer. He happened to meet Ko during the intermission of a performance of the Russian ballet and asked him to support the venture. Enchanted by both the beautiful ballerinas and wine, Ko agreed within minutes, and the project which resulted in the development of the Facom-100 (Fujitsu Automatic Computer) began.[20] Ikeda explained that, 'This wasn't a real decision from above to develop a computer. Rather, it took the form of something like; well, if there are some fellows within the company who are fond of computers let them go ahead. They won't do much harm.'[21]

This kind of approach appears to have been prevalent within the company, which was by then enjoying brisk business stemming from the ambitious expansion plans of the newly founded Nippon Telephone and Telegraph Public Corporation (NTTPC). Ikeda's computer group seems to have been regarded with paternalistic tolerance, and its members were given sufficient freedom to pursue their activities. There was apparently little opposition. This atmosphere of limited expectation and paternalistic protection proved to be ideal for Ikeda and his team. They were protégés, but few people seem to have taken them seriously. The general attitude prevailing within the company can best be illustrated by citing an example: at the time of the development of the Facom-100 machine, the group leader, Ikeda, was in the habit of gathering the other members of the team at his home. While listening to classical music, he would discuss the ongoing project until late into the night. Whereas the rest of the team would then be at work at nine o'clock the next morning, Ikeda himself would sleep until noon, then work at home until the late afternoon, showing up eventually at the company after five. Wages at that time were, however, paid on a daily basis, so Ikeda received no income and was forced to sell his library to a secondhand bookshop in order to make some money.[22] There were those in the company who demanded Ikeda's dismissal, but his direct superiors, Kobayashi and Omi, supported him. Indeed, they even changed his salary basis from a daily rate to a fixed monthly one.[23] However this episode is interpreted, the ability of the company to accommodate the eccentric behaviour of an extremely gifted engineer like Ikeda was remarkable. One wonders whether Fujitsu would have been able to nurture people like Ikeda and his computer team if the communications business had remained a part of Fuji Denki alongside its heavy electrical equipment division.

Going back to Fujitsu's transformation into a computer maker, it has to be stressed that the computers developed in the pioneering days were a technological, but not a commercial success. And although subsequent computers, such as the Facom 128, 128B, 138A, 318A, 415A, 514 and 524, received a positive reaction in the market, production facilities were both insufficient and inefficient. There was no factory exclusively assigned to the production of computers; their manufacture was dispersed throughout the Kawasaki complex. Moreover, Fujitsu used not only relays and transistors as components for its computers, but also 'parametron' components, which were based on a technology developed and employed only in Japan. As the trend towards transistors and, later, integrated circuits became clear, the parallel development of relay, parametron and transistor computers was abandoned in favour of concentration on the latter. However, this did not happen until the early 1960s.

This was the situation which existed within Fujitsu by the end of the 1950s. The company was still almost entirely dependent on its communications business, and hence on NTTPC's purchase programme. At the same time, it was manufacturing technologically advanced computers which were neither money-making nor solidly based within Fujitsu's strategy concept. Ikeda's 'crazy bunch', as they were referred to by the communications side of the company, existed, but they still remained outsiders.

All this changed dramatically when Kanjiro Okada became president of Fujitsu in November 1959. Already sixty-nine years old, Okada had formerly held the post of president of the board of Furukawa Mining Company, the central business within the Furukawa Zaibatsu. Immediately after the war, he had been forced to resign from all posts within the Furukawa group due to the purge conducted by the Supreme Command for the Allied Powers. Prior to his appointment at Fujitsu, he served for more than a decade as vice-president of the Ube Kosan (one of the large mining companies) in Yamaguchi Prefecture in southern Japan.

Okada had received his business education at Tokyo College of Commerce (now Hitotsubashi University) and had accumulated managerial expertise through practical business experience as president of Furukawa Mining and vice-president of Ube Kosan before and after the war. Fujitsu, facing a period of unprecedented expansion in its business activities, needed a person who would be able to represent a more business-orientated management approach than had hitherto been the company's style. However, this is not to say that Okada did not have a strong interest in technology. On the contrary, although not an engineer, and having little knowledge of the technological aspects of communications and computers, he nevertheless embarked on a thorough study of the principles of electronics soon after his appointment. In fact, this became a famous episode in the company, and young engineers to whom Okada turned for lectures on electronics and computer science seem to have received considerable encouragement from it.

Despite Okada's efforts to acquire an understanding of the technological aspects of Fujitsu's business, it may, in retrospect, be concluded that he was not entirely sure about the future prospects of the computer business. Not long after becoming head of the company, he reorganized it, introducing a kind of multi-divisional structure, with two major divisions – telecommunications and electronics. The electronics division did not have a computer department though. It was set up to deal with the whole range of the electronics business – electronic devices, semiconductors, and electronics machinery – but there was no specific mention of the computer.[24]

However, over time it became increasingly obvious that Okada regarded the computer and its related technology as the company's future mainstay, and the computer business as the market field with the most promising growth potential. He thus focused all his energy on turning Fujitsu away from its dependence on NTTPC and into an aggressive high-technology firm. It was in 1962 that an electric computing department was established within the electronics division. Okada made it clear that he considered this would be the future driving force behind the firm's development, yet he also required the computer department to operate with responsibility for the company's financial position and profitability. He was not, it seems, willing to tolerate the computer business running into debt. Okada was a businessman, not a computer maniac.

With the firm's future thus hinging on the development of the computer, Ikeda, Kobayashi, Yamamoto and the other people belonging to the original computer group, found themselves in an increasingly important position within Fujitsu. Members of this group, who had hitherto been treated as children playing with expensive toys and who had been developing computers without having to worry about the economic implications of their activities, suddenly had to take into consideration, and accept responsibility for, the performance of the entire company. Ikeda described Okada's significance for Fujitsu when he said that, 'In a managerial sense, the real start of Fujitsu's computers was the time when Okada was appointed president.'[25]

By the time Okada resigned as president, Fujitsu had become a quite different company from the one he had taken over eleven years previously. First of all, as mentioned above, its name had changed from Fuji Tsushinki Seizo Kabushiki Kaisha to 'Fujitsu', the partial elimination of 'Tsushinki' (communications equipment) from the new name reflecting the diminishing importance of the telecommunications division. Computers had become the main business activity, accounting for roughly 80 per cent of total sales. The company's image had changed too. Formerly regarded as a conservative supplier of telephones and switching systems to the NTTPC, the whole of Fujitsu came to be known as the 'crazy bunch', a term previously applied only to Ikeda's group.

Fujitsu had become Japan's foremost computer maker. Its share of the domestic market grew to surpass that of IBM Japan and it became able to compete with IBM in foreign markets as well. Fujitsu developed the Facom-230 series, which challenged IBM's 360 series and demonstrated technological superiority, the 230-60 machine proving to be the most powerful general purpose computer of its day. This had been achieved without any of the technological help from foreign companies on which Fujitsu's domestic rivals relied so heavily. The metamorphosis was made possible by a set of specific circumstances within the firm and the surrounding environment.

Firstly, Fuji Denki's decision to spin off its telecommunications department and establish Fujitsu, providing the expanding telecommunications business with the opportunity to pursue its business activities as a specialized company, was very important. Yet it was not really a well-planned decision, nor one based on a perfect understanding of the merits of decentralization. Although some people seem to have realized that the heavy electric equipment and switching systems businesses had little in common, and would be better separated into two different companies, there was certainly no clear plan or notion of the consequences. Rather the separation was the result of an external factor, and the historical environment. However, it was this separation that made Fujitsu's transformation possible. As already indicated, there was a clear difference between Fuji Denki's heavy electrical equipment and telephone businesses. There can be no doubt that there would have been much larger differences between heavy electric equipment, telephones and computers, and considerable difficulties if they had all been under one roof. The computer group, that 'crazy bunch', would not have had as much freedom had they been part of a large divisional organization.

Secondly, Fujitsu was fortunate in having someone like Toshio Ikeda, who has rightly been described as a computer genius. None the less,

Ikeda would not have been able to accomplish what he did without the backing of people such as Taiyu Kobayashi and Hanzo Omi. It was they who realized both the potential of computer technology and of Ikeda's genius, and the need to protect and promote Ikeda even when his eccentric behaviour violated the rules of company conduct.

Thirdly, there was Kanjiro Okada, who made the business decision to transform the company into a computer manufacturer on a broad scale. Ikeda and his group were passionate about computers, but it was not a business passion. Okada had the vision to turn computers into the breadwinning business of the company.

Endowed with capable and willing people, the group surrounding Ikeda was given sufficient freedom to pursue its ideas and develop them into real projects. Its members were able to become inventors, developers and entrepreneurs of a new technology within the existing company. They did not have to leave the firm in order to realize their plans, as, for example, did Gene Amdahl. He was forced to leave IBM and establish his own company when he was not given the leeway to realize his plans within IBM.

If this theory of externalization and decentralization as agents enabling innovative behaviour holds true, then why, it might be argued, did Fujitsu not spin off its computer business as an independent company, rather than setting out on the painful route of transforming itself into a computer maker? The answer is that a spin-off, in this case, would not have been possible since the computer business would have been unable to develop or survive, either technologically or economically, without the telecommunications business. It was the revenue flowing in from the booming telecommunications business, which was poured into computer research and development, that enabled Fujitsu to diversify into computers. The telecommunications side, consisting largely of business with the NTTPC, fostered the computer side and provided it with sufficient funds for its costly development activities. Furthermore, computer components were partially developed and produced with the help of technology obtained from telecommunications. Thus the telecommunications business functioned as a benevolent mother to the computer business. As Matsuro Umetsu of Fujitsu has pointed out:

> Fujitsu was founded as a company within the Furukawa group, which was known for copper, silver mining, transportation and other things, and when I joined Fujitsu in 1954, it was a totally humble company. There was Ikeda's group which was being referred to as 'the crazy bunch'. They were developing computers while generating enormous losses. Needless to say, the company's mainstay was

the telecommunications with NTTPC as the dominant customer, and this might not have been a business which could be called 'business', (since NTTPC's procurement was fixed in 5-year expansion plans).[26]

Fujitsu, which started as an independent company in 1935, as a spin-off from Fuji Denki's communications technology department, has grown to become the second largest computer maker in the world. During this period of continuous growth, Fujitsu has itself set up new companies. In 1990, the Fujitsu group consisted of 116 related and thirty-five affiliated companies in Japan and forty related companies abroad. The majority of these companies enjoy far-reaching independence from their mother company. They specialize in specific fields of technology, such as software engineering, thus enabling them to focus their resources and to achieve specialized knowledge and skills. This process seems to function much more smoothly in independent, spun-off companies than in huge multi-divisional concerns where technologically different businesses exist as groups under a centralized top management and are forced to compete for resources.

Attention will now be drawn to a company spun off by Fujitsu from one of its most profitable areas of business on technological, managerial and market-related grounds. This is the case of Fanuc, the leading manufacturer of numeric control devices and robotics.

FANUC: A SMALL GIANT

Fanuc's history, like that of its parent company Fujitsu, is the story of people who took the initiative in the development and application of a new technology. In the case of Fujitsu, Toshio Ikeda has been mentioned as the father of its computer technology. Similarly, Fanuc's history is closely connected with the name of its current president, Seiemon Inaba. There were further parallels. Like Ikeda, Inaba had, with a small group of young engineers, been undertaking research on numeric control, a new technology. They too were outside the mainstream of the firm, and they too were given enough freedom and patronage to enable them to pursue their research and development activities without being constrained by short-term financial goals.

The members of Inaba's group proved their competence as researchers and engineers by going on to develop the first numeric control (NC) in Japan in 1956, and the first continuous-path NC and the first electro-hydraulic pulse motor in the following year. The electro-hydraulic pulse motor, in particular, was a personal achievement of Inaba.

When Okada became president of the company in 1959, the position of Inaba's group began to change. From that time on, and here again there were parallels with Ikeda's group, they were no longer regarded as outsiders who could play around with technology without making any contribution to the company's performance. In 1962, Okada told Inaba, then head of the NC section, that, 'The basis of all business activity is profit. I would like to see your section in the black.'[27] Being made accountable for corporate profitability, the attitude of Inaba and his group changed from being solely concerned with developing technologically superior NC machines to becoming 'business-oriented'.

In 1965, Inaba managed to make his automatic control business profitable. Compared with Fujitsu's total sales of ¥152.6 billion in the fiscal year of 1970, the total sales of the automatic control section were only ¥10 billion, but the profit–sales ratio was more than 20 per cent while that of Fujitsu as a whole was only 6.7 per cent.[28] Given these figures, it is understandable that there was considerable opposition when a plan was put forward to make the automatic control section a separate company:

> The fruits of our long-term investment are finally about to ripen. At this point in time, there is no way to separate the NC business. On the contrary, the profit from the NC section should flow into computers which need any money they can possibly have. Making it a separate company would be absurd.[29]

These and similar opinions were frequently voiced within the firm. The president, Okada, was also negative about separation, but in 1972 he died suddenly from cancer. He had been succeeded as president in 1970 by Yoshimitsu Kora, and it was Kora who made the decision to establish Fanuc. Taiyu Kobayashi, Kora's successor, described the situation thus:

> President Okada's style was that of centralized control. In contrast to this, Kora favoured a decentralized management style. At the time immediately preceding the separation of the NC section, Fujitsu's business activity was heavily focused on computers. Thus, the chairman and other people involved in the decision, thought that computers and NCs, the technology and market structures of which are quite different, under the same management would be detrimental to both businesses.[30]

He explained further that,

> At a time of drastic technological change it is necessary to have a leader who is able to fully comprehend the technology involved. In

the case of NC technology, the only one within the company who understood this field was Inaba. Therefore, Kora decided that it would be better to have something like an 'Inaba NC Manufacturing Corporation'.

As can be seen from these accounts, the main promoter of the plan to establish a separate company was Kora himself. Indeed, the decision to go ahead was undertaken on his authority, in the face of strong opposition.

In December 1972, the NC section was established as a separate company named the Fujitsu Fanuc Corporation. The president of the new company was Kora himself, president of Fujitsu. But the person in real charge was Seiemon Inaba, then a board member.

From the time of its foundation, Fanuc emphasized its status as an independent company, and the influence exerted by its parent has since been in decline. For example, while Fujitsu initially owned 100 per cent of Fanuc's shares, this proportion has gradually fallen, to the present 34 per cent. As Inaba has observed, 'Fanuc is neither a subsidiary nor an affiliated company of Fujitsu. I dare say, Fujitsu is nothing more than the biggest shareholder and Fanuc is nothing more than a member of the Fujitsu group, that's all.'[31]

Kobayashi explained Fujitsu's attitude to the development of Fanuc as follows:

In order for Fanuc to continue to grow, I think it best to leave things to Inaba. If you have good people and money, you can manage any business, so it is said. However, for a company like Fanuc which is dealing with a completely new technology, this would not be enough. The top leaders have to be experts on the technology involved, as well as the conditions of the market in which the firm is operating. Thus, if the leader isn't quite a kind of superman, this would not be possible. Therefore, it is best to put such a person in charge and leave things to him. And Inaba is indeed the appropriate person for the job. From his days at Fujitsu onward, he has been responsible for technology development, manufacturing, as well as for sales.[32]

And regarding Fujitsu's relationship with Fanuc, Kobayashi stated that

it is desirable for Fujitsu to limit its role to that of a supplier of venture capital which has been invested in the venture business Fanuc. There have been voices saying Fujitsu shouldn't lower its shareholding below 50% and retain its status as a parent company, but I think this is not necessary and would not go beyond sheer formalism anyway.[33]

Ever since Fanuc was established, it's management have enjoyed wide-ranging independence in their decision-making activities. The firm has developed into a world leader of NC technology and robotics. Its profit–sales ratio for the fiscal year 1990 was a phenomenal 37.1 per cent, compared to Fujitsu's 6.0 per cent.[34] Such growth has been based first and foremost on the company's technological leadership, but Fanuc has been able to make full use of, and develop further this technology because it has been free to operate unfettered by the constraints of a multi-divisional concern. Inaba called his company 'Small Giant', and declared that his managerial principle was to increase sales without increasing the workforce.[35]

CONCLUSION

This chapter has analysed as an organizational pattern for innovative behaviour the spinning off of divisions within large business enterprises to form smaller, less bureaucratic, independent companies. It has focused on the corporate history of Fuji Denki, Fujitsu and Fanuc, and briefly described their historical development.

Although this chapter set out to discuss organizational strategy, it is clear that the most important driving force behind Fujitsu's trans-formation from a conservative communications equipment manufacturer into its present status as an all-round information technology company was its dedicated human resources, people like Toshio Ikeda, Taiyu Kobayashi, Shinsuke Shiokawa, Hanzo Omi, Kanjiro Okada and their like. Fanuc's emergence as the 'IBM of the numeric control industry', also, was initiated by the strong leadership of Seiemon Inaba. At the earliest stage of computer development within Fujitsu, a number of capable engineers around Ikeda formed an informal computer group which shared a common interest in automatic computing devices. Subsequently, this group started research into computer technology and developed the first relay computer in Japan, the Facom-100. Clearly their research and development activity was not part of the firm's strategy, nor had it been ordered from above. At the very beginning, Fujitsu's top management might not even have been aware of the group's existence. However, the group managed to obtain informal permission to continue its work from the president, Junichi Ko, although its members continued to be regarded as outsiders within Fujitsu until Kanjiro Okada became president. Ikeda and his group can be described as entrepreneurs within the enterprise. The same can be said of Inaba and his NC research and development group. They too staged a 'revolution from below', pursuing their activities without recognition from, and sometimes even without the consent of, management. Why and how did these informal groups survive within the existing organization? It is now necessary to return to the question of organization.

Smaller is better

When Fuji Denki separated off its communications business as a new company, those involved in the decision presumably did not realize its implications for the relationship between future innovative entrepreneurship and organizational size. Rather, the decision was part of a historical process. The crucial factor, however, was the size of the organization. When Fuji Denki spun off its telecommunications division as Fujitsu, it had 4,000 employees while Fujitsu had 700. In 1945, at the end of the Second World War, Fujitsu employed 4,119 in four factories, while Fuji Denki employed 15,200 in six factories. Although both companies had to trim their workforces in the chaotic period after the war, Fujitsu was sufficiently small and flexible to allow enthusiastic engineers to commit themselves to innovation. In other words, Fujitsu was more open towards new technology and less constrained by vested interests. As already mentioned, Fujitsu was able to keep its important human assets by changing, if necessary, its normal rules of work for them. Kobayashi changed the daily-rate wage to a fixed monthly one for Ikeda, whose attendance at his workplace was irregular. In a bureaucratic organization, this would not have been possible. In addition, the proximity of the corporate office and the factory site was important. Both Fujitsu's corporate office and its operational departments were at its Kawasaki factory site. This meant that a chief executive like Okada was not a remote figure, but was conscious of everything that was going on. When necessary, he talked to Ikeda and Inaba directly.

In order to pursue and adopt innovations, firms should be small and flexible enough to give their 'champions' freedom, even if this sometimes requires them to change their rules and regulations. This was also the story of Fanuc. Learning from practical experience, Fujitsu executives realized that the smaller an organization is, the more innovatively it behaves. Kora, then president of Fujitsu, delegated authority to Inaba to develop his beloved NC technology in a separated company, Fanuc. Furthermore, by reducing its ownership share, Fujitsu has given Fanuc almost total autonomy.

'The captain bites his tongue until it bleeds'[36]

At the same time, however, Ikeda's computer group and Inaba's NC enthusiasts were not totally on their own. Members of these two groups had the necessary informal support and promotion of their seniors. Omi and Kobayashi were the protectors, buffers and mentors of the creative youngsters. For innovative behaviour, both dedicated young people, the so-called 'champions', and protectors, the so-called 'executive champions', are necessary.[37] The expression 'the captain bites his tongue until it bleeds', describes how executive champions like Omi, Kobayashi and Kora felt when they delegated the authority to develop new products. However, to establish these two groups as business units, it was also necessary to have someone like Okada who could give them a feeling of responsibility as well as freedom. Both Ikeda and Inaba recalled that Okada had changed them from being mere technology fanatics into business-oriented leaders. Fujitsu was fortunate to have had all these talented people within the firm at the same time.

Whether Fujitsu would have become a computer company if it had remained a division of Fuji Denki is no more than a hypothetical question. Similarly, it is impossible to determine whether Fanuc would have been able to reach its current position as world leader in the NC and robotics markets had it continued to exist within the computer maker Fujitsu. However, it can be said that separating off as a smaller independent company that part of a firm which engages in a technology and market different from the core business, appears to be a strong means of enhancing innovative behaviour and technological change. In the case of industries characterized by rapid changes in technological innovations and consumer needs, in particular, the externalization strategy which has been examined in this chapter seems to be more effective than the traditional multi-divisional strategy.

The current discussion about corporate entrepreneurship focuses on this point. As Burgelman and Sayles state:

> Large, established corporations and new, maturing firms alike are confronted with the problem of maintaining their growth, if not their existence, by exploiting to the fullest the unique resource combinations they have assembled. Increasingly, there is an awareness that internal entrepreneurs are necessary for firms to achieve this.[38]

Regarding the growing significance of so-called 'intrapreneuring', they point out that:

> it seems to us that the development currently crystallizing in American business heralds an epoch-making change. . . . We believe

the change may well be of the same magnitude as the one that occurred during the first quarter of the 20th century, which led to the organizational innovation represented by the 'divisionalized firm' as brilliantly documented in Alfred D. Chandler's landmark study on strategy and structure.[39]

Interestingly, while this development is a current one in the United States and Europe, Japanese companies have been experiencing and practising intracorporate entrepreneurship for some hundred years.

NOTES

1 Alfred D. Chandler Jr, *Scale and Scope: The Dynamism of Industrial Capitalism*, Cambridge, Mass., Harvard University Press, 1990.
2 See Oliver Williamson, *Markets and Hierarchies: Analysis and Antitrust Implications*, New York, Free Press, 1975.
3 For the bureaucratic decline of the large multi-divisional corporations, see Gifford Pinciot, *Intrapreneuring*, New York, Harper and Row, 1985; and Robert Burgelman and Leonard Sayles, *Inside Corporate Innovation*, New York, Free Press, 1986.
4 Richard Florida and Martin Kenney, *The Break-through Illusion*, New York, Basic Books, 1990.
5 See Masaru Udagawa, *Shinko zaibatsu* (*New Industrial Zaibatsu*), Tokyo, Nihon Keizai Shinbunsha, 1984.
6 Fuji Denki Seizo Kabushiki Kaisha Shashi Henshu Iinkai (ed.), *Fuji Denki Seizo Kabushiki Kaisha Shashi* (*History of Fuji Denki*), Tokyo, Fuji Denki Seizo Kabushiki Kaisha, 1957, p. 2.
7 Fuji Tsushinki Kabushiki Kaisha Shashi Henshu Iinkai (ed.), *Fujitsu Shashi I* (*History of Fujitsu I*), Tokyo, Fujitsu Kabushiki Kaisha, 1964, p. 4.
8 Ibid., p. 12.
9 Ibid., p. 14.
10 Alfred D. Chandler Jr, *Strategy and Structure: Chapters in the History of the American Industrial Enterprise*, Cambridge, Mass., MIT Press, 1967, pp. 83–96.
11 *Fujitsu Shashi I*, pp. 23–35. Tokyo Denki established Tokyo Denki Musen (Tokyo Electric Wireless Corporation) in October 1935.
12 Ibid., p. 180.
13 Fujitsu Kabushiki Kaisha, *Yukashoken Hokoku-Sho* (Annual Report), 1990.
14 Gene Amdahl, 'Dr. Ikeda, The International Man' in Fujitsu Kabushiki Kaisha (ed.), *Ikeda Kinenronbunshu* (*Essays in Commemoration of Ikeda*), Tokyo, Fujitsu Kabushiki Kaisha, 1978, p. 229.
15 Hiroshi Matsuo, *Daitanna Chosen* (*Bold Challenge*), Tokyo, Aobashuppan, 1978, pp. 87–8.
16 Taiyu Kobayashi, *Tomokaku Yatte Miro*, Tokyo, Toyokeizaishinposha, 1983, pp. 41–4.
17 Hanzo Omi, 'Ikeda Toshio no Omoide' ('My Memories of Ikeda') in *Ikeda Kinenronbunshu*, pp. 224–5.
18 'Ikeda san no Kotoba' ('Ikeda's Words') in ibid., p. 202.

19 Kobayashi, *Tomokaku Yatte Miro*, p. 42.
20 'Ikeda san no Kotoba', pp. 202–3.
21 Ibid., p. 202.
22 Matsuo, *Daitanna Chosen*, pp. 112–15.
23 Kobayashi, *Tomokaku Yatte Miro*, p. 44.
24 *Fujitsu Shashi I*, pp. 162–3.
25 'Ikeda san no Kotoba', p. 208.
26 Matsuo, *Daitanna Chosen*, p. 201.
27 Akihiro Kano, *Fanuc-Joshiki Hazure Keieiho* (*Fanuc, An Unusual Business Approach*), Tokyo, Kodansha, 1983, p. 59.
28 Ibid., p. 77; and see Fuji Tsushinki Kabushiki Kaisha Shashi Henshu Iinkai (ed.), *Fujitsu Shashi III* (*History of Fujitsu III*), Tokyo, Fujitsu Kabushiki Kaisha, 1986, p. 44.
29 Kobayashi, *Tomokaku Yatte Miro*, pp. 64–5; Kano, *Fanuc*, p. 78.
30 Kano, *Fanuc*, p. 77.
31 Ibid., p. 79.
32 Ibid.
33 Ibid., p. 80.
34 Fujitsu, *Yukashoken Hokoku-Sho* (Annual Report), 1990, p. 25; Fanuc, *Yukashoken Hokoku-Sho* (Annual Report), 1990, p. 29.
35 Ken Mukui, *Kiiroi robotto: Fujitsu Fanuc no Kiseki* (*Yellow robot: The Miracle of Fujitsu Fanuc*), Tokyo, Yomiuri Shinbunsha, 1982, p. 75.
36 This is a naval expression used to describe the agonizing feeling of a captain when he entrusts a junior officer with bringing the ship alongside the dock for the first time, and can hardly prevent himself from intervening. See Tom Peters and Robert Waterman, *In Search of Excellence*, New York, Harper and Row, 1981, p.266.
37 Ibid., pp. 224–5.
38 Burgelman and Sayles, *Inside Corporate Innovation*, pp. 187–8.
39 Ibid., p. 191.

4   Canon: from camera to comprehensive office automation manufacturer

Takeshi Yuzawa

Generally speaking, most large Japanese companies are grouped under the historical ties of the *zaibatsu*, but there are some exceptions which have no special link with either *zaibatsu* groups or big banks. Canon, along with other big electrical or electro-mechanical companies like Matsushita and Seiko, is independent from the *zaibatsu* and from the control of any big bank.[1] In this sense, Canon is a representative of the new business powers which emerged after the Second World War, and as such may exemplify the essential nature of the modern Japanese firm.

CANON'S ORIGINS

In 1988, the Canon group, including its related companies, achieved total sales of one billion (million million) yen. It has a workforce of 38,000, of which one-third is foreign. In terms of total turnover, Canon is ranked seventy-first among the listed companies of the Tokyo Stock Exchange, and it has the largest share (23 per cent) of the Japanese camera market. At the same time, the company is diversifying rapidly into related fields, and is now one of the players in Japanese high technology industry.

The history of Canon is not so long as that of the *zaibatsu* companies, going back just over fifty years. All the major camera manufacturers were founded before the Second World War: Konika in 1874, Nikon in 1917, Olympus and Asahi Optical Industry in 1919, and Minolta in 1928. The last of these, Canon's predecessor Seiki Optical Institute (*Seiki Kogaku Kenkyusho*) was started in 1933 by Saburo Uchida, with the support of Goro Yoshida. Yoshida was involved in the film and projection industry, and often visited Shanghai, in China, where the most advanced mechanical and optical goods and parts were then to be obtained. Experiencing some difficulty in purchasing an expensive

Leica camera, he made an intensive study of it with the intention of manufacturing the same quality of camera for himself.

Yoshida consulted Uchida, a younger brother-in-law who was working at the Yamaichi Security Company after graduating from the Law Faculty of the University of Tokyo. Uchida supplied the money for the new venture, and Yoshida tried hard to produce a camera of as high a quality as the Leica. At first, the Institute had to ask Nihon Kogaku (Japan's largest producer of optical instruments at that time although after the Second World War it was to become, with the production of the Nikon, a major rival of Seiki Optical Institute) to supply it with lenses. In 1935, already a pioneer in the field of optical goods, Nihon Kogaku employed about 2,300 people, whereas the Seiki Optical Institute employed only ninety-five. The latter not only purchased lenses and other mechanical goods from Nihon Kogaku, but was also given engineering support by the larger company. Without the help of Nihon Kogaku, the Seiki Optical Institute would not have developed successfully.[2]

Seiki Optical Institute was formally launched in 1935 to produce and sell cameras with F35mm focal-plane shutters, the first of their kind in Japan. These cameras bore the trademark 'Kwanon', a word which originated from Buddhism and which was later the basis of the company's present name – Canon. The price of the Kwanon was approximately half that of the German-made Leica and Contax and its quality was said to be similar to that of these competitors. Indeed, the Kwanon was soon to earn a good reputation, not only from the general public but also from the military authorities.

In 1937, the Seiki Optical Institute was incorporated as a joint stock company, with a capital of one million yen, and its name was changed to Seiki Kogaku Kogyo Company Ltd (thereafter, Seiki KK). Uchida became managing director, representing the five directors who comprised the board. The post of president remained vacant. It is worth noting that two doctors, T. Mitarai and M. Atsugi, were brought into senior management as auditors. After this reorganization, the company produced four kinds of camera, all of which used the Nikkoru lens manufactured by Nihon Kogaku. The quality of the cameras was greatly appreciated overseas, as well as in Japan, making a particular impact at the 1938 Montreal exhibition in Canada.[3]

When the company started its business, the country was moving towards a wartime economy. Japan withdrew from the League of Nations in 1933, following the suspension of the gold standard, and depreciated the yen to a point at which its goods could be competitive in the world market. Seiki KK was able to make use of these circumstances to develop a domestic market: on the one hand, it became quite difficult to import foreign cameras, while on the other the military authorities required the company to produce instruments for military use, such as optical measures and binoculars. Cameras were required for military reconnaissance purpose. Demand was also rising for other optical goods, including telescopes, binoculars, periscopes and surveying instruments.

In addition to military goods, Seiki KK extended the range of its products from the standard quality camera to the lower grade camera, on the one hand, and to the higher grade camera, on the other. The company also followed the strategy of branching out into the manufacture of such accessories as enlargers, Arubada filters, and special tanks for developers. Around 1938, the company also began to manufacture its own camera lenses, with the assistance of Nihon Kogaku which lent it the services of able engineers.

It is noteworthy that Seiki KK also diversified into the production of X-ray cameras, urgently needed by doctors at the time because tuberculosis was then the single largest cause of death in Japan. The military authorities also made use of X-ray cameras in checking the health of the soldiers. As well as reporting a development, technologically, from the camera, the desire to manufacture X-ray cameras may have originated with the two doctors in senior management. During the Pacific War, Seiki KK's production shifted drastically to military goods, and in 1943 it came under the direct control of the Military and Navy Departments of the Ministry of Munitions.

In 1942, Takeshi Mitarai, a doctor of obstetrics and gynaecology, graduated from his position as auditor to become Seiki KK's first president. The company's presidency had been vacant since the start, though Uchida filled the role as representative managing director. After the war, Mitarai endeavoured to restore Seiki KK's plants and reorganize its structure for the production of high-quality cameras. His maxim was to 'catch up with and exceed the "Leica"'. In 1947, Seiki KK changed its name. Adopting the brand-name of its camera, it became the Canon Camera Corporation. Two years later, it was listed on the Tokyo Stock Exchange. The Canon Camera Corporation began to adopt aggressive strategies in three respects: firstly, it focused much more on the mass market for cameras, rather than on high-quality cameras; secondly, it decided to diversify into electrical and office automation machines; and, thirdly, it pursued a policy of multinational activity, by increasing foreign investment.[4]

In the case of the mass market, Canon moved from its established policy of focusing on high-quality products, to one of producing a much more popular camera. In 1960, against strong opposition from some elements of senior management, the company produced a new kind of camera called the Canonet, which was to be its first popular 35mm compact camera with automatic exposure. The Canonet was launched in January 1961, and within two and a half years had achieved world sales of more than one million units. The decision to target the mass market proved to be a good one because Japan was entering a period of high economic growth, and, in general, its people could afford to buy a popular camera of this sort. The AE-1 camera, which introduced electronic parts to automate its operation, was also quite successful. It achieved sales of three million units in only four years. The reasons for its success were to be found in the lower prices which mass-production methods made possible, and the simple design, which required fewer parts than before.

With regard to the policy of diversification, Canon was not always successful. For instance, the company began to manufacture and sell a new product called the 'synchro-reader'. This was a type of reading machine, with a sheet on which letters and pictures were printed that could be listened to on the machine at the same time as they were read. Following two years' research, it was introduced to the market with an extensive propaganda campaign, but the result was highly unsatisfactory. Its price was so high that it could not compete with the similar products of other companies which followed it. However, though the synchro-reader was not a market success, Canon was able to make use of the technology and other resources accumulated in the course of development, when it tried to branch out into electronics and other high-technology goods.[5]

In general, however, Canon's diversification attempts were successful, especially after the start in 1962 of its first long-term five year plan. The plan aimed at reducing the proportion of cameras in Canon's total sales from 95 per cent to 75 per cent. One of the items produced in 1964 was the world's first ten-key electronic calculator, the Canola 130. It marked the company's serious entry into the field of business machines. To begin with, the Canola 130 contributed enormously to Canon's revenue, maintaining a high level of market share by the introduction of successive innovations using integrated circuits and large-scale integration. However, senior management proved reluctant to sanction manufacture of the cheaper grades of electronic calculators, and eventually Canon was unable to compete with Casio's range of such products. The fierce competition among firms in this sector was indicated by the falling price of their products. Until 1970, prices fell by about 27 per cent every year; thereafter, they declined drastically by almost 50 per cent annually. Eventually, Casio succeeded in increasing its share of the electronic calculator market from 10 per cent in the mid-1960s to 35 per cent in 1973.[6]

The failure of the electronic calculator venture meant that in the first half of 1975 Canon suffered its first loss, because sales of the calculator amounted, at that time, to about 30 per cent of the company's total revenue. However, although the calculator itself was a casualty of the sales war, Canon was again able to make use of the technologies and other resources accumulated in the course of its innovation.

The Canon Camera Corporation became the Canon Corporation in 1969, signifying its intention to transform itself from a camera manufacturer into a comprehensive business machine and office automation manufacturer. From the beginning of the 1960s, the company had been considering whether it should enter the field of copying machines. Although Xerox possessed the exclusive patent for PPCs (plain paper copiers), Canon tried to develop a new PPC system avoiding Xerox's patents. Eventually it succeeded in manufacturing the Canon NP (New Process) system, which was able to produce copies of a similar quality to the Xerox system. In 1972, Canon introduced the NP-L7, which earned a good reputation for its quality and easy handling. In an epoch-making breakthrough in the history of Japanese copying machines, the know-how to produce the NP-L7 was licensed to the Saxon Company, an American office-machine maker, for one million dollars.[7]

After the introduction of the NP-L7, the copying-machine business boomed, and it now extends to various sectors of the market: the medium-grade NP-50 series was produced in 1977; and the NP-200 series, with the added benefit of toner-projection, and the PC-10 and PC-20 personal copiers, with replaceable cartridges, appeared in 1982. The latter series of copiers realized sales of two million machines in seven years. Gradually the share of copiers in Canon's total turnover increased – to 27 per cent in 1980 and 37 per cent in 1983. This looks like being a promising market for Canon. The laser-beam printer, developed in the copying machine department, is also now making a considerable contribution to the company's revenue, as are computer accessories. In 1984, sales of copying machines were 44 per cent of total revenue, whereas camera sales had fallen to 37 per cent. Four years later, in 1988, the proportion of Canon's camera sales had dwindled to 16 per cent of total revenue, in contrast to Olympus's 33 per cent, Nikon's 42 per cent, Minolta's 50 per cent and Asahi-kogaku's 53 per cent. Canon can thus be said to be diversifying more vigorously than the other camera manufacturers.

CHARACTERISTICS OF CANON'S STRATEGY

Takeshi Mitarai was Canon's first president when the company was still called the Seiki Optical Institute. He remained president until 1974. As already mentioned, he was a doctor and auditor at the time when the company was launched. He was succeeded by Takeo Maeda, who had been appointed vice-president following a career in sales and marketing. After only a short time in office, Takeo Maeda died in 1977. Canon's third president was the former managing director, Ryuzaburo Kaku, who had been responsible for promoting the Premier Company Plan. His term of office continued for ten years. In 1989, the vice-president, Keizo Yamaji, became president.

From 1978 a departmental organization came into being, with the introduction of the camera, office machinery, and mechanical optical machinery departments. The adoption of this organizational structure resulted in vigorous diversification policies, which resulted in sales of one billion yen in the 1980s on joint account with related companies.

The characteristics of Canon's strategy under its top management and in changing circumstances will now be examined.

Total Quality Control

One of the turning points in Canon's development after the oil shock of 1973–4 was the introduction of the Premier Company Plan. This was aimed at ensuring recovery from the deficit caused by the failure of electrical calculators and by the oil crisis, and at total renovation of the character and structure of the company. The Plan was instigated in 1976 and had a six-year term. It had five principal targets:

1 to establish a company image and promote it as a socially responsible public corporation;
2 to strengthen the Canon group companies and encourage them to co-operate with each other;
3 to develop and strengthen the creative technology;
4 to enhance, and make full use of, the abilities of the employees;
5 to overhaul totally Canon's structure and character.[8]

To realize this Plan, senior management established new committees which were responsible for the implementation of its goals. They also instigated a policy of reallocating factories and levelling-up production capacity with appropriate investment. The existing factories were relatively inefficient and were not concentrated on the production of specific goods. It was necessary to rationalize them and introduce specialization. Subsidiary companies were controlled much more rigidly, but were also encouraged to create new product lines. Two of Canon's subsidiaries, the Fukushima and Toride factories, were merged in order to control management and improve productivity.

Technology was essential to the ability to compete in this innovative industry. The Canon Development System was established in 1976, and was organized horizontally through every department. At the same time the Canon Production System was introduced, on the same lines as the Toyota production system, which reduced time and resources to the limit. The result of introducing the practice of Total Quality Control was that Canon developed three principles by which employees would be encouraged to work: 'self-motivation', whereby employees would try to find their own goals and challenges, and pursue these with self-awareness and self-reliance; 'self-awareness', whereby employees would try to understand the real needs and conditions of their society and the world; and 'self-reliance', whereby employees would accept responsibility for any decisions, actions and commitments made within the framework of the company. The intention was that this 'Canon Code' would help motivate the employees to work hard and devotedly for the company.

In the final stages of the Premier Company Plan, the high exchange rate of the yen impeded Canon's export policy. At the end of 1977, the rate was 230 yen to the US dollar; at the start of 1978, the rate was 200. It was estimated that at the 1975 level of the yen, losses were in the region of fifteen billion yen as a result of the yen's unfavourable exchange rate. Needless to say, the appreciation of the yen accelerated Canon's direct investment in foreign countries, and changed its export policy to trading in dollars. Canon had plans to increase the foreign share of its sales – in the United States and Europe – to twice the domestic share.

The strong yen also required the development of the domestic market, but Canon's sales policy in this market had been weak. Reflecting on past policy, which had been much more orientated to technological and product innovation, the company began to establish and strengthen its sales network. Top management decided to increase the number of chain stores by between 9 and 30 per cent. They also resolved that, in addition to an increase in the numbers of salesmen, the chain stores should be segmented according to the commodities sold in them, and that the amount of stock sold in the stores should be greatly reduced.

Canon's response to the oil crisis was typical of the behaviour of Japanese companies in confronting a business crisis. To start with, senior management resorted to spiritual appeals to employees to work in co-operation with them and overcome the difficulties. Then they devised various managerial innovations, including organizational reforms. But these managerial innovations would have been impossible to realize without the prior appeals for the co-operation of the employees. In the course of working together for the Premier Company Plan, for instance, workers reduced enormously the lead time for the preparation of parts for the assembly lines – from 240 minutes to seven minutes.[9]

After the six years of the Premier Company Plan, Canon had achieved a large increase in turnover, to over three and a half times its pre-Plan level, and, surprisingly, at operating profits which had soared to nearly thirteen and a half times their level in 1975 when the Plan had been proposed.

Vigorous diversification into related fields

Unlike American firms, which tend to diversify by way of takeovers and mergers, most Japanese companies have followed an in-house approach in developing new products and services. Of course, internal product diversification is more risky and time-consuming than restructuring through acquisitions. But an external acquisition in Japan means merging two closed and exclusive corporate families, each with its own well-established hierarchy and social system.[10]

Canon is a typical Japanese firm in this sense. The chairman, R. Kaku, explains the characteristics of Canon's diversification as follows:

There are some companies which specialise in one field. But if you do not diversify your business, you cannot expect to grow beyond a certain level. As diversification itself requires some risk, the first step should be to move into areas peripheral to existing operations. If you can expand using skills already accumulated in production and marketing, then there is very little risk. . . . my analysis is static, but clearly, by moving further and further into areas peripheral to existing operations, then the scope of the business can expand dramatically over time.[11]

Kaku's words describe the direction taken by Canon in the forty years since the middle of 1950. For ten years, from the middle of 1950, Canon ventured into the manufacture of 8mm cine-cameras, projectors and middle-range cameras using existing techniques, which were sold through established channels. In the next decade, from the middle of 1961, top management launched Canon into the fields of calculators and photocopiers, in which there were opportunities to make use of both existing techniques and established sales channels. This diversification was more risky than that of the former decade. From the middle of 1970, the company diversified by means of backward and forward integration. For instance, Canon started to produce semi conductors, and Canon USA began to control sales agents such as Bell & Howell directly. At first, therefore, Canon had attempted less risky diversification strategies, and then, with the increasing resources of the company, it ventured into bolder diversification strategies.

As already indicated, Canon has diversified from cameras into office automation machines and computer applicances. The process of this diversification seems to follow the theory of portfolio selection devised by the Boston Consulting Group.[12] Canon always looks for the 'star' which produces the pioneering goods and contributes profits to the company. Popular copy machines, targeted at the home user, and laser printers, which are being manufactured under OEM contracts with the big computer makers, are 'stars' for the company in this sense.

Indeed, the camera is now referred to as a 'mature' product. This means that it is quite a popular consumer item and that, while no longer expecting to experience a large boom in sales, Canon will not necessarily abandon its camera section. On the contrary, the company has now launched an attempt to recover the number one position in the camera field from Minolta, by selling the EOS 100 which is about half the price of Minolta's AE-1, has fewer parts, and is lighter in weight.[13] Far from abandoning the production of cameras, Canon is still endeavouring to make profits from this side of its business.

Aggressive strategy for the world market

In terms of internationalization and multinationalization, as early as 1951, Canon contracted to sell 70 per cent of its products to Jardine Matheson, the British trading company. After the expiry of its five-year contract with Jardine Matheson, Canon set up its own branch in New York in 1955 to promote sales of its cameras in the American market. In 1957, it established Canon Europe SA in Geneva, with the assistance of G. Lewbel, and reorganized the sales network, which covered thirteen countries and had originally been put in place by Jardine Matheson. In 1960, it was proposed that Bell & Howell should become the exclusive distributors for Canon's camera in the United States and Canada, and Canon entered into a five-year contract with this firm. However, in the case of the Canola, the world's first ten-key calculator, Canon tried to organize a dealer network in the United States itself. Following a different strategy from that of selling cameras, Canon USA controlled directly each American agent.

By the end of the 1960s, Canon had established three main bases for its overseas network: Canon USA Inc., Canon Amsterdam and Canon Latin America Inc. From the mid-1970s, Canon strengthened its overseas sales network by establishing new branches, reorganizing sales subsidiaries, and increasing its share in the equity of its agents. For instance, Canon Business Machines (UK) Ltd, controlled to the extent of 100 per cent·by the parent company, came into existence in 1976 to sell mainly office machines. In 1978, Canon increased its share in Canon Svenska AB to 90 per cent in order to sell all of the goods made by Canon in Sweden. In that year, too, Canon Italia SpA was established, with a 55 per cent shareholding by Canon, to deal with all the goods produced by it in Italy. In 1979, Canon Verkooporganisatie Nederland BV and Canon Copylux GmbH appeared in Holland and West Germany respectively, to sell mainly photocopiers. Thus, the marketing network was contrived so as to be able to adapt to the diversified policy of the parent company. In general, the marketing channels for cameras are not suitable for office automation machines, which require different selling methods. Canon prefers to exercise direct control over its sales network rather than to use sales agents, especially when there is severe cost competition, because, to the extent that sales agents are utilized in the market, there is a tendency to lose sight of flexible pricing policies and long-term strategies.

As foreign markets expanded, it was natural to establish a total service system so that local agents in each country could be supplied quickly with a range of parts. This necessarily led to direct investment by the parent company, and, especially in the 1980s, Canon sought vigorously for opportunities to construct factories overseas. After Canon Giessen GmbH, the largest overseas copier plant, was established in 1972 (adding a new factory in 1987), Canon Bretagne SA started operations in 1983 as France's first copier plant and is now expanding its range of products to include electronic typewriters, facsimile transceivers, and laser beam printers. In the case of the United States' market, sales of Canon copiers increased to the point at which the Company achieved top position in the sales league in 1986, with a dominating 26.8 per cent share of the market. Nevertheless, Canon Virginia was incorporated in 1986 to manufacture copiers, in addition to Canon Business Machines of California which had been incorporated in 1974 to produce consumables for copiers and electronic typewriters. Needless to say, Canon's direct investment was accelerated by trade friction between Japan and countries in North America and Europe. This policy of direct investment was a notable feature of the 1980s.

So far as Asia was concerned, Canon followed a policy of direct investment in Taiwan in 1970, comparatively earlier than in the West, in order to manufacture cameras. The reason was the high labour costs in Japan and the highly valued yen. In this sense, the motivation for the policy of direct investment was different as between Europe and America, and Asia. In the case of the former, Canon looked at its internationalization from the point of view of calming trade friction; the question of reducing costs came comparatively late in its multi-nationalization drive.[14] The company's idea was to reduce, as much as possible, the distance between consumers and producers, and to arrange local production at the most convenient locations near to the big consumer markets.

However, the multinationalization of the company required solutions to new problems. It became, for instance, more and more difficult for the parent company to control its foreign manufacturing and marketing subsidiaries. To address this problem, Canon imposed strict direct control over its foreign subsidiaries, communicating to them its policy and requiring that they should carry it out as planned. Thus in the early 1980s, the Head Office in Tokyo exercised direct control over Canon France SA, with its 1,500 employees and sales totalling 1.98 billion francs. Then it established Canon Europa NV, with 2,200 employees, as its sales centre for Europe and most of Africa and the Middle East. In 1982, Canon Business Machines (UK), with 1,100 employees and sales totalling more than £195 million, became Canon UK Ltd under the direct control of the Tokyo Head Office. Following this reorganization of its foreign subsidiaries, Canon Europa NV, for instance, was able to achieve in 1985 its largest turnover, with such policies as reducing unpaid sales credits and the amount of stock held.

At the same time, Canon promoted the localization of its subsidiaries, by transferring management to local people and by increasing the amount of production undertaken locally. For instance, the proportion of Canon Virginia Inc.'s production which was undertaken locally ranged from 35 to 80 per cent, though this differed according to the kind of product. But the parent company now aims for a much higher rate of local production, in order to be able to export products from the United States to European countries.[15] Production by foreign subsidiaries amounted to only about 20 per cent in 1988, but the then president, R. Kaku, forecast that it would exceed that of domestic plants and reach about 60 per cent of total production by the year 2000. Similarly, around two thirds of the total workforce was Japanese at the end of 1987, but at the beginning of the next century the situation will be completely reversed.[16] The localization of management is sought not only for the sake of local human resources, however, but also for local finance.

Canon is now quite active in raising money in foreign money markets, and in requiring its foreign subsidiaries to be listed by local stock exchanges. Research and development is also being transferred, in part, to foreign countries.

These organizational innovations have their roots in Canon's 1978 decision at home to adopt the matrix structure in order to realize the Premier Company Plan. The company introduced three new committees – for 'Development', 'Production' and 'Sales' – which began working effectively in 1979. Direct control by Canon's Head Office over its main foreign subsidiaries followed this innovation in Japan.

Since then, there has been vigorous direct and indirect investment worldwide, and, in consequence, the total amount of money invested in the Japanese market is getting, relatively, smaller and smaller. In terms of regional sales, in 1989 Japan shared in the 30.5 per cent market share of its region, Europe's market share was 31.4 per cent, North America's 30.6 per cent, and that of all the others together 7.4 per cent. In this context, Canon can be termed one of Japan's multinational companies. From 1970, and especially from the late 1970s, the company's total sales jumped: in 1970, they amounted to forty-five billion yen, exclusive of its related companies; in 1975, they were seventy-five billion yen; in 1980, 241 billion yen; and in 1985, 575 billion yen. The numbers of employees increased accordingly, from 4,702 in 1970 to 15,802 in 1985. Total assets rose from thirty-six billion yen in 1970 to 592 billion yen in 1985.

High rate of investment in R. & D. from the start

Whereas the average amount invested in research and development by Japanese companies is said to be about 4 or 5 per cent of total turnover, Canon invests 8.9 per cent of its total turnover in research and development. In the last ten years, Canon has already taken out more than 20,000 industrial patents, and more than 10,000 patents in the area of new technology, which puts it at the head of Japanese optical and business machinery companies. In 1980, it was ranked forty-fifth in the list of companies which applied to the American Patent Office, and fourth among Japanese companies.[17]

As already noted, one of the characteristics of Canon management, which has been supported by the engineering staff, is active diversification into related fields. By the end of the 1950s, research and development was focused on the development of the camera and its accessories. Computers were introduced to design their lenses and to improve and standardize their quality. In addition, research into camera materials was also an important theme. Canon developed the synchro-reader in conjunction with Tokyo Denki Kagaku (TDK) and launched it on the market in 1959. Although the synchro-reader proved to be unpopular, and unsuccessful as a business proposition, Canon's engineers learned about many new technologies – such as magnetic materials and magnetic heads – from its failure, which led to the company's new diversification attempts. In the 1960s, Canon concentrated on the manufacturing techniques necessary for the production of high quality cameras, introducing the 'Quality Control Circle' movement amongst its employees. It was able to achieve a good cost performance, with a high quality product.

In the 1970s, after the Canon Research Centre had been elevated to the status of a separate institute in 1969, Canon expanded the scope of its research greatly, to include electrical engineering, a new plain paper copying process, a laser-beam printer, and a video tape recorder. With the introduction of the Premier Company Plan in 1976, the Canon Development System Committee was established to make the development programme more efficient and to level-up its power. The Canon Production System Committee was also established, to ensure the production of high quality and low cost goods, and their rapid delivery: in short, to copy in Canon's factories Toyota's *kanban* production method, which sought to stock the least possible quantity of parts at any one time. In other words, the business environment of the 1970s, caused mainly by the oil crisis, required Canon's research and development effort to strengthen innovation in the manufacturing process. In this period, Canon started studying most of the technological fields which were to prove successful in production on a commercial scale in the 1980s.

What is remarkable, moreover, is that new products were sometimes born on the basis of mixed technologies – what is known as the 'synergy effect'. H. Yoshihara of Kobe University pointed out that there were three streams in Canon's technological development:

1 the high-grade camera → synchro-reader → electronic calculator → electronic office machine (e.g. the word processor and electronic typewriter);
2 the high-grade camera → duplicate copier → visual office machine (e.g. the facsimile and laser-beam printer);
3 the high-grade camera → mask aligner (printing machine for the semi-conductors) → optical machine.[18]

Canon's research and development policy is said to be based on five principles: 'first mover success', 'technologies should be guarded by patent', 'satisfaction of customer needs', 'high quality products' and 'good cost performance'. The company has always been ahead in the introduction of new products, such as digital colour copiers and laser-beam printers. In 1989, Canon made new applications to the Patent Bureau for about 1,000 patents, and its revenue from licensing patents to other companies was 9.1 billion yen, compared with 5.6 billion yen in 1988.[19]

The reason that Canon has been keen to invest in research and development is partly explained by the composition of its top management, which is largely dominated by directors who were previously engineers. Indeed, one of the characteristics of Canon management in general is the strong influence of its engineers, and it can be described as a typical technology-orientated company. In 1989, for instance, nineteen of its thirty directors were career engineers. It is true to say that precision industries probably require numerous engineering directors to launch new technological products, but Canon has a lot of engineering directors even in comparison with other such companies; Ricoh, for example, has eleven engineers among its twenty-seven directors, and Minolta has thirteen among its twenty-six directors.[20]

CONCLUSION

Canon is typical of the Japanese companies which diversify actively and branch vigorously into foreign markets. The performance of the company ranks it among the world's largest companies. According to *Fortune* Magazine's ranking of the world's biggest industrial corporations outside the United States, Canon's position has risen from 230th in 1981 to 125th in 1985 and 69th in 1990.

It is possible to point to several factors that have made Canon one of the most vigorous Japanese companies. Firstly, it has actively pursued rapid growth, expanding market share, and diversification. In this sense, Canon has been aiming at a fast growth rate rather than a steady one, with the focus on achieving technological advantage.

The second factor is an aggressive policy of diversification into fields relating to existing products, supported by a board of directors on which engineers have considerable influence. Engineers are advised not to worry about failure in research and development, and to challenge difficult problems. This attitude by senior management has turned the failures of the synchro-readers and the electro-calculators into the success of new products. The performance of the engineers is indicated by the number of patents, in Japan as well as in America.

The third factor is the Premier Company Plan, which was introduced at a time of crisis in the company to recoup its deficit and confront difficult business conditions. This was a kind of Total Quality Control movement, supported by the co-operation of the employees. Aimed at achieving the highly prestigious and honourable distinction of a Deming Prize for labour management, the movement was also introduced by such companies as Fuji Xerox who were confronting business crisis.

The fourth factor is the internationalization of the company, which transformed its strategy from an export-orientated policy to one of localization of management, the production of parts in local factories, and even the transfer overseas of research and development. The multinationalization of Japanese companies calls for a reconsideration of what is called 'Japanese management'. It requires a new idea of business management, which might be different from both existing Western-style management and traditional Japanese management.

NOTES

1 J.C. Abegglen and G. Stalk, *Kaisha: The Japanese Corporation*, New York, Basic Books, 1985, p. 190.
2 Canon, *Canon 50 nenshi* (*Canon's Fiftieth Anniversary*), Tokyo, Canon, 1987, pp. 2–5.
3 Ibid., pp. 11–16.
4 Ibid., ch. 3.
5 Hideki Yoshihara, *Senryakuteki Kigyo Kakusin* (*Strategic Managerial Innovation*), Tokyo, Toyokeizaishinposha, 1986, pp. 147–8.
6 Kazuhiko Imaoka, 'Canon wa OA senso ni kateruka' ('Does Canon Win the OA Competition?'), *President*, Tokyo, Purezidentosha, November 1984, pp. 228–9.
7 *Canon 50 nenshi*, pp. 79–84, 137–8.
8 Ibid., pp. 168–70.
9 *Bessatsu Daiyamondo* (Special Issue of Daiyamondo), Tokyo, Daiyamondosha, October 1978, p. 118.
10 A.M. Whitehill, *Japanese Management, Tradition and Transition*, London, Routledge, 1990, p. 234.
11 *Financial Times*, 3 December 1990.
12 Bruce Henderson, *The Logic of Business Strategy*, Cambridge, Mass., Ballinger, 1984, p. 56.
13 Kyoikusha (ed.), *Kamera Kogakukiki Gyokai no Keiei-hikaku* (*Comparative Analysis of Camera Companies*), Tokyo, Kyoikusha, 1989.
14 *Shukan Toyo Keizai* (weekly magazine of Toyo Keizai), Tokyo, Toyokeizaishinposha, 31 March 1990.
15 *President*, 1 October 1990, p. 455.
16 *Nikkei Sangyo Shinbun*, Tokyo, Nikkei Shinbunsha, 23–6 January 1989.
17 Abegglen and Stalk, *Kaisha*, p. 120.

18 Yoshihara, *Senryakuteki Kigyo Kakusin*, pp. 144–72.
19 *Shukan Toyo Keizai*, 31 March 1990.
20 *Yukashoken Hokokusho* (Official Company Reports to the Department of Finance), Tokyo, Canon, 1989.

5 Toray Corporation: seeking first-mover advantage

Tsuneo Suzuki

INTRODUCTION

It is said that the life span of a Japanese company can only be counted as thirty years. Certainly, we can see that the ranking of companies in Japan has changed drastically since the Meiji Era, when modern industry began in Japan. Even the Second World War did nothing to interrupt this tendency. In 1950, for instance, when the Korean War broke out, four cotton spinning firms were listed among Japan's top ten companies in terms of turnover; ten years later, in 1960, not only were there no cotton spinning firms among the top ten, there was only one in the top one hundred.[1] Observing the speed of these movements in and out of the ranking, it is hard to deny the brevity of the life expectancy of Japanese companies.

The synthetic fibre industry grew in Japan in the 1960s and 1970s, but its growth rate by the end of the period had slowed down. The 1960s, indeed, proved to have been a golden decade for the synthetic fibre industry as a whole. Although the growth rate was different for individual companies, the reasons for the industry's rapid growth in the 1960s in general, and comparative slow-down during the 1970s, will be analysed through examining the case of the Toray Corporation, the first company in Japan to produce both polyester and nylon. The problem will be considered from two points of view: first, the changing strategy from artificial to synthetic fibre, and second, the diversification from a fibre to a non-fibre industry.

Before starting to describe Toray, it is necessary to clarify what is meant by the strategy of diversification that makes a company grow faster than its rivals. Was the move from the manufacture of artificial to synthetic fibre a real diversification? Or was this merely a change of raw materials, from pulp to coal? While there were, indeed, many differences between artificial and synthetic fibres, there were also common elements in the technologies, such as the melting of the raw materials, the spinning of the fibre and the stretching of the yarn. In addition, as the products of the two technologies are sold in the same market, the difficulties of exploiting new markets, which usually accompany the introduction of new products, were not as great as usual. Synthetic fibre manufacturers were also able to move in similar directions to artificial fibre manufacturers with regard to the processing, dyeing, and making-up of cloth, though there were some differences between diversification from artificial to synthetic fibres and diversification from synthetic fibres to chemical products.

The Toray and Teijin companies expanded their turnover in the 1960s, while the Kurare, Toho Rayon and Mitsubishi Rayon companies did less well, because they were unable to exploit the 'first-mover advantage' in such fields as nylon and polyester, which have seen a more steady and stable development than other synthetic fibres. The case of the Toray Corporation thus seems especially suitable for analysis from the viewpoint both of first-mover advantage, which was the dominant strategy followed with regard to nylon and polyester, and of subsequent decline, caused by the difficulties of marketing new products, notably carbon fibres.

DEVELOPMENT OF THE SYNTHETIC FIBRE INDUSTRY

As indicated above, differences in turnover among artificial fibre firms in the 1950s were not as great as they were in the 1960s, when the synthetic fibre industry grew more rapidly than at any other time. Furthermore, in the 1960s, these differences arose not so much as a result of competition for greater market share, as from the strategy followed in entering the synthetic fibre industry and the choice of the synthetic fibre itself.

In Japan, the synthetic fibre industry started in earnest after 1949 when *Shoko Sho* (The Ministry of Commerce and Industry), predecessor of MITI (Ministry of International Trade and Industry), decided that it should be protected and fostered. To begin with, only the Toray and Kurare companies were permitted access to the nylon and vinylon industries which had started up in Japan during the Second World War. Initially, vinylon was expected to develop more quickly than nylon, but in fact the reverse was the case. Vinylon fibre was unable to exploit its potential market because it proved to be unsuitable for clothing. The different growth rates of the vinylon and nylon industries was a result not so much of technological innovation, therefore, as of the uncertainty surrounding the introduction of a new product.

There was no such protection in the case of other synthetic fibres. As there was no basic patent in the acrylic fibre industry, many companies entered the field, with products of differing quality and a variety of trademarks, such as Vonnel, Cashimilon and Exlan. Predictably, this resulted in such serious competition that there was no room for them to develop side by side. Rather, they fought one another to establish and then enlarge their plants, in order to cut costs and expand market share, the latter being the paramount aim of nearly all Japanese firms, taking precedence even over exploitation of their own markets. The consequence of this furious competition was that all the acrylic fibre companies made losses.[2]

By way of contrast, the Toray and Teijin companies entered the polyester industry in 1957 in co-operation with each other. They chose a common trademark – Tetolon – depicting the initial letter of both their names, which allowed them to work together to control the market as if they were a single monopolistic enterprise.[3] There were now three major synthetic fibres – nylon, acrylic and polyester – in production at the same time.

The introduction and development of three major fibres improved the image and value of synthetic fibres in general, and enabled them to become widely accepted. With the rapid development of the synthetic fibre industry, and expectations of continued future development, many other companies entered the field – cotton spinning as well as artificial fibre firms. While this resulted in a greater degree of competition in the synthetic fibre industry on the one hand, it encouraged faster development on the other. The extensive development of the 1960s was derived from the fact that the three major synthetic fibres were able not only to exploit their own fields, but to substitute for natural as well as artificial fibres.

At the beginning of the 1960s, production of goods made from natural fibres such as cotton still surpassed the production of goods made from both artificial and synthetic fibres, in terms of quantity. But in terms of growth rates, the production of synthetic fibre goods was developing faster than that of any other textile goods. It is, of course, true that the high rate of economic growth at this time led to an expansion in the production of the textile goods sector as a whole, but the development of the synthetic fibre industry was more rapid. As a result, production of synthetic fibres exceeded production of artificial fibres in 1966, and a year later, in 1967, outstripped production of cotton yarn as well.[4]

In the face of the rapid development of synthetic fibre, the cotton spinning and artificial fibre industries both made various improvements in quality and in productivity. However, their markets were restricted, in comparison with that of synthetic fibre, because while cotton yarn and artificial fibre were similar in having a single characteristic, synthetic fibre could claim a variety of characteristics, such as nylon, acrylic, and polyester.

Looking at the growth of Toray in the 1950s and 1960s, it is apparent that it changed specifically from being an artificial fibre producer to a synthetic fibre producer, rather than becoming a multiple producer of synthetic and artificial fibres. In the late 1940s, Toray had been merely an artificial fibre company, involved exclusively in the production of rayon as a result of of the increased demand for this fibre by the textile goods industry which had arisen under the control of the former wartime economy. In the prevailing circumstances, demand – not only for rayon, but for cotton yarns also – was such that it remained high even when the quality of the fibres being produced was unsuitable for textiles. Moreover, when the Korean War broke out in 1950, there was a sudden increase in the demand for rayon textiles, as well as for those made from cotton yarn, not only on the domestic front but also from the export market. There was little incentive, therefore, for companies to improve their efficiency, especially while the market for synthetic fibre remained small due to unfamiliarity with the product and problems with its quality. In these circumstances, with many artificial fibre companies and cotton yarn manufacturers steering clear of the synthetic fibre industry, Toray was able to develop and improve the production of nylon.[5]

Investigation of Toray's rapid growth in the 1940s and 1950s makes it very evident that the leading sectors of the textile industry changed during the course of development. In the late 1940s, its rayon division grew so fast that Toray was able to recover from the effects of war. However, in the 1950s, its nylon division expanded more rapidly than any other fibre division. As a result, Toray changed from an artificial to a synthetic fibre company, because in terms of turnover, production of nylon exceeded that of rayon. Furthermore, with the increase in the production of polyester during the early 1960s, Toray became one of the most prominent companies.

Stimulated by the rapid growth of Toray, many other artificial fibre companies, and cotton yarn manufacturers as well, tried to move into the production of not only nylon but also polyester, of which Japan has been and still is the second largest producer. As they tried to exploit markets adapted to the requirements of synthetic fibres and their substitute, cotton yarn, competition between synthetic fibres and cotton yarn became very serious. Such cut-throat competition resulted in expansion of the demand for fibre as a whole, and gave synthetic fibres a comparative advantage because of their competitive prices and qualities.

Through this competition and through market growth, synthetic fibre production grew faster than cotton yarn on the one hand, while on the other hand first-movers in the field made larger profits than latecomers. First-movers benefited from the following three advantages:

1 Unlike the many fibre-processing firms eager to participate in the synthetic fibre industry, but which were not as large or as stable in their performance as the synthetic fibre manufacturers, they could more easily form a business group, and thus make use of the better business opportunities provided by the trade organisation.[6]
2 They could diffuse their original brands throughout the markets more quickly and widely stimulating demand for their products.
3 Equally importantly, production was cheaper for first-movers than for latecomers because the costs of large synthetic fibre plants decreased in relation to their size, and the former were able to expand more rapidly.

Moreover, the industrial policy which MITI had initiated towards the synthetic fibre industry from the outset affected the development of first-movers by providing them with a monopoly market in order to avoid excessive competition at the start of the new industry. As a result, first-movers were able to reduce the risks entailed both in entering a new market and in adopting a new technology. As first-movers grew and their profits increased, and as the demand for synthetic fibres expanded, latecomers were inevitably attracted to the new and profitable market. The reaction of first-movers was to enlarge their plants. At this stage, MITI enforced another industrial policy, aimed not so much at fostering as at adjusting the supply of the new synthetic fibres. This policy permitted first-movers only, and not latecomers, to enlarge their plants. Thus MITI's industrial policies, both as to encouragement and as to adjustment, worked in favour of first-movers.[7]

This is one of the main reasons why so many artificial fibre and cotton spinning firms were keen to launch the new synthetic fibre – polypropylene – which was invented after nylon, acrylic and polyester had been developed. The manufacture of polypropylene, and its full exploitation, are the most vital issues facing companies in their efforts to increase profitability and growth.

Most synthetic fibre companies expressed an interest in the technology of polypropylene when Montecatini announced that it had developed this new product. Some, however, hearing of the new silk-like fibre – Qiana – developed by Du Pont, decided to explore this route. As a result, there was intense competition in the early 1960s between the introduction of polypropylene and the development of a new silk-like fibre.

Such business activity can be explained in terms of a kind of risk aversion strategy, rather than entrepreneurship. If an enterprise is unable to introduce or to develop new products in the first place, it faces the prospect of always being subordinate to first-movers in circumstances of continuous and rapid technological innovation. In Japan, if an enterprise falls behind its rivals, and/or does not introduce new products, it is held to be inferior to its rivals. A policy of following blindly is therefore a kind of risk aversion, and it makes competition among companies all the more serious.

Toray was able, in co-operation with other companies, to introduce Montecatini's polypropylene patents to Japan, and became the first-mover in this field. However, although Toray made great efforts to improve the technology over many years, the company found that polypropylene was inherently unsuitable as a textile fibre for clothing manufacture. Although its chemical and physical properties were good, it proved to be of inferior quality as a fabric because of difficulties of holding dye and because of its inflammability. Toray found that far from being a dream fibre, polypropylene was a nightmare. Qiana, on the other hand, with its silk-like nature, proved to be an excellent fibre for clothing manufacture. But because its research and development costs were much greater than for other fibres, in terms of both money and time, it was too expensive either to substitute for other synthetic fibres or to achieve popularity in the mass market.[8]

The upshot was that the development of a fourth synthetic fibre proved to be impractical and undesirable. This was the main reason why the growth of the synthetic fibre industry in the 1960s was not as rapid as before.

START OF DIVERSIFICATION

At this stage, whether or not they were involved with the introduction of polypropylene, enterprises started to process nylon, acrylic fibre and polyester in order to develop new products. They had, of course, already been processing synthetic fibres in order to penetrate the markets for clothes, carpets, tyre-cords and so forth, but now they attempted to develop new products rather than merely to improve the production process. They tried to make new fibres by combining different yarns; twisting fibres heavily; creating fibres with various sections – for example, triangular or star-shaped; manufacturing hollow fibres; and producing very fine yarns.[9]

Toray endeavoured to create new products by developing such technologies.[10] It started to produce polypropylene in February 1969. The following year it created a new fibre, made from polyester but with a non-round section, which, for the first time, was similar to silk. During the 1960s it produced a number of new fibres, with such strongly advantageous characteristics as a woollen-like feel or the appearance of solidity. But although this strategy of developing different products succeeded to some extent, it could not substitute for nylon, acrylic fibre and polyester.

Compared with the markets for nylon and polyester, those for the new products were so small that the synthetic fibre industry, as a whole, was unable to grow as fast as before. In the early 1960s, as the late-comers started to operate their plants and supply more synthetic fibres, competition between the first-movers and the latecomers became more intense and, for the first time, prices began to fall. Moreover, an economic depression in 1965 also inhibited growth in the industry.

Toray took three decisive steps to cope with these circumstances. Firstly, in order to reduce costs, it decided to produce raw materials such as xylene, toluene and benzene. Secondly, it realised the import-ance of export to Asian markets as a substitute for the domestic market. Thirdly, it adapted its polymer technology in order to diversify into non-fibre areas such as chemicals.[11] The first of these strategies was to impose a heavy burden on Toray because the oil shocks of the early 1970s led to an increase in the prices of raw materials and a decrease, therefore, in the expected advantage to be gained from their pro-duction. In addition, the dollar shock of 1971 offset competitive prices in Asian markets.

Shigeki Tashiro, Toray's president, made the decision to move into the production of plastics, by applying polymer technology and using the company's own raw materials.[12] On the basis that any products developed by Du Pont were bound to be excellent and experience quick growth, Toray began to study what Du Pont had evolved and was exploiting. The result was that Toray entered the artificial leather market, which Du Pont was already exploiting with its product Corfam.[13] Manufactured by coating fabrics with nitrocellulose or polyvinyl chloride, Corfam was brought to Japan after 1964. Many firms – such as Kurare, Teijin and Toyo Rubber, for example – started to produce this artificial leather, expecting it to become another nylon in scale.[14]

In the 1950s, Toray had developed an artificial leather product with the Toyo Cloth Company, and had manufactured, in 1959, the new product Delacoule from nylon resin. This was processed for bags but, because of its nature, not used for clothes or shoes. Stimulated by the import of Corfam, Toray tried to develop a new synthetic leather, suitable for shoes. With Toyo Cloth Company, Toray incorporated a new company, Hi-Telac Co., in 1966, in order to produce the synthetic leather named hi-Telac, and production of hi-Telac began in earnest the following year. However, because of intense competition and the difficulties of finding suitable markets, hi-Telac was not as successful as expected.[15] The greatest obstacle to its popularity in the market was the inability to develop hi-Telac for shoes. Even Corfam was too expensive to find a market that would yield profits. Having experimented with the production of hi-Telac, and investigated its quality and marketing, Toray decided in 1970 to cut its losses and abandon this avenue of approach.[16]

In its efforts to emulate Du Pont, Toray had thrown human resources as well as money into its technical rather than marketing divisions, in order to develop and exploit the first-mover advantage. There were, for example, more directors from technical divisions than from non-technical divisions, and nearly all of the firm's presidents came from the technical side. Toray was able to concentrate much more of its energy on producing superior technology than on exploiting the market, because from the outset sales of its products had proved to be a great success. Although the company had initially experienced some difficulty in gaining market acceptance for nylon, it was later able to generate large profits from its sales. Moreover, the demand for nylon increased so rapidly that Toray was unable to supply enough to meet it. As a result, Toray was able to to establish and sell nylon easily without having to strive to market it. The company was in a position, in short, to focus more on the development of technology than on the strengthening of its marketing skills.

Toray's strategy was successful in the 1950s and early 1960s, because it was able to exploit fully its first-mover advantage when, in turn, the demand for nylon and polyester increased. But when Toray started to produce acrylic fibre, and after that plastics, it had to face the problem of marketing. A latecomer in the acrylic fibre field, the company had to cope with serious competition, and thus to establish new methods for the manufacturing process and for gaining sales know-how.

While the Japanese economy enjoyed prosperity and grew faster than before in the second half of the 1960s, the growth rate of the synthetic fibre industry was not as great as for the economy as a whole. In addition, in the 1970s, there were two major shocks to the economy which reduced the scope for exports and the potential of the synthetic fibre industry. The first of these was the dollar shock of 1971, which made Japanese synthetic fibre companies unwilling to export to Asia and America because of the revaluation of the yen. The second was the oil crises of 1973 and 1979, which reduced demand for synthetic fibres, because they raised the prices of raw materials such as petroleum products, in particular, but also of energy.

DIVERSIFICATION TOWARDS NON-FIBRES

When the news that the Union Carbide Corporation (UCC) had developed a carbon fibre was reported in Japan in 1959, Akio Shindo, a research worker at *Osaka Kogyo Shikenjo* (the Institute of Osaka Industrial Laboratory), was the first to respond. He too developed a carbon fibre, of high strength and elasticity, by using acrylic fibre as the raw material, initially oxidizing it at 190–200°C, and then burning it in an inert gas such nitrogen or argon over a period of ten to twenty hours at 800–1,000°C. In 1961, when he had perfected the process, he reported in English on his carbon fibre.[17] Introducing the technology developed by Akio Shindo, and with acrylic fibre obtained from the Asahi Kasei Corporation, the Nippon Carbon Corporation produced a strong and elastic carbon fibre for the first time.

Although Toray had developed and improved acrylic fibre, as a latecomer rather than a first-mover it could neither exploit acrylic fibre fully nor make much profit from it. In the circumstances, Tsuguhide Hujiyosi, then president of the company, decided that Toray should enter the carbon fibre industry, and Masatoshi Ito, managing director and later president of the company, launched into the development of a carbon fibre by applying the technology and know-how of acrylic fibre.[18] By 1969, Toray was in a position to develop a carbon fibre of a reasonable quality because of its long experience as a synthetic fibre company, but it had not been able to master fully such technologies as burning and engineering.

Although UCC had been the first company worldwide to produce a carbon fibre, and had perfected technologies like burning and engineering, it needed a good acrylic fibre as raw material instead of the rayon it had been using. In April 1970, Toray and UCC began working in concert with each other, the former developing an improved acrylic fibre, and the latter refining its burning and engineering technologies.[19] Then, in August 1971, Toray set up a pilot plant with a production capability of a ton of carbon fibre per month; in December, it was named

Toraca.[20] As the pilot plant was small, and the cost of production was therefore very high, it was decided in November 1979 that, in order to reduce this cost by applying economies of scale, another plant should be constructed, capable of producing five tons per month. This plant, constructed in March 1973, possessed such integrated operations as the polymerizing of acrylic fibre, the spinning and burning of yarn. It was the first to produce a carbon fibre which had high tension and high elasticity.

In the early 1970s, there was, however, almost no demand for carbon fibre in Japan. Even in America, the largest market for carbon fibre, there was only a demand for some four or five tons a year, so that UCC produced a mere fraction of a ton a month. Because Toray had built a much larger factory, and therefore produced a greater tonnage of carbon fibre, it was forced to expand and exploit the market for carbon fibre. For example, Toray began to supply fibres for heat-proof materials, for the wicks of oil stoves, for the absorption of electric waves, and for the fuel nozzles of rockets. Initially, demand remained small, since carbon fibre products proved too costly to substitute for products used hitherto. However, Toray was tenacious in its efforts to penetrate markets, taking advantage of the special qualities of carbon fibre to promote its use for the manufacture of such products as golf clubs, tennis rackets, fishing rods, and aircraft materials. Certainly demand in the latter market increased to some extent; carbon fibre's strength and lightness meant that aircraft made from them could be operated more economically than aeroplanes made more extensively from duralumin. In addition, the demand for golf clubs made from carbon fibres grew slowly but surely. But the markets for golf clubs and aircraft remained very small in comparison with the market for clothes.

It was difficult, therefore, for Toray to recoup what it had expended on the development and exploitation of carbon fibre. The company was sure that carbon fibre was a good material for some of the products mentioned above, but the demand for these products was small because of the nature and spread of the markets themselves. For the first time, Toray found itself facing difficulties of marketing, not of technology. Toray has always sought a first-mover advantage, and with nylon and polyester it succeeded. In entering the carbon fibre industry, however, it found itself with a first-mover disadvantage. The experience taught Toray that technical superiority does not always result in good products, and that marketing is no less important than research and development. The company also learnt that diversification into new markets is much more difficult than it seems.

CONCLUSION

Synthetic fibre was a new product, developed by applying polymer technology, and it struck a blow at the artificial fibre industry. It was expected to substitute for natural fibres as well as artificial ones. In addition, synthetic fibre technology was so similar to that of artificial fibre, apart from its use of polymer technology, that nearly all artificial fibre-producing companies were seriously concerned with the advent of synthetic fibre. Toray had started to develop synthetic fibres, especially nylon after Du Pont announced its invention in 1936.

The demand for synthetic fibres increased in the 1950s and 1960s, not because they were able to create new markets but because they substituted for artificial and natural fibres. Furthermore, after nylon had penetrated markets, acrylic fibre and polyester were developed in quick succession. So began the process of substitution, and the demand for synthetic fibres grew even greater. Toray had obtained a first-mover advantage in this process, and in the 1960s it became one of the most prominent companies. However, the growth of the synthetic fibre industry slowed down when it was found that polypropylene, the fourth synthetic fibre to be developed, was not a good material for clothes.

At this stage, diversification started in earnest in the synthetic fibre industry. Toray launched itself into the manufacture of products such as chemicals and artificial leather, aiming to become a Japanese Du Pont. However, it was unable to produce an artificial leather which was suitable for shoes, which eventually led it to cut its losses and retire from this field. On the other hand, while Toray was able to develop and improve carbon fibre in order to exploit the first-mover advantage, the company found that it then had to find suitable markets for carbon fibre, and create channels for its processing and sale. Moreover, it found that the market for carbon fibre was much smaller than the market for synthetic fibres. Toray had, therefore, to attend to marketing as well as technology on the one hand, and to diversify vigorously, on the other, because of the small size of the new markets.

Even though there were some differences, of raw material and polymer technology for instance, between the artificial and synthetic fibre industries, they exploited the same markets. Toray invested managerial resources in its technical division in order to resolve these problems. However, diversification from a fibre to a non-fibre industry was diametrically different. Although the technology and materials of the synthetic fibre industry resembled those of the chemical fibre industry, the markets of the former were different from those of the latter. This is one of the main reasons why Toray was able to develop quickly, but then gradually had to slow down.

NOTES

1 Nikkei Business (ed.), *Kaisha no Jumyo* (*A Life of a Company*), Tokyo, Shinchosha, 1989, pp. 174–89.
2 Minoru Tanaka, *Nihon Gosei Seni Kogyoron* (*The Problem of the Japanese Fibre Industry*), Tokyo, Miraisha, 1967, pp. 88–99.
3 Masu Uekusa and Turuhiko Nanbu, 'Gosei Seni' ('Synthetic Fibres') in Kumagai Hisao (ed.), *Nihon no Sangyo Soshiki* (*Market Organization in Japan*), Tokyo, Chuo Koronsha, 1973, pp. 193–4; Shin Aochi, *Yakusin Monogatari: Toray* (*A Story of Progress: Toray*), Tokyo, Nihon Kogyo Shinbunsha, 1963, pp. 165–72; Kunio Hukumoto (ed.), *Kagirinaki Yumeno Punranto – Toray* (*The Eternal Dream Plant*), Tokyo, Fuji International Consalutanto, 1961, pp. 47–50; *Nikkei Sangyo Shinbun*, 1, 4, 5, 8, 9 January 1990.
4 Nihon Kagaku Seni Kyokai (Association of the Japanese Artificial Fibre Industry) (ed.), *Showa 49 nen Kagaku Seni Tokei* (*Artificial Fibre Statistics in 1974*), Tokyo, Nihon Kagaku Seni Kyokai, 1975, pp. 1–6.
5 Toray Co., *Toyo Rayon Shashi* (*A History of Toray*), Tokyo, Toray Co., 1954, pp. 294–304; *Nikkei Sangyo Shinbun*, 10–12 January 1990.
6 Tsuneo Suzuki, 'Goseiseni' ('Synthetic Fibres') in Shin'ichi Yonekawa, Koichi Shimokawa and Masaaki Yamazaki (eds), *Sengo Nihon Keieishi I* (*A Business History of Post War Japan I*), Tokyo, Toyokeizaishinposha, 1991, pp. 126–7; Kazukuni Okuda, *Gosei Seni: Ito Iko ni okeru Kigyou Keiretsu* (*Synthetic Fibre: Business Group Organization down to Fibres*), Tokyo, Nihon Choki Shinyo Ginko, 1960, pp. 189–219.
7 Tsuneo Suzuki, 'Seni Sangyo no Kozo Kaizen' ('Structural Reform of the Fibre Industry'), in Tsusho Sangyo Seisakushi Hensan Iinkai (ed.), *Tsusho Sangyo Seisakushi 10* (*A History of Trade and Industry Policy 10*), Tokyo, Tsuinsho Sangyo Chosakai, 1990, pp. 396–403; Minoru Tanaka, *Wagakuni Goseiseni Dokusenno Seimitukenkyino* (*A Detailed Study on Monopoly in the Japanese Synthetic Fibre Industry*), Osaka, Nihon Seni Kenkyuukai, 1969, pp.86–94.
8 Toshihiro Higashise, '70 nendai no Gosen Sangyo no haihatu Senryaku' ('The Developing Strategy of the Synthetic Fibre Industry in the 1970s'), *Kagaku Keizai*, October 1973, pp. 52–8; *Nikkei Sangyo Shinbun*, 16 January 1990.
9 Hideo Ohe, 'Hukugoshi no Kaihatsu to Kongo no Tenbo' ('Development in and Views on the Future of Conjugate Yarn'), *Kagaku Keizai*, May 1965, pp. 34–9; Tatsuya Motomiya, *Nyu Seni no Sekai* (*The New World of Fibre*), Tokyo, Nikkan Kogyo Shinbunsha, 1988, pp. 68–90.
10 Nihon Kagaku Seni Kyokai (Association of the Japanese Artificial Fibre Industry) (ed.), *Nihon Kagaku Seni Sangyoshi* (*A History of the Japanese Artificial Fibre Industry*), Tokyo, Nihon Kagaku Seni Kyokai, 1974, pp. 964–74.
11 Toray Co., *Toray 50 nenshi* (*Fifty Years of Toray*), Tokyo, Toray Co., 1977, pp. 153–6, 176–82; Hoshimi Uchida, *Gosei Seni Kogyo 'Shinteiban'* (*A Synthetic Fibre Industry 'Newly Revised'*), Tokyo, Toyokeizaishinposha, 1970, pp. 225–30.
12 Shigeki Tashiro, *Tore to Tomoni* (*Along with Toray*), Tokyo, Toray Co., 1972, p. 99.

13 David A. Hounshell and John Kenly Smith Jr, *Science and Corporate Strategy: Du Pont R. & D., 1902–1980*, New York, Cambridge University Press, 1988, pp. 536–9; *Nikkei Sangyo Shinbun*, 18 and 19 January 1990.

14 Yukio Kawarabayasi, *Yomigaeru Shinwa* (*The Revival of a Myth*), Tokyo, Nihon Seni Syuppabsha, 1990, pp. 12–14.

15 Toyo Cloth Co., *Toyo Cloth 70 nenshi* (*Seventy Years of Toyo Cloth*), Osaka, Toyo Cloth Co., 1990, pp. 308–13.

16 Toray Co, *Toray 50 nenshi*, pp. 198–9.

17 *Nikkei Sangyo Shinbun*, 14 December 1976; Akio Shindo, 'Studies on Graphite Fibre', *Report of the Government Industrial Research Institute*, Osaka, December 1961, No. 317.

18 Ibid., 15 and 16 December 1976, and 17 January 1990.

19 Ibid., 17 January 1990.

20 Ibid., 17 and 18 December 1976.

Part II

Traditional and restructuring industries

6 Anatomy of a Japanese steel firm: NKK – its strategy and performance against the tide, 1951–1990

Etsuo Abe

INTRODUCTION

A typical example of the 'Japanese miracle' is the case of the steel industry. The facts speak for themselves – Japan's spectacular growth from its ruinously damaged position following the Second World War, to become the world's largest steel producer after Russia. Several Japanese steel companies contributed to this rapid growth. The most important of these in terms of output was the Japan Steel Corporation, closely followed by Nippon Kokan KK (which changed its name to NKK in 1988). NKK is now the seventh largest steel company in the world, and, like Bethlehem Steel of the United States and the Broken Hill Proprietary Company (BHP) of Australia, it also has a shipbuilding section. This is unusual. Few steel-producing companies have shipbuilding yards as well. Moreover, NKK's shipbuilding operation is substantial and the company is the fifth or sixth largest shipbuilder in Japan. However, while the strategy and performance of NKK in the post-Second World War period will be analysed in some detail here, its shipbuilding activities will be excluded.

Before proceeding further, it will be helpful to review briefly the earlier history of NKK. The company was established by several entrepreneurs, engineers and iron merchants in Kawasaki, near Tokyo, in 1912. Foremost among its founders were Motojiro Shiraishi, a businessman; Kaichiro Imaizumi, a leading technical specialist; Eiichi Shibusawa, a famous company promoter; and Soichiro Asano. The last-named played a particularly important role. The object of setting up NKK was to manufacture steel pipe, as its former name indicates: *Kokan* meaning steel pipe in Japanese.[1] There was only one large and modern steel works in Japan before the formation of NKK, the Yawata Iron and Steel Works which was owned and run by the state. NKK became the first private steel firm with a manufacturing capacity capable of producing a variety of steels. According to one steel analyst, this was one of the three most important milestones in the history of the Japanese steel industry, the other two being the formation of the Yawata Iron and Steel Works in 1901, and the building of the Chiba Steelworks by the Kawasaki Steel Corporation in 1951.[2] Since NKK was, in the main, established by the financial power of Asano, who was the founder of a middle-ranking *zaibatsu*, NKK was thought to be an Asano Zaibatsu company and thus closely linked with one of the great *zaibatsu*, Yasuda, ranked fourth in Japan. However, this was a mis-apprehension. NKK had numerous shareholders from the outset, and had, to some degree, the character of an independent firm.

Shortly after NKK's formation, the First World War broke out. NKK made huge profits as a result of the war, and was able to set a course for rapid growth. Nevertheless, the company was unable to avoid the effects of the post-war depression; it suffered large losses and was forced to reduce its capital. Despite this considerable setback, NKK not only managed to survive the crisis of the early 1920s, but turned itself into an integrated works by building a blast furnace in 1936 – previously, it had had only open hearth furnaces and rolling mills. Before the Second World War, there were only two such integrated firms in Japan, the Yawata Iron and Steel Works and NKK. Moreover, NKK continued the process of development, acquiring its shipbuilding section through merger with the Tsurumi Iron and Shipbuilding Company, also an Asano company, in 1940. Immediately after the merger, however, Japan entered the Pacific War, with ultimately disastrous consequences for Japanese industry.[3] NKK's Kawasaki Works was bombed repeatedly and totally destroyed. This marked the end of an era and the start of a new chapter in the history of NKK.

DYNAMICS OF THE RAPID GROWTH OF THE JAPANESE STEEL INDUSTRY AND NKK

The development of the Japanese steel industry

After the War the output of the Japanese steel industry shrank to 557,000 metric tons in 1946, from a peak of 7,650,000 tons in 1943. Faced with this drastic decrease, and works which had been virtually decimated, nobody expected that it would be an easy task to rebuild the industry. However, as Table 6.1 indicates, the output of the Japanese steel industry grew rapidly in the 1950s and 1960s. By the early 1970s, production had reached 100 million tons, making Japan the world's third largest steel producer after the (then) Soviet Union and

the United States.[4] Japan also became the largest exporter of steel
products across the world. The international competitiveness built up
thereby provided Japan and the United States respectively with considerable amounts of surplus and deficit in the steel trade.[5]

Table 6.1 NKK: production, market share and number of employees

| | Steel ingots (10,000 tons) | | | Employees[d] |
	NKK[a]	Japan[b]	Share[c]	
1951	81	650	12.5	26,453
1955	116	941	12.3	25,374
1960	221	2,214	10.0	30,243
1965	429	4,176	10.3	35,385
1970	1,288	9,333	13.8	40,292
1975	1,444	10,161	14.2	40,217
1980	1,345	10,739	12.5	31,754
1985	1,260	10,528	12.0	33,295
1989	1,202	10,791	11.1	23,869
1990	1,221			22,824

Sources: *Yukashoken Hokokusho* (Annual Report to the Finance Ministry); *Nippon
Kokan Kabushikikaisha 70 nenshi* (70 years of Nippon Kokan); ibid., *60 nenshi, 50 nenshi.*
Notes:
a 1951–70: calendar year; 1975–90: financial year ending at the end of March
b Calendar year
c NKK's share in total steel production of Japan (%)
d 1951–60: at the end of December
1965–90: at the end of March

Why then was Japan's rapid growth possible, and what factors
contributed to it?

On the demand side, it was beneficial to growth in the steel industry
that the overall annual economic growth rate (GNP) was in excess of 10
per cent during the 1950s and 1960s. The steel industry's growth rate
was usually higher than 10 per cent over the same period, although there
were deep recessions from time to time. In addition to the growing
domestic market, the export market was open to Japan, specifically the
South-East Asian countries and the United States. The free trade system
after the Second World War, realized through the GATT-IMF arrangement, enabled Japan to export freely. As a result, in general terms, Japan
was able to export a third of all steel products, proceeds from the sales
of which were just about equivalent to the costs of importing the coal
and ore necessary for production. If indirect steel exports, such as
electrical appliances, automobiles and so forth were to be included, the

export ratio amounted to nearly 50 per cent of Japan's total steel output. These demand-side factors were favourable to the development of the Japanese steel industry.[6]

The free trade system was also one of the supply-side factors contributing to Japan's growth, being conducive to the import of iron ore and coal. The best quality ore and coal were to be found in Australia, and Japanese steel firms were able to utilize them partly because Japan had almost no raw materials of its own and partly because the free trade system was in operation. This was the kind of basic condition imperative for the growth of the steel industry. Ironically, Japan was perhaps fortunate in not having indigenous raw materials for steel production. Other countries which did have these resources were often at a disadvantage because, despite their raw materials not necessarily being of the best quality, their steel industries were under considerable political pressure to make use of them. In addition, Japanese steel firms were very aggressive and shrewd with regard to technological innovation. In their adoption of LD converters (basic oxygen furnaces) and the continuous casting process, their choices were quick and correct, as the ratio of these innovations to the whole plant illustrates. For instance, while the ratio of LD converters in Japan was 79 per cent in 1970, in the United States and European Community it was only 48 and 43 per cent respectively.[7] Similarly, Japan led the way in the adoption of continuous casting, with a ratio of 60 per cent in 1980 compared to 21 per cent in the United States and 47 per cent in West Germany.[8] And it was the same with the enlargement of blast furnaces. In 1978, there were just fifteen blast furnaces in the world which had an interior furnace capacity of over 4,000 cubic metres. Of these, twelve were in Japan, while France, Italy and the Soviet Union had one each.[9] As late as 1988, the United States had only seven blast furnaces with an interior furnace capacity of 2,000 cubic metres, although Japan had as many as thirty-four (representing 26 per cent of the worldwide total of large blast furnaces in existence that year).[10] Japan's share of world pig iron production was 15 per cent. Finally, special ships were designed and built exclusively to transport raw materials from overseas, which substantially reduced transportation costs. The building of special ships for the specific purpose of transporting coal and iron ore, leaving such vessels cargoeless for the outward journey from Japan to Australia, was an epoch-making innovation in the history of maritime transportation. Hitherto, it had been taken for granted that it was crucial for cost-saving to keep the periods when a ship was empty as short as possible. The discovery that the use of large dedicated ships actually made the cost of transportation cheaper reversed accepted opinion about shipping.

In order to take advantage of all these factors, steel firms built completely new steel works in coastal areas. Good seaports were needed for the import of raw materials from Australia and elsewhere, because Japan has always been heavily dependent on imported raw materials. It also proved necessary to build greenfield works so that full use could be made of new technology. With good quality materials, special ships, large blast furnaces, efficient LD converters and continuous casting, and new works with the most modern and efficient layout and state-of-the-art equipment available, Japan was successful in becoming the world's most efficient producer of steel.[11] In the early stages, Japan also benefited from cheap labour costs, though this advantage was lost later on.

The strategy adopted by Japanese steel firms proved effective. However, the development of the industry was not dependent on this strategy alone; management techniques also played an important part. The organizational structure of steel firms is relatively flexible, without rigid job demarcation. This allows firms to have freedom of job designation or allocation, thereby making possible a quick response to the kind of technological changes which can sometimes lead to serious resistance from employees. From this point of view, Japanese steel firms were in a much easier position than those of the United States and Europe. Management techniques such as OR (operations research), QC (quality control) and IE (industrial engineering) were introduced from the United States and developed in a Japanese way.[12] These scientific management methods helped the modernization process and improved the performance of firms. In particular, the introduction of computer systems in offices and works led to higher productivity and improvements in the quality of products. Computer control in blast furnaces, steelmaking and rolling mills enabled the production of high-quality products, such as sheet for automobiles, which increasingly demanded high-grade bending and curving attributes. These techniques were originally invented in the United States, but it was in Japan that they were to be used to the best advantage, and now Japan is said to be more advanced than any other nation in the computer control of production.[13]

Another characteristic of Japanese steel firms is the wide use of subsidiaries and associated firms (actually subcontracting firms). Such firms can often number anything from twenty to several hundred. Moreover, even large steelworks have many employees from associated firms working in them; when there is a recession, these employees are the first to be laid off. There is thus a certain latitude for decision-making in the labour management policy of Japanese steel firms.

All these factors so contributed to the strengthening of Japan's international competitiveness that it was able to emerge as a world leader in the cost and quality of steel products.

A number of integrated steel firms were responsible for the development of the industry. Now there are just five large, integrated firms: Japan Steel Corporation, NKK, Kawasaki Steel, Sumitomo Metals, and Kobe Seiko (*seiko* means steelmaking). Each has somewhat different traits and traditions – for example, Kawasaki Steel has some advantage in sheet production, Sumitomo Metals in pipe, Kobe Seiko in engineering, and so on. However, since similarity or homogeneity is one of the basic characteristics of Japanese steel firms, it is hoped that the decision to focus on the growth and development of NKK will shed some light on the experience of other steel firms.

The growth pattern of NKK

NKK's Kawasaki Works (not to be confused with the company, Kawasaki Steel) was severely damaged by bombing during the Second World War, but, as was the case with nearly every Japanese company, it was the post-war financial confusion which precipitated crisis. Yet NKK managed to weather such storms as the Dodge Line, the stringent monetary policy instituted by the American financial adviser Mr Dodge. And the outbreak of the Korean War in 1950 provided the opportunity of recovery from the depressed post-war conditions.

At about that time, NKK's engineers read in the German technical journal, *Stahl und Eisen*, about LD converters, a new steel-making process invented in Austria.[14] They immediately recognized the potential of the new process, partly because as early as 1938 NKK had been the first company in Japan to adopt the Thomas converter process, which had some technical similarities to the LD process. NKK saw that the LD converters would improve productivity and profitability because they could produce good quality steel in an efficient way. Also, they did not require scrap, which was in very short supply in Japan at the time. Soon after, Yawata Iron and Steel, too, began to examine the new process. In order to avoid the inevitable competition among Japanese firms over securing patents, NKK, Yawata and MITI (the Ministry of International Trade and Industry) consulted together and decided that NKK should become the only licensee for the new process in Japan, but that other Japanese steel firms should be in the position of sub-licensees on the basis of relatively cheap sub-licence fees. Eventually, Japan's licence fees for the process were very low in comparison with the value of LD converters. Rather surprisingly, the MITI section manager flew to

Austria with NKK's delegates to support their negotiation with the Austrian company. Furthermore, probably under MITI's guidance, joint technical meetings were arranged to enable engineers from the large steel firms to study LD converters, and this kind of technical information exchange helped to diffuse their use.

The introduction of the LD converter process, including the guiding role of MITI, exemplifies the functioning of co-operation among Japanese firms, another notable facet of Japanese industry.[15] It is equally clear that Japanese firms were very assiduous in their study and introduction of new foreign techniques. Over the course of time, LD converters were adopted more quickly and readily in Japan than elsewhere, and were a major cause of Japan's ability to increase productivity. It was the same story with the continuous casting process; as described above, NKK was quick to adopt this vital new technique. However, when it came to the building of a new works – a crucial element for the rapid development of both an individual firm and the steel industry as a whole, NKK was rather slow off the mark. In this respect, Kawasaki Steel was the first mover.[16] Kawasaki began to build the Chiba Steelworks in 1951, which resulted in its becoming Japan's fourth-ranked integrated steel company.

Before the Second World War, there had been only two integrated steel firms in Japan, NKK and Japan Steel. After the war, on the orders of GHQ (General Headquarters of the Army of Occupation), Japan Steel was split into two companies, Yawata Iron and Steel and Fuji Steel. Then, Kawasaki was elevated to the status of an integrated firm through its ownership of blast furnaces, and this had the effect of stimulating firms which only had open-hearth steel furnaces to follow its example. Thus Sumitomo merged with Kokura Steel, and Kobe Seiko took over Amagasaki Iron, in order to acquire blast furnaces. The result of all this was that there were six major integrated firms post-war, and NKK's market share of steels fell from 12.5 per cent in 1951 to 9.2 per cent in 1959.

Maintenance of market share is of supreme importance to Japanese firms. A company's status in its industry is determined by output rather than profits, and is crucial for its management who are, for the most part, salaried managers. Because the firm's social reputation and that of its managers depended on it, NKK tried to recover its market share by building the Mizue Works next to the Kawasaki Works. But the addition of this plant only enabled NKK to regain a bare 1 per cent of market share. Further expansion was necessary. The other steel firms were also expanding, however, through the establishment of greenfield, coastal, completely integrated steelworks. In the 1950s, in addition to Kawasaki Steel's Chiba Works, mentioned above, Yawata built its Tobata and Sakai Works, Fuji Steel erected the Nagoya Works, Sumitomo Metals the Wakayama Works, and Kobe Seiko the Nagahama Works.[17] Already overtaken by Kawasaki Steel, NKK's response was the decision to establish a new works on a grand scale. The Fukuyama Works, with a production capacity of sixteen million tons of crude steel, was built in 1965. It was equipped with state-of-the-art machinery, and is still the largest steelworks in the world. As Table 6.1 demonstrates, the erection of the Fukuyama Works enabled NKK to win 14.2 per cent of market share in 1975, the peak of the post-war period.

Along with the co-operation between steel firms, mainly on the technical side, mentioned above, there is strong competition to retain or increase market share. This tendency is strengthened by homogeneity. When a firm comes up with a new project, or branches out in a new direction, rival firms are quick to follow it and adopt a similar strategy, resulting in intensified competition. The two distinguishing characteristics of Japanese industry are thus on the one hand competition, specifically for market share, and on the other hand co-operation, mostly in terms of technical information exchange.

The enlargement of blast furnaces continued. Fuji Steel erected a blast furnace with a capacity of 2,000 cubic metres at its Nagoya Works in 1964. NKK's Fukuyama Works had the first 3,000 cubic metre capacity blast furnace in 1969.[18] Coupled with this increase in cubic capacity, was the introduction of computer control at converters and blast furnaces around 1964. Computer control is one of the comparative advantages which the Japanese steel industry enjoys. In this context, it is interesting to note that the USSR's steel industry failed to make full use of computers, although it did succeed in enlarging facilities. This might well explain the relative inefficiency of the USSR's steel industry, in spite of its very large steel output.[19]

Over the years, NKK restructured its old works, and by 1968 the Kawasaki, Tsurumi and Mizue Works had been consolidated into the Keihin Works. It was then decided that the Keihin Works should be moved to newly reclaimed land, several miles offshore. The new complex, called the Ogishima Works and costing about one trillion yen, began to operate in 1976, after the oil crisis which radically changed the circumstances in which the steel industry operated. The Ogishima Works will, it is said, be the last completely new steelworks in Japan, at least until the end of this century. With the somewhat late advent of the Ogishima Works, the Japanese steel industry entered its second phase.

THE AGE OF STAGNANT DEMAND: WHAT STRATEGY SHOULD BE FOLLOWED AGAINST THE TIDE?

Production in the Japanese steel industry grew to an unprecedented level, though it occasionally experienced cyclical ups and downs. It reached the peak of its output – 120 million tons – in 1973, a record never since surpassed. Indeed, it seems clear that after the rapid growth of the first two post-war decades, the Japanese steel industry entered a period of stagnant demand. Table 6.2 demonstrates that since the early 1970s the steel production of not only Japan but also other developed countries has either remained constant or decreased. West Germany, France and Japan managed to avoid any great drop in production, but the United Kingdom and the United States suffered serious setbacks. Broadly speaking, it was inevitable that the output of developed countries should level out or fall. World output of steel continued to increase to some degree, but the increase was accounted for by the production of developing countries such as South Korea, Taiwan and China. For Japan, matters were made worse by the protectionist policies followed by developed nations like the United States and the members of the European Community. Domestic demand did not increase sufficiently, and the export market narrowed. Prospects for the immediate future did not appear particularly bright and it became increasingly obvious that the 1970s and 1980s were going to be very different from the 1950s and 1960s. While the latter could be characterized as years of growth, the former looked set to be years of stagnation.

A financial analysis of NKK

Like other steel firms, NKK's profitability declined in the 1970s and 1980s. However, because of its shipbuilding division, its profits fell even more steeply, the shipbuilding industry if anything, experiencing even greater difficulties than steel. For the first time in its post-war history, NKK made a loss in 1984; a second loss followed in 1987. As Table 6.3 demonstrates, both losses were heavy, the 1987 one in particular amounting to the exhorbitant sum of a little over 110 billion yen in real *keijo* profits. *Keijo* profits are those profits remaining after financial income and payments such as bank interest have been subtracted from operating profits; *toki* profits are the profits left after the subtraction of extraordinary income and losses from *keijo* profits; and real *keijo* profits are *keijo* profits before taking into account the proceeds from sales of securities. By any of these measures, NKK's profitability fell drastically.

Table 6.2 Crude steel production by countries (million metric tons/calendar year)

	UK	West Germany	France	USA	USSR	South Japan	Korea	Taiwan	China	World
1950	17	12	9	88	27	5				190
1955	20	21	12	106	45	9				273
1960	25	34	17	90	65	22				341
1965	27	37	20	119	91	41				460
1970	28	45	23	119	116	93				596
1975	20	40	22	106	141	102	2	1	24	647
1980	11	44	23	101	148	111	9	3	37	716
1985	16	40	19	80	155	105	14	5	47	717
1989	19	41	19	89	160	108	22	9	61	783

Sources: *Tekko Tokei Yoran* (Key Statistics of Iron and Steel), for 1990, 1980.

Table 6.3 Profitability of NKK

	Profits (keijo)^a ¥ m.	Profits (toki)^b ¥ m.	Profits (toki)/ sales (%)	Profits (toki)/ net worth (%)
1951	–	916	3.7	13.1
1955	–	1,805	3.9	8.6
1960	–	4,666	5.4	11.4
1965	11,979	11,979	5.8	13.2
1970	31,313	18,227	3.6	18.2
1975	44,878	20,292	1.7	13.5
1980	50,890	25,178	1.9	12.6
1984	−12,257	−11,074	−0.8	−4.1
1985	37,582	19,568	1.3	7.1
1987	−7,823	−13,948	−1.3	−5.3
1988	41,497	12,665	1.2	4.7
1989	101,058	42,013	3.3	14.4
1990	82,081	30,847	2.4	6.8

Sources: See Table 6.1
Notes: Financial year ending in March
    ^{a} Operating profits plus regular financial profits and losses
    ^{b} net profits

Over the long term, NKK's profit rate was unmistakably in decline. In the 1950s and 1960s the rate of *toki* profits on sales averaged 4.84 per cent and 4.85 per cent a year respectively; in the 1970s and 1980s the rate was 1.29 per cent and 1.37 per cent. The contrast between the former decades and the latter is evident. If the rate of *toki* profits on net worth is taken as the measure, the result is the same. The average annual rate was 12.5 per cent in the 1950s, 13.8 per cent in the 1960s, 8.0 per cent in the 1970s, and 6.7 per cent in the 1980s.[20] The downward tendency is clear. Moreover, the building costs of the Ogishima Works were a heavy burden for NKK, on top of the losses incurred in shipbuilding. NKK was thus in a worse state than the other major steel firms.

Another reason for NKK's critical condition was its habit, very typical of Japanese firms in general, of relying heavily on loan finance.[21] As Table 6.4 indicates, the company's financial structure after the Second World War depended on borrowed capital, especially loans from commercial banks. Before the war, such financing was virtually unknown to Japanese firms, but the rapid post-war growth of private manufacturing companies led them to borrow money to invest in their factories. Steel firms like NKK were no exception. In 1980 NKK's net worth was only 10 per cent, but the level of its borrowed capital was as high as 90 per cent. Like many other firms, therefore, NKK had to pay huge amounts of interest. In times of prosperity or growth, it is relatively easy to sustain such interest charges, but when times are hard it can prove very difficult indeed. As the years of rapid growth levelled off and gave way to a period of relative stagnation, it was widely urged that firms should reduce their borrowed capital and, conversely, increase their net worth. But the repayment of loans, and consequent reduction of borrowed capital, was easier to prescribe than achieve during a period of low or zero growth.

Table 6.4 Financial structure of NKK

Year/ Month	Net worth (%)	Borrowed Capital (%)	Debenture and loan (%)
1912/11	100	0	0
1915/11	60	40	7
1920/11	53	47	33
1925/11	45	55	44
1930/11	42	58	49
1935/11	67	33	17
1940/10	69	31	8
1945/ 3	40	60	36
1950/ 3	40	60	19
1955/ 3	31	69	37
1960/ 3	30	70	43
1965/ 3	30	70	44
1970/ 3	13	87	43
1975/ 3	11	89	47
1980/ 3	10	90	56
1985/ 3	11	89	53
1986/ 3	11	89	-
1987/ 3	11	89	-
1988/ 3	12	88	-
1989/ 3	13	87	-
1990/ 3	20	80	49

Source: See Table 6.1

During the growth years of the 1950s and 1960s, profit rates were relatively high so that the pay-out ratio (i.e. the percentage of dividend out of profits) could be kept low. When profitability is low, however, the pay-out ratio has to be higher, and NKK's pay-out ratio was increasing, as the following figures demonstrate. During the 1950s the ratio was 31.6 per cent, during the 1960s 53.7 per cent, and during the 1970s

105.5 per cent. No ratio can be calculated for the two years in the 1980s
when losses were made. If those years are excluded, the pay-out ratio
would be 61.5 per cent, but the actual ratio was almost certainly far in
excess of 70 per cent. It is therefore fair to conclude that, in comparison
with the 1950s and 1960s, NKK would have found it very difficult to
invest in its operations out of profits since it had to devote a greater
proportion of these to the payment of dividends (see Table 6.5).

Table 6.5 Dividend and capital structure of NKK

	Dividend (%)	Dividend/ profits (toki) (%)	Paid-up capital ¥ bn.	Gross capital ¥ bn.	Net worth ¥ bn.
1951	22.5	25	1.0	21	7
1955	15	42	5.0	67	21
1960	9	29	22.5	139	41
1965	10	64	76.4	299	91
1970	10	42	76.4	782	100
1975	10	50	102.1	1,590	150
1980	8	47	146.9	2,377	200
1985	10	80	156.9	2,531	275
1990	10	55	233.5	2,230	454

Source: See Table 6.1
Note: Financial year ending at the end of March

Since the early 1970s all Japanese steel firms, including NKK, have
been faced with a tough situation. In earlier years, steel firms were able
to grow rapidly by virtue of expanding demand, and of splendid
entrepreneurship in terms of the technological choices made, the
expansion of facilities, and other similar devices. Exports reached thirty
million tons annually, which was equivalent to a third of production.
Imports of steel products were negligible. By January 1991, however,
and in sharp contrast, imports had overtaken exports. Coming mainly
from NIEs (newly industrializing economies) such as Korea and
Taiwan, imports for that month reached 1,243,000 tons, surpassing
exports by 12,000 tons.[22] Moreover, forecasts suggested that imports
would prove to have been greater than exports throughout 1991. This
had never happened before, except during the short and turbulent period
just after the Second World War. Steel exports remained at thirty
million tons a year until 1986, but since then there has been a
precipitous decline, to seventeen million tons in 1990. On the other

hand, imports of steel products increased from about three million tons in 1985 to thirteen million tons in 1990.[23] While one of the reasons for this could be that the export drive was not very strong because domestic demand was so solid, the real reason was that steel production was stable at the 110 million ton level. One way or another, taking a long-term view, it is evident that the beleaguered steel industry faces a number of problems.

Future policy

What strategy should NKK have adopted to overcome these difficulties? There were, in fact, three possible avenues of approach – firstly, rationalization, including the manufacture of higher value-added products; secondly, diversification; and thirdly, internationalization.

As demand has stagnated since the early 1970s, NKK has tried to make its steelworks more efficient. Large sums have been expended on rationalization. Although it became impossible to build new works, or even to erect new blast furnaces in the 1980s, NKK improved the operation of its existing works and enlarged blast furnaces, utilizing the idling time which recurred at regular four or five yearly intervals. Now all but one of NKK's blast furnaces have an internal capacity of over 4,000 cubic metres. Every conceivable measure has also been taken to trim costs.[24] The workforce has been reduced in order to increase labour productivity; as the figures in Table 6.1 indicate, whereas there were around 40,000 employees in the early 1970s, there were only half that number in the 1980s. In addition, separation by products has been undertaken. NKK has two operations, the Fukuyama Works and the Ogishima (Keihin) Works. Although the latter is the newer, it is also the smaller of the two, with an annual production capacity of six million tons of steel, as compared with the sixteen million tons of the Fukuyama Works. For this reason, while production of general steels is concentrated at Fukuyama, manufacture of higher quality products such as special steels is concentrated at Ogishima.[25] In fact, labour productivity at Fukuyama is higher than at Ogishima, the annual steel output per worker being 841 tons at the former and 577 tons at the latter.[26] At the present time, four out of six blast furnaces are in operation, one at Ogishima and three at Fukuyama. NKK is thus actively pursuing rationalization in a variety of ways. Older and smaller blast furnaces are being left idle; production is being specialized at each works; the workforce is being reduced; incremental improvements are being sought, such as the yield ratio at each production stage, including the comprehensive use of robots; job combination schemes related to the integration of workshops are proceeding further; and so forth. Furthermore, it is also policy to increase the ratio of higher value-added products, such as electrically galvanized steel sheet, stainless sheet, and steel specially coated with silicon, the demand for which is increasing.[27] On the other hand, NKK is attempting to reduce its ratio of such cheaper and simpler products as hot coils, sections, bars and rails, because of severe competition from Japanese mini-mills using the electric furnace process, such as Tokyo Seitetsu Company, and manufacturers from the NIEs.

The second strategy is to diversify outside the steel industry. The demand for the steel products is not growing so sharply that expansion of production can be relied upon. As shown in Table 6.6, NKK's sales have remained at virtually the same level of 1,200 to 1,500 billion yen since 1975. Growth-orientation is a notable characteristic of Japanese firms, along with homogeneity (the tendency to adopt similar or identical strategies), co-operation, and competition for market share. It is not considered good practice for a firm to remain the same size, from the viewpoint either of growth or of employees' morale. Steel firms have therefore had to diversify into other fields such as general engineering, new materials, electronics, biotechnology and integrated community development. NKK pursued this diversification strategy, and, not surprisingly given the homogeneous character of Japanese companies, other steel firms pursued almost the same course. In contrast, the response of steel companies in the United States to stagnant demand has differed from firm to firm.

As stated earlier, NKK was unique in having a shipbuilding division. In this sense, it is true to say that NKK had been diversified for a long time. But this diversification was of the old type since the shipbuilding and steel industries fall into the category of so-called 'old industry', and over the long term precipitate growth in the shipbuilding industry cannot be assumed. Table 6.6 indicates that the sales ratio of NKK's steel division has been fairly stable, at 73 to 88 per cent, over the years represented. The first statistics distinguishing shipbuilding from engineering appeared, so far as it has been possible to determine, in 1971.[28] According to these, the sales ratios of both the shipbuilding and the engineering divisions were 9 per cent in that year. Thereafter, however, the sales ratio of the shipbuilding division decreased steadily, while that of the engineering division increased. In these circumstances, NKK came up with an ambitious programme called 'New Future Vision', which anticipated the diversified routes the company might follow. It was forecast, for example, that the composition of NKK's sales in the year 2000 would be as follows: steel (50 per cent); general engineering, including shipbuilding (25 per cent); community development (12.5 per cent); and new materials, electronics, and biotechnology (12.5 per cent).[29] Of these categories, NKK can be reasonably certain of achieving the forecast ratio for engineering, a field with which it has long been familiar. Community development may also prove a successful venture as it is intended that land which NKK already owns near a big city, Yokohama, will be used. However, in the fields of new metals (technically advanced, complex non-ferrous metals), electronics and biotechnology, success is more difficult to predict. As far as electronics is concerned, while it is true to say that NKK is one of the largest users of computer systems, so that it has accumulated an enormous amount of know-how and has established business links with Massachusetts Computer Incorporated and Convex Computer Corporation,[30] the fact remains that there are so many competitors in this field that it does not seem possible to achieve success on a substantial scale, even in the production of semiconductors. A move into biotechnology will be even more difficult. The manufacture of new metals might, however, offer greater opportunities for success, since the technology already accumulated by NKK in steels is not dissimilar.

The third strategy is internationalization. Interestingly, NKK was the first mover here. It is a well-known fact that NKK acquired a 50 per cent shareholding in the National Steel Corporation of America in 1984.[31] This was the first large-scale international joint venture in the steel industry, as National Steel was the sixth largest steel-producing firm in the United States. Moreover, before this there were no multinational

Table 6.6 Sales of NKK: percentage share of divisions

	Sales ¥ bn.	Steel %	Engineering %	Shipbuilding %
1951	25	88		12
1955	46	80		20
1960	86	85		15
1965	206	85		15
1970	513	88		12
1971	587	81	9.5	9.4
1975	1,192	79	10.3	10.7
1980	1,311	84	11.4	4.6
1985	1,501	73	20.2	6.8
1989	1,261	75	22.3	2.7
1990	1,278	79	17.8	3.2

Source: See Table 6.1
Note: Financial year ending at the end of March

steel companies operating large works in a number of countries. All steel firms, whether Japanese, American or European, were localized in their own country. It is therefore worth examining this Japanese-American joint venture in more detail.

National Steel, a subsidiary of National Intergroup Incorporated (NII), was faced with a number of problems. Its equipment was out-of-date through lack of sufficient investment over a long period. Consequently, profitability was low or negative. NII had lost the incentive to manage National Steel, concentrating instead on developing opportunities in finance and distribution, and was looking for a buyer for the company. At one time, US Steel made an offer for National Steel, but this was blocked by the United States Department of Justice as an infringement of anti-trust legislation. NKK was more successful. It was able to purchase half of National Steel's equity, at a cost of $293 million. Despite the fact that NII retained the remaining 50 per cent, it was expected that the actual management of the company would be undertaken by NKK's representatives. At first, National Steel's chairman was Howard Love of NII, and its president was also an NII man, the Japanese vice-chairman being NKK's most senior representative in the company. But in time this position altered, National Steel acquiring first a Japanese president, and then a Japanese chairman. In 1990, NKK increased its interest in National Steel to 70 per cent – finally achieving majority control.[32]

The apparent reasons for NKK's purchase of a share of National Steel in 1984 were in part alarm at the rise of protectionism in the United States, and in part a response to the fact that Japanese automobile firms had begun to manufacture there. But the fundamental reason is almost certainly to be found in the previously mentioned growth-orientated motivation of the company. Over the period of a decade or so, NKK's sales were so stagnant that expansionary tactics seemed called for. A move overseas was an appropriate response, especially given that continuing growth was one of the major goals of Japanese firms. The case of National Steel appears also to symbolize recent trends among American firms – in their case, deindustrialization and a move into finance or commerce. As well as its purchase of 50 per cent of National Steel's equity, NKK invested $800 million in the five years following its participation in order to modernize outdated equipment and build such new facilities as an electric galvanized line. This was a continuous casting process which enabled National Steel to trim costs and stabilize operations, as well as to raise its yield ratio of finished steel from crude steel to 96.7 per cent.[33] NKK did not merely confine itself to the modernization of National Steel's plant and equipment, however; it also began to restructure the latter's organization and to change its industrial relations, imbuing the American workforce with new ideas. In other words, NKK started to introduce the so-called Japanese management style into the American company, experimenting with such innovations as harmonious co-operation between management and workers, a no-lay-off policy (more precisely, a no-readily-lay-off policy), the creation of fewer job categories through job combination, and so forth. Despite all this, National Steel's performance continued to be less than satisfactory, in the opinion of the American business journals, since its profitability was still below that of other large American steel manufacturers.[34] However, this criticism seems to be somewhat wide of the mark, especially if it is considered that National Steel's main product, steel sheet for automobiles, is notorious for low margins. Meanwhile, the fusion of Japanese and American business styles remains an attractive prospect from the viewpoint of both real management and academic study.

NKK AT THE CROSSROADS: SOME CONCLUDING REMARKS

Looking back on the post-Second World War history of the Japanese steel industry, it seems clear that the period can be divided into two distinct parts, the 1950s and 1960s, and the 1970s and 1980s. The former was a period of rapid growth, the latter one of stagnation. While the growth rate of steel output, and profitability, are quite different in each period, there are nevertheless some characteristics common to both. Although these have been touched on already, it is worth emphasizing them. In the first place, Japanese firms are homogeneous by nature and in their behaviour. If one company forms a strategy, other companies immediately follow suit. This was true of the adoption of LD converters and continuous casting, the enlarging of blast furnaces, and the building of coastal, greenfield, integrated works. It was also true of the strategies of rationalization, diversification and internationalization during the 1970s and 1980s, when all major steel firms followed similar policies in these three directions. It is a pattern of behaviour which leads to fierce competition between Japanese firms, often called 'competition with excessive fighting' (*kato kyoso*); 'excessive fighting' came to be a feature of Japan's business environment, as is indicated by the maxim, 'If you win in Japan, you will be able to win all over the world'. This competitive structure is very similar to that described by Michael Porter.[35] The competitive interrelationship amongst firms was what gave the advantage to Japanese firms. It is possible, however, that this particular characteristic may lead to difficulties with regard to the strategy of internationalization. At the present time, all the major Japanese automobile firms (eight of them) have moved into the United States and have begun to manufacture cars there. As a result, it is predicted that in a few years there will be an over-supply of cars. Following the automobile firms, all Japan's major steel companies have established joint ventures with United States steel manufacturers – NKK with National Steel, Japan Steel Corporation (re-established in 1970 when Yawata and Fuji merged again) with Inland Steel, Kawasaki Steel with California Steel and Armco, Sumitomo Metals with LTV, and Kobe Seiko with US Steel.[36] This level of penetration into the United States market may cause friction in the future through excessive production.

Secondly, co-operation between firms, and between firms and government (specifically MITI), is crucial to the understanding of Japanese business. It can be divided into two categories: co-operation regarding the exchange of technical information, and co-operation over price, production quotas, investment and the like, which has not been examined here. The latter sort of co-operation often leads to the formation of cartels.

Thirdly, there is the competition, often fierce, for market share, and fourthly, there is growth orientation, both of which have already been discussed.

Finally, let us examine the current position of the strategies of rationalization, diversification and internationalization. Thanks to across-the-board rationalization, the Japanese steel industry has partially recovered its international competitiveness. In the case of relatively simple products such as hot coils, Japan was under severe pressure from South Korea and Taiwan, because of the wide gap in manufacturing costs. However, this gap is diminishing, even with low-quality products, and analysts now observe that Japan has inversely regained the cost advantage in regard to coated steel plate.[37] In fact, NKK's recent profits emanate partly from high prices and partly from rationalization. In this context, it should be noted that although NKK's steel production capacity is twenty to twenty-two million tons, actual production is only twelve million tons. Around 40 per cent of productive capacity is thus idle. Nevertheless, NKK continues to make profits.

So far as internationalization is concerned, some possibility of success still exists.

Diversification is a more difficult prospect because the fields of electronics and biotechnology are uncharted waters for steel firms like

NKK. Moreover, the problem arises of how to organize and control diversified activities. Generally speaking, Japanese firms have tackled this by spinning off a diversified division from their main business, once it has reached a certain size, in order to provide it with effective control. Size is the operative factor. As a diversified division grows larger, the centrifugal forces become stronger and it becomes more and more difficult to retain the new business within the parent company. So a separate subsidiary is set up; and eventually a group of companies – a *keiretsu* – is created.[38] However, difficulties may still arise. If a subsidiary is too successful, this may cause friction with the parent. To cite an example, in 1957 Sumitomo Metals spun off Sumitomo Light Metals as a subsidiary whose main business was the refining of aluminium; but it was not long before Sumitomo Light Metals was challenging the authority of its parent. It would be rash to draw specific conclusions as to the merits or otherwise of diversification at this juncture, but it is certain that, as the experience of American steel firms suggests, this strategy carries with it a number of difficulties.

In conclusion, there appear to be two fundamental considerations facing NKK. Can it retain its position as a steel firm, domestically and internationally? And will the strategies of diversification and internationalization succeed? These are still open questions.

NOTES

1 *Nippon Kokan Kabushikikaisha 70 Nenshi* (*70 Years of Nippon Kokan*), 1982, pp. 1–12; see also *Nippon Kokan Kabushikikaisha 60 Nenshi*, 1972, and *Nippon Kokan Kabushikikaisha 50 Nenshi*, 1962. The position and characteristics of NKK are quite similar to Mannesmann in Germany or Stewarts and Lloyds in Britain.
2 Takeo Fukushima, *Moeru Tekko* (*The Vigorous Iron and Steel Industry*), 1991, p. 202.
3 *Nippon Kokan 50 Nenshi*, pp. 119–219.
4 As regards the long-term history of the steel industry, see E. Abe and Y. Suzuki (eds), *Changing Patterns of International Rivalry: Some Lessons from the Steel Industry*, Tokyo, University of Tokyo Press, 1991. Also useful is Thomas K. McCraw, 'Steel since 1850: Varieties of Competition and Industry Structure', *Annual Bulletin of Research Institute for Social Science*, Ryukoku University, 1988, no. 18, supplement.
5 See Paul Tiffany, *The Decline of American Steel*, New York, Oxford University Press, 1988.
6 Regarding the analysis from the viewpoint of both the demand and supply side, see E. Abe, 'Introduction' in Abe and Suzuki (eds), *Changing Patterns*.
7 Donald Barnett and Louis Schorsch, *Steel: Upheaval in a Basic Industry*, Cambridge, Mass., Ballinger, 1983, p. 55.

8 Japan Iron and Steel Federation, *Nippon no Tekkogyo, 1989* (*The Iron and Steel Industry in 1989*), 1989, p. 28.

9 Japan Iron and Steel Federation, Tekko Tokei Iinkai Hen (compiled by the Committee for Iron and Steel Statistics), *Tekko Tokei Yoran* (*Abstracts of Iron and Steel Statistics*), 1978, pp. 214–17.

10 *Nippon no Tekkogyo, 1989*, p. 28.

11 Kenichi Iida, *Nippon Tekko Gijutsushi* (*A History of Japanese Iron and Steel Technology*), 1979, pp. 377–87.

12 Ibid., pp. 426–8.

13 Regarding the technical aspects of computer control, see Yasuo Nosaka (ed.), *Tekkogyo no Computer Control* (*Computer Control in the Iron and Steel Industry*), Tokyo, 1970.

14 Iida, *Nippon*, pp. 423–6. For a comparison of the adoption process of LD converters in Japan as compared with the USA, see Leonard Lynn, *How Japan Innovates: A Comparison with the US in the Case of Oxygen Steelmaking*, Boulder, Colo., Westview Press, 1982.

15 For a description of the role of MITI in co-operation between firms in the Japanese iron and steel industry, see T.K. McCraw and Patricia O'Brien, 'Production and Distribution: Competition Policy and Industry Structure' in McCraw (ed.), *America Versus Japan*, Boston, Mass., Harvard Business School Press, 1986, pp. 86–100.

16 For the case of Kawasaki Steel, see S. Yonekura, 'Sengo Nippon Tekkogyo niokeru Kawasaki Seitetsu no Kakushinsei' ('Innovative Behaviour of Kawasaki Steel in Post-War Japanese Industry'), *Hitotsubashi Ronso*, 1983, vol. 90, no. 3; see also, *idem*, 'The Postwar Japanese Iron and Steel Industry: Continuity and Discontinuity' in E. Abe and Y. Suzuki (eds), *Changing Patterns*. As mentioned above, Kawasaki has some advantage in the production of sheet for automobiles. In this regard, it may be of interest to highlight the fact that Toyota Automobile, the largest car manufacturer in Japan, did not buy steels from Kawasaki for almost forty years because Kawasaki had stopped supplying sheet steel to Toyota in the 1950s when the latter suffered a serious financial crisis. It was, in fact, hardly surprising that Kawasaki should stop the supply of steel sheet, since Toyota had been unable to pay. However, after recovering from the crisis, Toyota took its revenge; although it bought steels from all other major steel companies, it boycotted Kawasaki steel until quite recently. Toyota only started to buy from Kawasaki again in 1990, because the latter does have some advantage in sheet steel for automobiles. This anecdote serves to illustrate the importance of long-term trust in Japanese business relations.

17 *Tsusho Sangyo Seisakushi* (*A History of Trade and Industry Policy*), 1990, vol. 10, ch. 5, section 4, especially p. 139.

18 Iida, *Nippon*, p. 382.

19 A more careful and detailed study of the Soviet steel industry between the 1950s and 1970s is needed in order to ascertain the reasons for success and failure.

20 The percentages are calculated from the annual figures, which do not appear in the Tables. This also applies to the pay-out ratio.

21 See Kenichi Iida, Shuji Ohashi and Toshio Kuroiwa (eds), *Gendai Nippon Sangyo Hattatsushi*, Dai 4 kan, *Tekko* (*The Development History of Modern Japanese Industry*, vol. 4, *Iron and Steel*), 1969, part 6, ch. 3.

22 *Nihon Keizai Shinbun* (*Japan Economic Times*), 9 February 1991.

23 Naoki Komatsu, 'Tekko' ('Iron and Steel'), *Kogin Chosa* (*Bulletin of the Industrial Bank of Japan*), no. 246, p. 3.

24 Masaaki Fukuma, 'NKK, Kyuchitsujo Hakai e "peresutoroika" no Gekido' ('Radical change to destroy the old stability in NKK'), *Shukan Toyo Keizai*, 12 November 1988, p. 49.

25 Fukushima, *Moeru Tekko*, pp. 82–3.

26 Masahiro Moritama, 'Gorika, Kohukakachikade Shuekiryoku Takamaru Koroote' ('Profitability Increase of Major Integrated Steel Firms by Rationalisation and a Shift to Higher Value-Added Products'), *Nikko Research Centre Toshi Geppo*, October 1989, p. 37.

27 Masaaki Fukuma, 'Fine Busosuru "sekai saikyo" tetsu no gundan' ('Army of steel firms of the strongest power in the world through the production of fine metals'), *Shukan Toyo Keizai*, 22 April 1989.

28 *Nippon Kokan Kabushikikaisha 70 Nenshi*, Shiryo, p. 20.

29 Fukushima, *Moeru Tekko*, p. 87.

30 *Fortune*, 1 August 1988, p. S-45.

31 'Steel Forges a Japanese Connection', *Business Week*, 7 May 1984; 'Nippon, National Steel Set Deal, Japan Company to Buy 50% of US Firm', *The Washington Post*, 25 April 1984.

32 'Bonuses for Steelworkers? (National Steel Corp.)', *Forbes*, 27 April 1987; 'Nippon Official Named President of National Steel', *Wall Street Journal*, 2 July 1986; 'National Steel's Robert D. McBride Resigns Two Posts', *Wall Street Journal*, 23 May 1986; 'National Intergroup Plans Either to Sell or Spin off 50% Stake in National Steel', *Wall Street Journal*, 5 March 1986; *Tekko Shinbun* (Iron and Steel Times), 26 April 1990; *Nikkei Sangyo Shinbun*, 28 June 1990.

33 Fukushima, *Moeru Tekko*, p. 92. For joint ventures of Japanese steel firms with American firms, see L. Lynn, 'America ni shinshutsusuru nihon tekkogyo' ('Japanese steel firms which move into the USA'), *Business Review*, Hitotsubashi University, 1987, vol. 34, no. 3.

34 'The Weak Weld at National Steel-NKK', *Business Week*, 24 July 1989.

35 Michael Porter stresses that fierce domestic competition brings about the strong international competitiveness that enables companies in such countries to compete successfully in overseas markets. Michael E. Porter, 'The Competitive Advantage of Nations', *Harvard Business Review*, March–April 1990. See also, *idem*, *The Competitive Advantage of Nations*, London, Macmillan, 1990. His explanation of the competitive structure of Japanese industry, in this book, is quite persuasive, emphasizing as it does the domestic rivalry of Japanese firms. However, Patricia A. O'Brien, 'Industry Structure as a Competitive Advantage: The History of Japan's Post-war Steel Industry', *Business History*, 1992, vol. 34, no. 1, stresses the role of MITI in the development of the steel industry in Japan.

36 Moritama, 'Gorika', p. 39.

37 Ibid., p. 36.

38 Kazuichi Sakamoto and Masahiro Shimotani (eds), *Gendai Nihon no Kigyo Group* (*Company Groups in Modern Japan*), 1987, especially ch. 4.

7 Competitive advantage in the Japanese shipbuilding industry: the case of IHI

Shin Goto

INTRODUCTION

Before the Second World War, many of the Japanese heavy and chemical industries were no better than import-substituting industries, and protective measures by the government against foreign competition were important for the maintenance of their domestic markets. After the war, however, during the reconstruction of the Japanese economy, almost all these industries were able not only to obtain domestic markets by themselves but to attain a strongly competitive position in the world market. In a short time their export activities had become responsible for the rapid growth of the Japanese economy. The Japanese shipbuilding industry, to be discussed here, is one of the industries that underwent the transformation from a protected to an export-oriented industry shortly after the war.

This chapter will focus on the technical innovations that were the most important factor contributing to the international competitiveness of the post-war shipbuilding industry, and to its rapid growth. The case of a large shipbuilding firm will be examined for this purpose, and its post-war technical strategy traced. The firm selected for study is IHI (Ishikawajima-Harima Heavy Industries), which was incorporated in 1960 on the merger of Ishikawajima Heavy Industries Company and Harima Shipyard. IHI was a pioneer in technical innovation in post-war Japanese shipbuilding, and became one of the top shipbuilders in the world. The first two sections below will trace the pattern of IHI's technical strategy from around the time of merger, and in the last section the features and implications of IHI's technical strategy will be summed up.

MODERNIZATION OF BUILDING METHODS

At the time of their merger, Ishikawajima Heavy Industries and Harima Shipyard were among the larger shipbuilders in Japan, although far from being the largest. Ishikawajima Heavy Industries[1] had already diversified its business into non-shipbuilding fields, and shipbuilding sales were only a quarter of the total sales of its aggregate business activities. Ishikawajima's building capacity was rather small relative to its competitors; even the largest building berth in its Tokyo Works had a capacity of only 22,000 gross tons (grt).[2] Moreover, the possibility of any great extension of this building berth was limited by its unfavourable location inside the Bay of Tokyo. Thus, in order to expand, there was no other alternative than to find a new site or to buy out another shipyard.

Harima Shipyard, on the other hand, had two berths, each with a building capacity of 40,000 grt, and was recognized as being one of the larger shipbuilders.[3] Harima's shipbuilding specialization meant that it was dependent on uncertain orders from shipping companies and industrial carriers, and its performance was therefore volatile. At the time of the merger, Harima was in financial difficulties due to the severe shipbuilding depression which followed the Suez boom, and it was looking for new business in non-shipbuilding areas.

The merger of the two companies was thus an accord between Ishikawajima's wish to expand its building capacity and Harima's desire to diversify the range of its business. It not only enabled them to achieve balanced growth as a general heavy engineering enterprise, however, but also provided better opportunities for further expansion in the shipbuilding field. The newly incorporated company, by combining efficient construction methods and numerous competent engineers trained in shipbuilding techniques, grasped the chance of becoming a top-ranking performer in the Japanese shipbuilding industry.

Technical innovation, the principal distinction between pre- and postwar shipbuilding, is said, in general, to consist of such changes in construction methods as electric welding rather than riveting in the joining of steel plates, and the use of the block system and pre-outfitting in the building process, rather than erection in the building berth and onboard outfitting. Much research still remains to be undertaken into the ways in which these innovations from abroad were introduced into the post-war Japanese shipbuilding industry. However, it is surely possible to point to NBC's shipyard at Kure, in Hiroshima Prefecture, as being one of the more influential routes for the diffusion of new technology. In 1951, an American shipping company, NBC (National Bulk Carriers) Corporation, came to an agreement with the Japanese government which enabled it to lease part of Kure, a former Japanese naval dockyard, to build its own merchant vessels. NBC's shipyard employed many Japanese engineers and workers, including Hisashi Shinto, a former employee of Harima Shipyard and later to be general manager of the shipbuilding division and president of IHI, who was appointed as chief engineer.[4]

While he was at NBC's Kure Shipyard, Shinto introduced new building techniques, which he had learned from aeroplane production during the war, into the shipbuilding process. The main thrust of the new methods was to attach importance to 'how to build', as well as to 'what to build', and to draw up a plan showing the procedures, materials and personnel allocation necessary for every stage in the process of the building of a vessel. Thus hull construction, for example, was divided into several stages – moulding, marking, cutting, bending, sub-assembly, assembly and erection – and a file issued, recording the equipment, working hours and workforce necessary for each stage, on the basis of which the whole building programme could be scheduled.[5] As for outfitting, such conventional methods as drawing up a plan and fitting on a functional base were gradually replaced by new techniques of composite drawing, unit assembly and the installation of auxiliary equipment.[6]

It is difficult to ascertain whether Shinto's innovations at NBC's Kure Shipyard were the result of his own basic ideas or merely a transplantation of the construction methods used in the USA in the mass-production of 'Liberty Ships' during the war. Whatever the truth of their origins, the important factor was that these innovations in the building process were openly accessible to and rapidly absorbed by many other Japanese naval architects. Their diffusion in this way contributed to a general increase in the technical level of the Japanese shipbuilding industry, at a time when it was endeavouring to augment its international competitive capacity in the world market.[7]

With the merger of Ishikawajima and Harima in 1960, Shinto left NBC's Kure Shipyard to become general manager of the shipbuilding division at IHI. He was soon to discover that there was a technological gap between the NBC operation and IHI. In particular, the old system of functional outfitting remained in use at the Aioi Works, the main shipyard (in Hyogo Prefecture) at the time of the merger.[8] Shinto lost no time in introducing NBC's construction methods at Kure into the IHI works. This process of technical transfer required many difficult adjustments, both outside and inside the works. Around the Aioi area, he had to organize and foster a host of technically specialized suppliers to deliver various parts to the shipyard 'just in time'. And he had to retrain the skilled workers as well as the technical staff in order for them to understand and accept the new construction system.[9]

Thus, after a two-year period of trial and error, various innovations that had been tried out and elaborated at NBC's Kure Shipyard, in particular construction methods on the basis of composite drawings, took root at the Aioi Works, resulting in a great reduction of man-hours. For example, total man-hours per deadweight ton employed in hull construction at the Aioi Works were reduced from 36.7 hours in 1961 to 25.6 hours in 1965 in the case of an oil tanker, and, during the same period, from 69.7 to 32.5 hours in the case of a bulk-carrier.[10] At the same time, IHI innovated in the field of hull construction suitable for large-size vessels. Its first innovative vessel was the *Ajia Maru*, built at the Aioi Works in 1961. By shortening the beam–length ratio to 6.72, less than the conventional ratio of 7.0, and leaving void space in the midship section, it was possible to reduce the weight of steel plates by 6.2 per cent and raise the deadweight tonnage by 252 tons, in comparison with the conventional design of a vessel.[11] The reduction of hull weight and increase in carrying capacity meant a lower ship price per deadweight ton. Vessels constructed on the basis of this sort of hull design, which became a typical hull design for large vessels, came to be known as 'economy' class ships, or 'Shinto's vessels'. Boosted by the development of an 'economy' class ship design and the introduction of the new building methods mentioned above, IHI's Aioi Works was able to raise its productivity substantially. As a result, during the period from 1962 to 1964, when the Japanese shipbuilding industry encountered the second export boom, the Aioi Works succeeded in securing orders from many shipowners, both foreign and domestic, and achieved world records in new shipbuilding for three consecutive years.[12]

PRODUCT DEVELOPMENT

As already indicated, the development of the Japanese shipbuilding industry after the war owed much to technical innovations in the building process. Since the 1960s, however, most of the effort has been directed towards improving existing technology, rather than towards producing innovations. Japanese competitive advantages, such as the low price of a vessel and a quick delivery time, which were established in the 1950s, were maintained very successfully thereafter. But the most important factor leading to the remarkably rapid growth of the Japanese shipbuilding industry from the late 1960s was product innovation, rather than improvements in the construction process. In the case of IHI, product development went in two directions: one focused on increasing the size of specialized cargo vessels such as tankers and bulk-carriers, and the other on the mass production of standardized cargo vessels. IHI's product development will be described in the following sections.

The increasing size of vessels

Since the war, there has been a developing tendency towards increasing the size of specialized cargo vessels, especially oil tankers, and by the early 1950s the age of the supertanker of over 40,000 deadweight tons (dwt) had already arrived. The Suez crisis further accelerated this trend, with the appearance of the so-called mammoth-tanker of over 80,000 dwt and the even larger tanker of over 100,000 dwt.[13]

The initiative to increase the size of vessels was said to lie initially with Japanese shipbuilders, who inherited the large building berths of the former naval dockyards. However, IHI was slow to increase ship size, owing to the capacity constraints of its existing berths. As already indicated, at the time of the 1960 merger, IHI's largest building berth was the third berth in the Aioi Works and its maximum capacity was 55,000 grt. This was an up-to-date berth, specializing in the construction of large vessels, which had been extended just before the merger. And, in 1961 and 1965 respectively, the supertanker *Ajia Maru*, and the *Takasago Maru*, a 100,000 dwt class vessel, were built at this berth (see Table 7.1). Nevertheless, IHI was still considered to be some five years behind the world's leading shipbuilders in the trend towards increasing size of vessels, at a stage when a five-year time lapse corresponded to a doubling in tanker size. In these circumstances, even a modern shipyard like the Aioi Works was exposed to the danger of rapid obsolescence.

Moreover, at the end of the 1960s, the trend towards increased size received a further spur. This time the impetus came not from Japanese shipbuilders, but from shipowners and shippers in Japan and elsewhere. As regards oil tankers, in particular, the development of the central terminal system for oil shipments, and the extension of oil transportation distances as a result of the third Middle East war in 1967, which closed the Suez Canal, made it profitable for shipowners and shippers to own larger and larger oil tankers. This meant that only those shipbuilders who were able and willing to respond to requests for big specialized cargo vessels were in a position to take orders. Needless to say, it was necessary to expand building capacity to be in this position. Orders for the massive vessels were therefore concentrated on those shipbuilders who were prepared to undertake large-scale investment in the expansion of their facilities. It was the positive attitude of Japanese shipbuilders to the requests of shipowners and shippers for ever larger vessels that boosted the expansion of the Japanese shipbuilding industry from the late 1960s.

Almost all the bigger Japanese shipbuilders began to construct very large building docks at this time. It was not unusual for these new docks to have a building capacity of more than 800,000 dwt. Basically, the rush to construct them was the result of severe competition among shipbuilders. However, the fact that the Ministry of Transport had the right to permit new construction or the extension of building capacity was also an accelerating factor. It was essential for shipbuilders at least not to be outstripped by rivals in applying to the Ministry for permits for new construction, since any tardiness might earn Ministry disapproval and lose them the opportunity for future expansion. Japanese shipbuilders were thus pushed into filing applications for expansion, whether or not it was immediately necessary. IHI, like its peers, took part in this contest for capacity expansion, and its progress can be divided into three stages.

The first stage was the construction of a new shipyard in addition to the two it already had – the Tokyo and Aioi Works. Thus, in January 1961, IHI decided to establish a new shipyard on reclaimed land at Negishi Bay in Yokohama, and in August of the same year construction began on a new dock.[14] This new yard, later called the Yokohama Works, in which 9.9 billion yen had been invested by 1966, had an area of about 250,000 square metres, with some 45,000 square metres for a building site.[15] The Yokohama Works was at first intended for the continuous construction of oil tankers of 80,000 dwt; the first vessel to have its keel laid down at the Works in October 1964 was that size.[16] Immediately after its launch, however, the original plan was revised to cope with the increasing size of vessels, and the modifications to the plant layout, enlargement of the conveyor systems, and expansion of facilities necessary to increase the building capacity, were carried out.[17] As a result, IHI was able not only to overcome its early disadvantage regarding the size of vessels but to regain and retain the record for building the largest vessels in the world. As shown in Table 7.1, *Tokyo Maru*, a tanker completed in January 1966, was the first vessel in the world to exceed 150,000 dwt. This was followed in December of the same year by the *Idemitsu Maru*, the first tanker to exceed 200,000 dwt, and then, in September 1968, *Universe Ireland*, the first tanker of over 300,000 dwt, was completed at Yokohama Works. The ability to produce such vessels as VLCCs (very large crude oil carriers, exceeding 200,000 dwt) and ULCCs (ultra large crude oil carriers, exceeding 300,000 dwt) meant that IHI was able to take its place among the world's foremost builders of very large vessels.

The second stage was the expansion of the production facilities of an acquired firm. In March 1968, IHI merged with the Kure Shipyard Company. This firm, which changed its name to the First Works of

Table 7.1 Large ships built by IHI, 1961–75

Year built	Ship's name	Type	dwt	Shipowner	Place of registration	Place where built
1961	Ajia Maru	oil tanker	48,284	Nitto Shosen	Japan	Aioi
1962	Andes Maru	ore carrier	52,744	Nippon Suisan	Japan	Aioi
1963	Tonegawa Maru	oil tanker	73,415	Kawasaki Kisen	Japan	Aioi
1964	Tashima Maru	oil tanker	89,962	Nippon Yusen	Japan	Aioi
1965	Takasago Maru	oil tanker	102,758	Nippon Yusen	Japan	Aioi
1966	Idemitsu Maru[a]	oil tanker	209,302	Idemitsu Tanker	Japan	Yokohama
1968	Universe Ireland[b]	oil tanker	326,585	NBC	Liberia	Yokohama
1969	Universe Korea[c]	oil tanker	326,676	NBC	Liberia	Yokohama
1971	Nisseki Maru[d]	oil tanker	372,698	Tokyo Tanker	Japan	Kure
1973	Globtik Yokyo[e]	oil tanker	483,664	Globtik Tanker	UK	Kure
1973	Globtik London[f]	oil tanker	484,337	Globtik Tanker	UK	Kure
1975	Nissei Maru[g]	oil tanker	484,337	Tokyo Tanker	Japan	Kure

Sources: compiled from IHI, 1986, 5–7∼26 and Lloyd's Register of Shipping: Annual Summary of Merchant Ships
Notes: [a] largest ship completed in 1966
[b] largest ship launched in 1968
[c] largest ship launched in 1969
[d] largest ship launched in 1971
[e] largest ship launched in 1972
[f] largest ship launched in 1973
[g] largest ship completed in 1975

Kure, had been related to Harima Shipyard, one of IHI's predecessors.[18] Just before the merger, in November 1967, Kure Shipyard had started an extension to its dock, to add a maximum of 130,000 dwt to its capacity.[19] This extension, costing two billion yen, was finished in February 1969, and its completion gave the dock a total maximum building capacity of 400,000 dwt.[20] Moreover, in November 1969, soon after the expansion of the existing dock was complete, IHI decided to construct a new building dock, gaining the necessary permit from the Ministry of Transport in 1970. This new dock, which had a maximum capacity of 800,000 dwt, was finally completed in March 1973.[21] By virtue of this expansion at the acquired shipyard, IHI was able to achieve new oil tanker records in the world shipbuilding industry, with the completion of the *Nisseki Maru* in 1971, and the *Globtik Tokyo* and *Globtik London* in 1973 (see Table 7.1).

The last of the three stages was the plan to construct a new dock, with a building capacity of one million dwt, at a new site. As already indicated, IHI had been able to secure a lot of orders for large specialized cargo vessels, such as VLCCs and ULCCs, from both home and abroad, owing to its policy of positive expansion of its building facilities. On the other hand, it became apparent that the Yokohama Works, the most up-to-date of IHI's shipyards, had already reached the limits of its building capacity, being equipped with only one dock.

By the early 1970s, it was apparent that the third Japanese export boom, which had begun in 1965, was of an unprecedented magnitude.[22] In the short period 1970–1, IHI received orders for twenty-five VLCC and ULCC vessels.[23] The need to bridge the gap between these vast orders and the limitations of its existing building capacity undoubtedly promoted IHI's plan for further large-scale expansion of its facilities. The aim was to construct a new shipyard with a building dock capacity of one million dwt at Chita, in Aichi Prefecture, the total expenditure on the production facilities being estimated at twenty-five billion yen.[24] The building dock, designed to be at its most efficient when five tankers or bulk-carriers of a 250,000 dwt class were being produced consecutively per annum, represented the peak of IHI's response to the trend for large vessels. Construction of the new shipyard, later called the Chita Works, was rapid; it began in October 1971, and in June 1973 the keel of the first ship was laid down.[25] However, the Chita Works was unable to fulfil IHI's expectations of becoming the main yard for the production of large vessels. The oil crisis of October 1973, and the consequent great imbalance of energy supply and demand, fundamentally upset the break-even point in the operation of large tankers; this drastic change in business circumstances brought to an end the era of the VLCCs and ULCCs. The long-term plan for the expansion of building capacity therefore collapsed, and a reconsideration by IHI of its shipbuilding division has recently brought an end to large building docks, and the closure of its modern yards, including the Chita and Yokohama Works.

The mass production of standardized vessels

It can be said that, in general, the shipbuilding industry is based on made-to-order production and, unlike the automobile industry, is thus unsuited to mass production with standardized parts. Indeed it is vital for a shipbuilder to meet the particular requirements of each shipowner. In the case of one specific type of a vessel, however, IHI broke away from conventional methods, whereby the specifications for each vessel were altered in line with the varied requests of an individual shipowner, and was thus able to undertake a certain degree of mass production. The specific vessel concerned was the standardized general cargo vessel, known as the 'F' series, which played a vital role in the transition from made-to-order production to mass production of general cargo vessels in the Japanese shipbuilding industry.

This vessel was originally designed to replace the Liberty ship, the wartime standardized cargo vessel built in the USA. Some one thousand Liberty ships remained in operation after the war, and these were not due to become obsolete until the mid-1960s. IHI predicted that, if just half of these Liberty ships were to be replaced by their owners, it should secure orders for fifty vessels on the basis of its share (10 per cent) of the world market for new shipbuilding. If the price of a new vessel was estimated at two million US dollars, therefore, IHI thought it could be looking at a one hundred million dollar project.[26]

The *Freedom*, the first vessel of the 'F' series, was designed in 1965–6 in collaboration with G.T.R. Campbell, a Canadian consultant. Its keel was laid down at IHI's Tokyo Works in November 1966, and it was completed in September 1967.[27] The 'F' series ships, including the *Freedom*, were a resounding success, not only in meeting replacement demands as originally intended, but also in opening up a new market. As shown in Table 7.2, IHI in fact contracted to build more than three hundred 'F' series vessels between 1966 and 1984. This great achievement resulted from several new developments in design, production and sales activities. Referring mainly to the *Freedom*, the first of the 'F' series ships, the most important of these developments will be described below.

Table 7.2 The 'F' series: descriptions and records of the principal ships built, 1966–84

'F' Series	Type	Year developed	dwt	Speed (knots)	Nos of vessels built	Nos of vessels (ordered)
Freedom	Multi-purpose cargo ship	1966	14,800	13.6	124	(124)
Freedom Mark-II	Multi-purpose cargo ship	1976	16,600	14.5	29	(34)
Fortune	Multi-purpose cargo ship	1969	22,000	15.0	62	(63)
Friendship	Multi-purpose cargo ship	1975	22,800	15.0	10	(10)
Future 32	Bulk carrier	1975	37,550	14.2	35	(35)
Future 32-A	Bulk carrier	1983	38,800	14.3	16	(32)

Sources: compiled from IHI, 1986, 5–30, and Machida, 1988, p.43p.

Ship design

IHI determined the basic design of the Freedom ship in advance, although a shipowner could request the addition of various options when the order was passed. The conventional approval of a plan by the shipowner in advance was therefore abolished. The Freedom ship was a twin-deck, multi-purpose cargo vessel, similar to the American Liberty ship. It was designed, however, to emulate the performance of a single-deck vessel in the loading of bulky cargo. This design concept was particularly appropriate at a time when the demand for a cargo combination of industrial goods on an outward voyage from Japan and such bulky cargo as wheat flour on a homeward voyage to Japan was gradually increasing, and it created considerable demand for the Freedom ship.[28]

Further improvements in the building process

As already mentioned above, basic innovations in the building process had been introduced into IHI's works in the first half of the 1960s. But this did not preclude further improvements in the process. A series of new production methods was developed and introduced from the latter half of the 1960s through the continuous building of standardized vessels of the 'F' class. The semi-tandem construction method, whereby one and a half vessels were constructed on the same building berth or dock; the fixed-stage method, which was devised to rationalize work arrangement and to save time at the assembly stages; and thorough pre-outfitting and the adoption of large unit assembly techniques; these were but a few of the new methods introduced at the Tokyo Works at this time.[29] Further similar improvements in production techniques, in order to raise productivity and rationalize work, amplified the effect of continuous building of standardized vessels. In 1968, the first year of mass-production of the 'F' series ships, thirteen vessels were built at the Tokyo Works; then fourteen vessels were built continuously each year from 1969 to 1971.[30] During the same period, the time of hull construction was reduced by 25 per cent, the time of outfitting by 45 per cent, and the total man-hours per vessel by 48 per cent.[31]

Astonishingly, IHI was able to achieve this great improvement in productivity without any further expansion of its shipyard. Originally, IHI had planned that when the new Yokohama Works was complete it would close down most of the production facilities at the Tokyo Works, where the 'F' series ships were to be built.[32] As a result, the building berths at the Tokyo Works – even the largest berth which, although extended after the merger, had a capacity of only 45,000 grt – remained unchanged until after the first vessel of the 'F' series had had its keel laid. Of course, surface tables for assembly had had to be laid for continuous construction, and large cranes had had to be built for the increase of carrying capacity consequent on the adoption of large unit outfitting and prefabrication.[33] However, the costs of carrying out this work were considerably less than would have been the case if the building capacity itself had been extended. Thus, without any large-scale investment in the building capacity, the Tokyo Works could claim a great achievement – by 1971, when it moved to the production of Fortune class ships, the next series of mass-produced vessels, it had launched a total of no fewer than fifty-six vessels of the Freedom type.[34]

Sales

Those who ordered a standardized vessel of the 'F' series, including the Freedom ship, were mainly foreign rather than Japanese shipowners, who perceived the price of the Freedom ship as being relatively high. At the end of 1965, when it had succeeded in making a provisional contract with a Greek shipowner for the first four Freedom ships, IHI set up a sales section in its shipbuilding division solely to promote sales of the 'F' series. At first, the selling price of the Freedom ship was 2.5 million dollars (about 900 million yen), whereas a bulk-carrier of the same size as the Freedom (15,000 dwt) would cost Japanese shipowners about 1.95 million dollars (700 million yen), a difference of close to 200 million yen.[35] In these circumstances, Japanese shipowners preferred to charter the standardized vessels from foreign shipowners, rather than build them on their own account. It was a preference, moreover, that was prompted by IHI's sales methods. These were directed at obtaining assurances from Japanese shipowners that they would charter the Freedom ships, and then notifying foreign shipowners accordingly, so that building orders from overseas could be more readily procured. Influential charterers of this sort included NYK, OSK, Kawasaki, YS Line, and Iino.[36] Through the formation of such linkages between Japanese charterers and foreign shipowners, IHI was able to increase the number of its contracts to build the Freedom ship, and, by the end of 1967, raise the price of each vessel to 2.9 million dollars.[37]

CONCLUSION

As demonstrated by the pattern of IHI's growth after the war, technical innovation was essential to the development of the Japanese ship-building industry. Two kinds of innovation can be detected: one was process innovation, relating to 'how to build a vessel', chiefly developed and refined in the period from the end of the war to the 1960s; the other was product innovation, relating to 'what to build', which has borne much fruit since the latter half of the 1960s.

In the case of process innovation, it has been stressed that, generally speaking, the Japanese shipbuilding industry contrived only to catch up with the technologically advanced countries in Europe and the USA. However, as is abundantly clear from the experience of IHI, catching up did not only have the somewhat negative meaning of the industry overcoming its earlier backwardness in technology, but the more positive meaning of further innovating the building process itself. When technical innovations from overseas, such as electric welding and the block system, were introduced into Japan, they were married to the original Japanese production system which required that a vessel should be built as far as possible in accordance with the flow process. The new building process which developed in Japan as a result contributed greatly to Japanese competitive advantage, in terms of low ship prices and rapid delivery times. Had there not been such innovative development in the building process, Japanese comparative advantage might have relied solely on low-wage labour, which could have given the country's shipbuilders only temporary international competitiveness.

After the 1960s, the tendency towards the increasing size of vessels was accelerated. Japanese shipbuilders responded vigorously to this by extending their productive facilities and by producing a new original design suitable for large vessels. As a result, Japanese shipbuilders virtually monopolized orders for very large vessels worldwide. While the positive reaction to the increasing size of vessels was undoubtedly prompted by the fact that the Ministry of Transport had the right to permit the extension of private shipbuilding facilities, its fundamental cause was the vigorous competition among Japanese shipbuilders. On the one hand, IHI met market requirements for the increasing size of vessels by extending its existing facilities and by constructing new shipyards. However, using its existing production facilities, IHI also succeeded in exploiting and developing a new market for standardized ships such as the 'F' series. IHI thus proved that a medium or even small shipbuilder could grow in the age of the large vessel, after the 1960s. Furthermore, its experience demonstrated that a medium or even small shipbuilder could mass-produce standardized vessels on a continuous basis. What was absolutely essential for competitive advantage, whether building large vessels or not, was that the vessel was a new product, based on IHI's original design, and very well suited to market needs.

Through their contributions to process innovation, therefore, and by creating market demand for a new type of vessel, Japanese shipbuilders have been able to grow continuously since the war. And IHI has always been among leading shipbuilders in the formation of Japan's competitive advantage.

NOTES

1 Ishikawajima Heavy Industries can trace its origin back to Ishikawajima Shipyard, which was established in 1853 by the Tokugawa Shogunate to build a Western-style sailing vessel. After the Meiji Restoration, this shipyard was transferred to private management, and between the two World Wars Ishikawajima had already diversified its business into the automobile and aircraft industries as well as civil engineering. See Ishikawajima Jukogyo Kabushiki Kaisha, *Ishikawajima Jukogyo Kabushiki Kaisha 108 nenshi (A One Hundred and Eight Year History of Ishikawajima Heavy Industries Co., Ltd)*, Tokyo, IHI, 1961.
2 The Ministry of Transport, *Zosen Yoran (A Survey of Shipbuilding)*, Tokyo, Kaiun Shinbunsha, 1960, p. 80.
3 Ibid., pp. 83–4. Harima Dock Co., predecessor of Harima Shipyard, was formed in 1907 at Aioi in Hyogo Prefecture, and after several transfers of its property right, established its reputation as a builder of oil tankers. See Harima Zoshensho, *Harima Zoshensko 50 nenshi (Fifty Years of Harima Shipyard)*, Tokyo, the firm, 1960.
4 Kure Zosensho, *Fune wo tukutte 80 nen (Eighty years in Shipbuilding)*, Tokyo, 1968, pp. 56–7; H. Shinto, *Zosen Seisan Gijyutu no Hatten to watashi (The Development of Naval Architecture and Me)*, Tokyo, Kaiji Press, 1980, pp. 18–19.
5 Shinto, *Zosen Seisan Gijyutu*, p. 24.
6 Ibid., pp. 32–4.
7 At the same time, in the first half of the 1950s, several institutions for joint research were formed in order to improve technologies for welding and the development of steel plates suitable for welding; their members, who participated voluntarily, were drawn from a wide range of competent associations, including the Society of Naval Architects of Japan, and the national institutes for ship research and steelmakers as well as shipbuilders. The results of joint research and experiments carried on at these institutions were immediately taken back to the private shipyards, in order to gain practical experience. Besides the innovations introduced at NBC's Kure Shipyard, the improvements in technology for welding and in the quality of materials also contributed to the development of the Japanese shipbuilding industry. See Nippon Zosen Gakkai (SNAJ: Society of Naval Architects of Japan), *Showa Zosen Shi (A History of Shipbuilding in the Showa Era)*, Tokyo, Hara Shobo, 1973, vol. 2, pp. 1–2, 21–4; M. Yoshiki, *Un Don Kon (Fortune, Caution and Spirit: Three Conditions for Success)*, private edition, 1987, pp. 207–9.
8 Shinto, *Zosen Seisan Gijyutu*, pp. 69–71.
9 Ibid., pp. 72–3.

10 IHI Sempaku Kaiyo Jigyohonbu, 'Sempaku Kaiyo Jigyohonbu 25 nenshi' ('Twenty-five years of the Ship and Marine Division'), (typescript), 1986, 1–89.

11 Ibid., 1–121; Shinto, *Zosen Seisan Gijyutu*, pp. 91–3; Nippon Zosen Gakkai, *Showa Zosen Shi*, p. 314.

12 The tonnage of merchant vessels launched at the Aioi Works from 1962 to 1964 was as follows: 287,713 grt in 1962, 346,149 grt in 1963, and 484,649 grt in 1964. IHI, *Sempaku Kaiyo Jigyohonbu*, 1–71.

13 E. Kaneko (ed.), *Zosen (Shipbuilding)*, Tokyo, Kojyunsha, 1964, p. 457.

14 IHI, *Sempaku Kaiyo Jigyohonbu*, 2–118.

15 Ibid., 2–122.

16 Ibid., 2–122, 242.

17 Ibid., 2–243, 244.

18 Kure Shipyard's predecessor was Harima Shipyard's Kure Dock, which had opened in 1946 at the site of the former Kure naval dockyard. In 1954, the Dock became Kure Shipyard Company, separate from Harima Shipyard, but wholly financed by the latter. In 1962, Kure Shipyard took over all the facilities and employees of NBC's Kure shipyard in order to establish itself as one of Japan's large shipbuilders. See Kure Zosensho, *Fune wo tukutte 80 nen*.

19 IHI, *Sempaku Kaiyo Jigyohonbu*, 2–182.

20 Kure Zosensho, *Fune wo tukutte 80 nen*, pp. 82–3; IHI, *Sempaku Kaiyo Jigyohonbu*, 2–183.

21 IHI, *Sempaku Kaiyo Jigyohonbu*, 2–186, 188, 190.

22 Nippon Zosen Kogyokai (SAJ: Shipbuilders' Association of Japan), *Nippon Zosen Kogyokai 30 nenshi (A Thirty-Year History of the Shipbuilders' Association of Japan)*, 1980, pp. 164–72. See also, Nippon Sempaku Yushutsu Kumiai (Ship Exporters' Association of Japan), *20 nen no Ayumi (Twenty Years of the Ship Exporters' Association)*, 1966, pp. 50–2.

23 S. Machida, *Sempaku Yushutsu Monogatari (The Whole Story of the Export of Vessels)*, Tokyo, Kaiji Press, 1988, p. 95.

24 IHI, *Sempaku Kaiyo Jigyohonbu*, 2–126.

25 Ibid., 2–127.

26 Ibid., 2–11.

27 Ibid., 2–213.

28 ibid., 2–14.

29 Ibid., 2–174, 196.

30 Ibid., 2–168.

31 Ibid., 2–174.

32 Ibid., 2–166.

33 Ibid., 2–129.

34 Ibid., 2–278.

35 Machida, *Sempaku Yushutsu Monogatari*, p. 52.

36 IHI, *Sempaku Kaiyo Jigyohonbu*, 2–14.

37 Machida, *Sempaku Yushutsu Monogatari*, p. 53.

8   The growth and limitations of Idemitsu Kosan: gentleman-merchant management

Tomoaki Saito

INTRODUCTION

Japan's pre-war Petroleum Industry Law was, it is often said, a tragedy, while the post-war Law is a comedy. The petroleum industry is a peculiar one, regulated as it is even now by laws that are held up to ridicule as anachronistic. Whereas Japan's automobile and electric industries were able to become internationally competitive after the war, its petroleum industry was unable to achieve independence even in the domestic market, and excessive competition and debt management became trademarks of the industry. This has been the miserable state of affairs within Japan's petroleum industry in the period since the Second World War.

The main reason why Japan's petroleum industry was unable to become internationally competitive can perhaps be ascribed to the overwhelming strength of its competitors – to differentials in scale, technology and profit structure. Yet, if one takes size as a factor and maintains that Japan's petroleum industry could not possibly stand up against the 'majors' (the giant international oil companies) because of its smaller size, then General Motors, by the same reasoning, should have dominated Toyota. Moreover, so far as technology is concerned, the industry started introducing foreign technology at the same time as other industries, and there were numerous technical links with independent refining-technology companies. Thus the argument that the industry was at a disadvantage in this regard in competition with the majors cannot be sustained.

More persuasive is the argument that Japan's petroleum industry cannot be competitive because of the competitive superiority of the majors in the crude oil sector. Having adopted the strategy after the war of refining and selling Middle East crude oil at the point of consumption, and achieving a vertical integration of refining and sales, the majors came to control the lion's share of the market, even in Japan, by means of foreign capital tie-ups.[1] The existence of enterprises with foreign capital tie-ups that were based on the domestic market, something not found in other industries, limited the growth of enterprises that were not tied up with foreign capital.

Still, can it be said that opportunities for these latter enterprises to grow were not available during the nearly fifty years since the end of the war? I think not. In the circumstances of worldwide over-supply of crude oil that have prevailed from the latter half of the 1950s, enterprises without foreign capital ties were not placed at a competitive disadvantage in regard to securing crude oil. The competitive superiority in the crude oil sector enjoyed by the majors was not in respect of stability of supply, but in stability of earnings. There was no disparity in crude oil costs between enterprises with foreign capital tie-ups and those without such tie-ups; it was in the market that the battle was decided.[2] When we discuss the post-war rise of new enterprises such as Idemitsu or Kyodo Oil Company, we cannot overlook these changes in the management environment.

Why has Japan's petroleum industry remained at its present level? One of the answers to this question lies in MITI's petroleum policies. It is true that MITI support is the reason why Japanese enterprises attained international competitive ability. But it is a mistake to think that MITI made a positive contribution to policies in all industries. The petroleum industry is a case where MITI blundered.

The role of MITI was one of protecting and nurturing domestic industries by establishing preparation periods during which these industries could become competitive. In the case of the petroleum industry, however, it could not impose tariffs on products, since the refineries of the enterprises with foreign capital tie-ups were located within Japan itself. And the petroleum industry, because it is a highly capital-intensive process industry, was not involved in the push to adopt production techniques that occurred in other manufacturing industries: *kaizen* (improvement); skill-mastery training; integration of development, production and sales; co-operation with group suppliers. The protection and nurture that MITI could provide was to impose a licensing system on refining, regulate production plans, and protect the market from a monopoly of foreign capital. MITI's objectives in doing these things were to nurture the growth of enterprises that were financed by Japanese capital, secure for them a fixed share of the market, and weaken the influence of enterprises financed by foreign capital. Instead of nurturing the Japanese-financed enterprises through free competition among private companies, however, MITI put into place policies built around the idea of a government-run amalgamation of enterprises funded by Japanese capital, and it established Kyodo Oil Company, Ltd. Idemitsu,[3] an enterprise funded by Japanese capital and second in size to Nippon Oil, was not considered a desirable party to MITI's scheme. The reason was that Idemitsu had criticized MITI's regulating activities and had continued to argue for free competition. In order to assess the present state of Japan's petroleum industry (including the policies of MITI), therefore, it will be meaningful to examine Idemitsu's struggles and the process of its growth under the Petroleum Industry Law.[4]

IDEMITSU'S UNIQUENESS

In its corporate structure and management philosophy, Idemitsu is in a class by itself among Japan's large enterprises. In the 1989 list of profit-making legal bodies it ranked 118th,[5] but, like Takenaka Komuten (ranked seventy-second), it is one of the very few joint-stock corporations whose shares are not offered publicly. This non-public aspect of its structure is based on the management philosophy of its founder, Sazo Idemitsu.[6] Idemitsu's rapid growth is a product of Sazo's pre-eminent management ability and his management philosophy, which is not just a simple Japanese-style paternalism but also contains aspects of modern rationalism. Now, while the main reasons for Idemitsu's growth are to be found in Sazo's philosophy, the company's limitations stem from it as well, for there is no guarantee that the narrow-minded value system one tends to find in a family business that is the product of the founder's strong individuality can continue to hold good in a changed management environment.

There are three points which single Idemitsu out in the petroleum industry. The first is that, from being a special agent of Nippon Oil before the war, it has grown since the war into a refining and sales enterprise that is ranked in scale on a par with such companies as Nippon Oil, Mitsubishi Oil, Esso-Mobil (formerly, Stanvac), and Shell (formerly, Rising Sun) – giants from the pre-war era. The second is that, when the Petroleum Industry Law was enacted in 1962 and the industry came under MITI regulation, Idemitsu was the only company to oppose and challenge that regulation from beginning to end. And the third is that it has set up overseas offices, in the same way as the trading companies, and it engages in its own trading in crude oil supplies without any third-party mediation.

THE MANAGEMENT PHILOSOPHY

When Sazo Idemitsu graduated from *Kobe Koto Shogyo Gakko* (later to become Kobe University), he did not seek employment in a large trading company, as his classmates did, but worked in a retail shop, where he acquired the know-how of individual management. In 1911 he founded the Idemitsu Shokai in Moji City, and began selling machine oil to the Kita-Kyushu industrial area as a special agency (retailer) for Nippon Oil. From the beginning, Sazo Idemitsu proclaimed his management ideals as 'respect for people', 'big-familyism', 'independent autonomy', 'don't be a slave of money', and 'from producer to consumer'. The main tenet, 'respect for people', concerned the development of the human being through business activities. 'Respect for people' meant respect for the workers; it was linked to treating them as members of the family ('big-familyism'); giving them freedom and independence and letting them manage branch offices ('independent autonomy'); considering people as assets, and the development of the business through them as of primary importance, with capital accumulation as secondary ('not being a slave to money'); and eliminating intermediate, exploitative wholesalers and striving for a smooth supply of products ('from producer to consumer').

Idemitsu has adopted labour policies that are different, even within the context of Japanese enterprise. 'Big-familyism', according to which employees are all members of the family, led to the adoption of the unique policy of no attendance records, no fixed retirement age, no dismissals, no publication of salary figures, and no labour union. 'Independent autonomy' led to the handing over of complete authority, so that branch office management is entrusted entirely to branch staff. And 'don't be a slave of money' extolled the value of achieving a worthwhile business, rather than simply a lucrative one.

Among all Idemitsu's guiding business principles, the idea given most weight is that of 'from producer to consumer'. This means that, to ensure that the objectives of the company are to the advantage of society (i.e. of producers and consumers), the company puts in place tradesmen whose function it is to aim at a direct link between producer and consumer, the fine-tuning of supply and demand, and the mutual advantage of producer and consumer; the company eliminates the customary intermediate margin-squeezing and speculative transactions. Essentially, this idea developed into one of a 'large regional retail trade', whereby a large number of branch offices and agencies were set up over a large region of the country and retail trade was carried on in direct contact with consumers. The idea was given full scope in the form of direct sales to consumers after the war, when the company became a wholesaler and began to acquire its own refineries. However, despite the fact that the concept of a 'large regional retail trade' presupposes a policy of direct sales to consumers, filling stations were managed both by Idemitsu directly and by agents under special contract. Operating through the latter was against Idemitsu's principle of direct sales to consumers, but it was more efficient than direct management and more in the interests of consumers in terms of cost. In this sense, therefore, it conformed to the spirit of Idemitsu's consumer-first principle. In line with its policy of 'big-familyism', Idemitsu changed the term 'special agency' to 'sales outlet', giving these sales outlets exactly the same treatment as its own directly managed filling stations – in regard to petrol delivery prices as well as all other matters.

Because his management philosophy could not be carried through if outside capital were brought into the picture, since this might permit managers to shirk their management responsibilities (in case of bankruptcy, the salaried manager simply resigns and that is it), and since the profits earned by the workers would only flow out as dividends, Sazo Idemitsu did not adopt the joint-stock company structure. The method he chose to gather funds from the general public was that of borrowing from banks.

Despite his preference for an individually owned shop structure, and his desire to avoid in principle the structure of a joint-stock company, Sazo Idemitsu finally had to adopt the latter form. The reason was the taxation system, which worked to the extreme disadvantage of individually owned business. The capital of 1,000 million yen (as of 1991) is divided into shares owned by the Idemitsu family and the Workers Shareholders Association; these shares are not offered to the public.

DEVELOPMENT IN THE PRE-WAR PERIOD

The history of Idemitsu Kosan began with Sazo Idemitsu's establishment of Idemitsu Shokai in 1911 in Moji City, and his involvement in the sale of petroleum products. Two years later he expanded to Shimonoseki, where he sold fuel oil for motor-powered fishing boats. He expanded outlets to Manchuria in 1914 (with the sale of axle oil to the South Manchurian Railway), to Korea in 1920, and to Taiwan in 1922. In 1935–6 he expanded to the Chinese mainland, with outlets in Peking, Tientsin, Shanghai and Canton. In view of the fact that Nippon Oil was to set up a Taipei branch in Taiwan in 1927, a Seoul branch in Korea in 1930, and to expand operations to Manchuria through joint investment in the Manchurian Oil Company in 1934, Idemitsu's search for overseas locations for its activities was comparatively early. In view of the promulgation of the 1934 Manchurian Oil Monopoly Law, the spread of economic control within Japan, and the need for business policies inside China, the individually owned shop structure entailed too many difficulties. In consequence, a partial structural change was introduced into the joint-stock company in 1939. The result was as follows:

Idemitsu Shokai:	parent company – domestic operations;
Idemitsu Kosan Co:	capital, ¥4 million – operations in Japan, Taiwan, Korea, Kwantung Province;
Manchuria Idemitsu Kosan Co:	capital, ¥1.5 million – operations in Manchuria;
Chuka Idemitsu Kosan Co:	capital, ¥12.5 million – operations in mainland China.

In 1939 petroleum distribution controls were put into effect in Japan, so that wholesale and retail sales came under a unitary distribution system and it became impossible to sell freely. Anticipating this move, Idemitsu shifted its sales overseas, imported petroleum directly from the United States, and sold imported goods to meet the demands of the private sector. Idemitsu Shokai (head office in Moji) had a branch office in Nagoya, and five agencies; Idemitsu Kosan (head office in Tokyo) had branch offices in Seoul, Taipei and Dairen, and ten agencies; Manchuria Idemitsu Kosan (head office in Changchun) had a branch office and six agencies; Chuka Idemitsu (head office in Shanghai) had branch offices in Peking, Chingtao, Tientsin, Canton and Hankow, and twenty-six agencies. Idemitsu employed 103 people within Japan, and 375 overseas.[7] As a result of Japan's defeat in the war, the whole of this overseas sales organization was lost to Idemitsu. Its sales capabilities and reputation at the time were such that Idemitsu was nearly contracted by Texaco Oil as sales representative for the latter's Shanghai branch office;[8] and entered into tie-up negotiations with Caltex after the war although eventually Caltex tied-up with Nippon Oil.[9]

POST-WAR DEVELOPMENT: EXPANSION INTO REFINING, TRANSPORT, AND SALES

During the Japanese petroleum industry's post-war conversion from importing petroleum products to refining at the point of consumption, Idemitsu steadfastly maintained that the importing and refining of crude oil was not necessarily linked with savings in foreign currency. Sazo Idemitsu suggested to the government that it adopt as policy, (1) the rational revival of refineries along the Pacific coast, and (2) the freeing of the Japanese market from monopoly and the importation of petroleum being dumped at low prices. The suggestion was ignored. The government's perception of savings in foreign currency, and the Japanese market's function as an outlet for the Middle East crude oil of the majors, represented a coincidence of benefits, so refining at the point of consumption was in fashion. Before the war 70 per cent of petroleum imports had been refined products and 30 per cent crude oil, but after the war this ratio was reversed. Sazo, swimming against the current, considered a ratio of 30 per cent for crude oil imports to be reasonable and argued that the construction of new refineries was irresponsible. He voiced publicly the bold view that the importation of petroleum products would lead to savings in foreign currency. The grounds for his argument were that if, by raising the proportion of gasoline obtained in the refineries, the production of heavy oil was decreased, the deficiencies could be made up by importing products, leading to savings in foreign currency; consumer prices would also fall. He came to this view after studying the prices of products in the United States. Idemitsu's management strategy immediately after the post-war revival was nationwide sales based on product imports.

In 1947, Idemitsu returned to the petroleum industry when it was named a designated sales trader of the Petroleum Distribution Public Corporation. This public corporation was abolished in January 1949, however, and the government decided in April that it would thereafter designate wholesale traders. A condition of being so designated was that the potential wholesaler 'held oil tanks at the import base and possessed sales capability'. Idemitsu had anticipated this move very early, and in December 1948 had purchased import tanks (in Nagasaki and Moji) from the former Mitsui Head Office. From being a special agency, Idemitsu thus rose to the rank of wholesaler. (Of the ten such wholesalers at the time, all save Idemitsu and Nichimo had enjoyed that position from pre-war days.) Under eight controlling branch offices (in Fukuoka, Shimonoseki, Marugame, Osaka, Nagoya, Tokyo, Sendai and Sapporo), Idemitsu set up subordinate branch offices, agencies, and sales outlets. The wholesalers were each allotted quotas of the amount of petroleum products they could distribute. Even though Idemitsu has never exceeded the 10 per cent quota it was allotted in April 1949, it has maintained the largest share of the market among those companies financed by Japanese capital.

Private trading was permitted from October 1950. Since, under the policy of refining at the point of consumption, foreign currency was allotted for crude oil, and only crude oil, up to January–March 1951, Idemitsu, a simple wholesaler without a refinery of its own, was unable to secure the full quantity of petroleum products it could sell. In these adverse circumstances, Idemitsu shifted its strategy from the importing and sale of petroleum products to expansion into refining and the tanker sector. In July 1949, it planned the construction of a refinery on an old fuel depot site in Tokuyama. The following March, it received a partial disposal of this government property. However, the Korean War interrupted the disposal plans, and, in 1954, the government, pressured by a British government antagonized by the oil problem in Iran, disposed of one-third of the site to the Shell Oil subsidiary, Showa Oil. As a result, Idemitsu's expansion into refining did not materialize. However, in August 1955, when changes were made in the foreign currency quota system, the Tokuyama site problem was ironed out, whereupon the complete site was sold by disposal to Idemitsu.

The management of foreign exchange through the foreign currency quota was a system that kept restrictions on imported goods in order to save foreign currency and ensure its efficient use. With the idea of allocating enough foreign currency to purchase the crude oil necessary for refining all petrol domestically, and distributing the other 30 per cent for purchasing petroleum products, a ratio of seven-tenths for crude oil and three-tenths for petroleum products was decided upon. This ratio was changed to nine-tenths and one-tenth in 1955, in line with a single foreign currency system that decided upon the same foreign currency standard for both crude oil and oil products (actual quota totals and actual import quantity). The principal reason given was that domestic refining capacity had expanded, with the result that the need to import products had diminished. There is no denying that the foreign currency quota system served as a powerful force in support of the point-of-consumption refining system. The government had narrowed the range of activities of those traders importing products (Idemitsu, Shell Oil and two other companies) and had prompted their entry into refining. This was part of the background to the government's disposal of the Tokuyama site to Idemitsu.

Sazo Idemitsu set about having architects' plans drawn for the construction of a refinery, procuring crude oil supplies and raising funds. In the autumn of 1955, he went to the United States and engaged the architectural firm of UPO, and he entered into contracts with Esso and Gulf. To raise funds, he borrowed 3,600 million yen from Bank of America in January 1956, after which Japanese banks also gave him loans. Work began on the Tokuyama refinery in May 1956, and construction work that would normally have taken two to three years was completed in ten months. By March 1957 the plant was operating at a capacity of 40,000 barrels a day (b/d).

To meet growing demand, the company hastened to expand its refining capacity. It did this by raising the capacity of its Tokuyama refinery (to 80,000 b/d in 1959, 100,000 b/d in 1960 and 140,000 b/d in 1961) and, in addition, by building refineries throughout the country. Acquiring a site for a refinery in Chiba in May 1961, it set its sights on the market in eastern Japan. The Chiba refinery was fitted out in 1963 with a capacity of 100,000 b/d.

In the context of the industry as a whole, Idemitsu's refining capacity was a mere 7 per cent in 1957. However, by 1959 this had increased to 12.8 per cent, outstripping Maruzen Oil, and by 1963 Idemitsu's capacity had risen to 16.2 per cent, putting it ahead of Nippon Oil and second only to Toa Nenryo. This rapid expansion in refining capacity showed the ability of Idemitsu to make quick decisions involving business expansion. But government policy also played a part. Having, from 1955 on, directed foreign currency quotas solely towards crude oil, and driven wholesalers to move into the refining sector, the government decided to dispose of old fuel-storage sites.

Because it was difficult to charter Japanese-registered tankers, and foreign-registered tankers were expensive to charter, Idemitsu embarked at the end of 1950 on the construction of a tanker, and, in September 1951, *Nissho Maru II* was launched. Idemitsu was thus the first Japanese oil company to transport oil in its own ship. In April 1951, because of a shortage in Japan, the government gave permission for heavy oil to be imported, and Idemitsu imported heavy oil from the United States. But the selling price of heavy oil was low at this time, and the government was soon forced to permit the import and sale of petrol, and lubricating oil as well. Within a month of obtaining the government's permission in April 1952, Idemitsu was importing high-octane petrol from the United States.

These imports served to show that domestically produced petrol was a half-finished and overpriced product, and led to a drop in petrol prices as well as to Idemitsu's capture of a greater share of the market. From 1953 to 1955, its refining company took the step of installing high-octane petrol manufacturing equipment (catalytic reformers, catalytic crackers and so on). In 1953, also, Idemitsu showed the world its independent spirit by importing large quantities of petrol from Iran, which was, at the time, involved in an international conflict over the nationalization of its petroleum industry.

As for Idemitsu's sales organization, a new branch office was opened in Hiroshima in 1957, bringing to seven the number of controlling branch offices. Its distribution network expanded in step with its refinery capacity: its market share of filling stations, which was 8.6 per cent of the total in 1956, had risen to 13.4 per cent by 1961, second only to Nippon Oil. This rapid expansion was due to the energetic construction of filling stations to keep up with the growth in capacity provided by its new Tokuyama refinery. Whereas Nippon Oil's filling stations were already in place, Idemitsu, as a new entrant in the field, was able to build numerous filling stations on favourably located sites. Its share of sales rose from 10.7 per cent in 1955 to 14.7 per cent in 1961, putting it in third place behind Nippon Oil and Shell Oil. Thus, by reducing the shortfall of refining capcity to sales from 5.6 per cent in 1957 to 1.8 per cent in 1961, in line with the expansion of its sales and refining capacities, Idemitsu created a healthy enterprise structure. (In the fine-tuning of a vertical integration flow, it is desirable to have a balance in the shares of refining and sales.)

The import of high-octane petrol from the United States in May 1952, and of petrol and light oil from Iran in May 1953, were a brilliant achievement. These operations were made possible by Idemitsu's overseas information gathering activities, by means of which it kept in constant touch with world trends and movements in the petroleum market, thus enabling it to purchase and import petroleum independently, from anywhere in the world. To these ends, Idemitsu had opened offices in Los Angeles (June 1952), Teheran (March 1953) and New York (1955).

PRODUCTION REGULATION AND IDEMITSU'S WITHDRAWAL FROM THE PETROLEUM ASSOCIATION

The Petroleum Industry Law gives the Minister of International Trade and Industry the authority to advise modifications in plans for the production or importation of petrol products whenever obstacles arise to the carrying out of petroleum supply plans, or if there is the possibility of this happening. In practice, such modification plans are carried out through autonomous regulation of production within the petroleum industry, under MITI guidance. In order to avoid any criticism of bureaucratic control, MITI administrators have entrusted the determination of production frameworks and their fulfilment to the Petroleum Association, in the form of autonomous regulation under administrative guidance.

In the second half of 1962, the production plans of all companies exceeded petroleum supply plans by about 25 per cent. As a result, regulation of production was carried out at the direction of MITI officials. Opinion was divided as to the standard for production regulation, with the Japanese-owned small and medium-sized companies opting for plant capacity, and the giant companies insisting on a standard weighted towards sales performance. In late 1962, MITI presented a compromise plan that would give even weight to three factors: actual sales performance, actual crude-oil treatment figures, and crude-oil treatment capacity. Autonomous regulation based on this plan was put into effect from October to December 1962, though in reality the plan was distorted by the inclusion of countermeasures put forward by small and medium traders.

Since it sought to overcome the worsening of market conditions solely by way of production regulation, MITI linked this with the establishment of a standard price in November 1962. The production regulation, with its three-point formula and an agreement that the disparity between production and sales was to be overcome by joint measures by the wholesalers, was put into effect on the understanding that it would only be for the latter half of 1962. However, MITI then applied the same formula to the first half of 1963 as well. Idemitsu reacted to this broken promise by presenting its own production plans to MITI at the start of 1963, but out of deference to the appointment of a new head of the Mining Bureau, it reluctantly submitted to production regulation for that period. ·

For the second half of 1963, Nippon Oil proposed regulation of the petrol base. This was supported by Idemitsu, but opposed by Maruzen Oil and MITI, so the proposal was rejected. When the Petroleum Association proposed that the same production regulation be followed for a third time, Idemitsu withdrew from the Association in November 1963 and embarked on independent production, in keeping with its own sales base. In its public announcement of its withdrawal, it stated:

> A petroleum company is supposed to 1) respect the freedom of purchase of the consumer and formulate future refining and sales plans in accordance with the policy that each oil company is to manufacture as much as it can sell. But this company has been forced, because of an incomprehensible production quota, to buy high-priced products from the market and pass these on to the consumer. . . . The original aim of the Petroleum Industry Law was stability of demand and price, and traders were to ensure a ready supply. Also, stability of price is something traders themselves should be seeing to. We cannot agree to a way of doing things that prevents us from doing what we

are supposed to do by limiting production, and that imposes burdens on the consumer.[10]

Part of the background to this statement was the fact that the capacity (100,000 b/d) of Idemitsu's Chiba refinery, completed in January 1963, was not incorporated in MITI's production formula.

Idemitsu's sales capacity had always been greater than its refining capacity, and this was remedied by the start of operations at the Chiba refinery.[11] To bring the rate of operation at the Chiba refinery to the proper level, Idemitsu increased production there from April 1963. The result was that its refining capacity in 1963 (240,000 b/d) surpassed that of Nippon Oil (226,000 b/d), which provided Idemitsu with the opportunity to exceed Nippon Oil in sales share as well. By October–November, the two companies were suddenly nearly even in the sales volume of fuel oil, excluding lubricating oil, with only an average difference of 10,000 kilolitres a month; the speed of this change can be judged by the fact that the previous year, Nippon Oil's fuel-oil sales, excluding lubricating oil, had exceeded those of Idemitsu by a monthly average of 92,000 kilolitres. A glance at the actual 1963 results of the two companies shows that it was Nippon Oil that had overproduction, and the gap between its production and sales was slightly greater than Idemitsu's. Though the latter was unable to overtake Nippon Oil, it did succeed in greatly reducing the gap in production share (from 5.8 to 2.3 per cent) and the gap in sales share (from 4.4 to 1.6 per cent). Idemitsu's withdrawal from the Petroleum Association was thus motivated not only by the contradiction between production regulation and its own management philosophy, but also by its desire to capture some of Nippon Oil's sales share through expanded refining capacity.

The price-cutting war that developed after Idemitsu's withdrawal from the Petroleum Association, which included a battle for market share between Idemitsu and Nippon Oil, only made market conditions worse, however. In the second half of 1963, the industry's average current profit ratio on sales fell 0.45 per cent lower than in the first half, to end at 1.29 per cent. For Idemitsu and Nippon Oil, the average current profit ratio on sales for the second half of 1963 was 0.86 per cent and 1.1 per cent respectively – below the average for the industry as a whole – attesting to the liveliness and ferocity of the battle between the two giants. A comparison of the working profit ratio on sales shows that, while Idemitsu's was around 5 per cent for both halves of the year, Nippon Oil's dropped below 1 per cent in the second half of the year. In other words, Idemitsu won the sales race, but because of its weaker constitution financially – payments on loan interest were four times those of Nippon Oil – it paid no dividends for the first half of 1963, and was still unable to beat Nippon Oil in terms of its current profit ratio on sales in the second half of 1963.

Reflecting its concern about Idemitsu's withdrawal from the Petroleum Association, MITI organized a conference in January 1964 with the Minister of International Trade and Industry, the president of the Petroleum Council and Sazo Idemitsu. Idemitsu set out as its conditions the early abandonment of the practice of joint use, of production quotas, of the licensing system for the construction of refineries, and of the standard price; the administrative authorities, on the other hand, demanded compliance with production regulation in return for their acceptance of these conditions. When the government made the following announcement, Idemitsu agreed to the authorities' terms:

> We will do our best to do away with production regulation as soon as possible. In consideration of the position of consumers, we will come up with a petroleum supply plan proposal that has some latitude. From January 1964 crude oil will be treated according to a production regulation proposal presented by the president of the Petroleum Council.[12]

As a result, from January 1964 to September 1966, production regulation was taken out of the hands of the Petroleum Association, and MITI, acting on the advice of the Petroleum Council, directly allotted to each company the amount of crude oil it was to refine.

Despite these efforts by MITI to ameliorate market conditions, they did not recover, for companies did not always comply with either production regulation or the standard price. In April 1964, the Minister for International Trade and Industry issued a warning that 'the petroleum industry should be conscious of its social responsibilities and cease excessive competition, and should observe production regulation and the standard price'. The administrative authorities also indicated market countermeasures. The market did show signs of recovery in the first half of 1965, however, and all companies had improved results in the second half the year, so the standard price was abolished in February 1966, and production regulation in October of the same year.

Idemitsu's sales organization grew from seven controlling branch offices and twenty-one branch offices in 1963 to seven and twenty-four, respectively, in 1972. In 1982, with a view to a more closely controlled sales system, all were reorganized into twelve controlling branch offices. During this period, the sales share maintained its position in third place.

Though new refineries were built in Hyogo in 1970, in Hokkaido in

1973 and in Aichi in 1975, Idemitsu had to be content with fourth place in terms of refining capacity, because Kyodo Oil, with powerful support from MITI from 1968 on, increased its share.

In the development of its subsidiaries, Idemitsu proceeded along the road of diversification – with Idemitsu Tanker Company in 1962, Idemitsu Petrochemical Company in 1963, Idemitsu Sea of Japan Oil Development Company in 1971 and Idemitsu Geothermal Development Company in 1979.

New overseas offices were opened in 1973–4 in Beirut, Kuwait and Riyadh, and a branch office in London in 1975. Internationalization of Idemitsu's business was promoted through the addition of overseas subsidiaries: Idemitsu Apollo Corporation (New York) in 1971, Idemitsu International (Asia) Pte Ltd (Singapore) in 1977, Idemitsu Internacional-America Latina Industria e Comercial Ltda (Rio de Janeiro) in 1978, and Idemitsu Uranium Exploration Australia Pty Ltd in 1980.

LIMITATIONS OF THE MANAGEMENT PHILOSOPHY AND THE TASKS AHEAD

The driving force behind Idemitsu's development into a large enterprise after the war was the management philosophy proclaimed by Sazo Idemitsu. That philosophy was reflected in such positive and bold business activities as the importing of Soviet crude oil in 1960 (one of the principal factors leading to the enactment of the Petroleum Industry Law), the consistent opposition to that Law from the time of its enactment and the 1963 withdrawal from the Petroleum Association (because of opposition to MITI's production regulation). And the reason Idemitsu was able to develop a nationwide sales network so rapidly was that, in line with Sazo's philosophy, it entrusted heads of branch offices with authority.

However, that management philosophy also has a negative side. The Idemitsu labour policy contains elements that could equally be described as pre-modern, even feudal, such as treating employees on the same level as family members. This attitude differs conspicuously from the general practice. And, when employees who cannot accept Idemitsu-ism are forced to leave, the image is presented of a closed company.

In addition, because its shares are not publicly offered, Idemitsu's equity capital (¥1,000 million in capital funds) is low. Investment for growth has, therefore, to be financed through loans, thus worsening the financial constitution of the company. In this regard, we can compare it with, for example, Nippon Oil. Idemitsu's operating profit for 1984 was

¥77,000 million more than Nippon Oil's,[13] but because its non-operating expenses totalled ¥85,000 million, it ended up with a current profit below that of Nippon Oil. As is patently clear from Idemitsu's long- and short-term loans of ¥1,110,200 million as against Nippon Oil's of ¥121,800 million, and from Idemitsu's equity capital of ¥39,500 million as against Nippon Oil's of ¥231,800 million, not offering its shares to the public and not hesitating to borrow for the sake of expansion are weak points stemming from Idemitsu's management philosophy. This raises some fundamental doubts about that management philosophy.

Table 8.1 Comparison of Idemitsu and Nippon Oil, 1984 (¥ m)

	Nippon Oil	*Idemitsu*
Sales	3,083,414	2,583,289
Operating profit	1,626	79,390
Non-operating revenue	37,116	14,766
Non-operating expenses	24,137	85,175
Current profit	14,690	8,981

Sources: Annual Reports of Nippon Oil and Idemitsu.

NOTES

1 The majors had followed the strategy of exporting refined products to the end-user market before the war. Shell and Stanvac established a distribution network by making an exclusive agency contract in Japan. Mitsubishi Oil Co. had formed a tie-up with Associated Oil in 1931.
2 Indeed, independent foreign oil companies were willing to loan a large amount of money at a low interest rate to any enterprise without foreign capital ties which planned to expand refining capacity.
3 For information on Idemitsu, this chapter relies principally on: Idemitsu Kosan Co., *Idemitsu 50 nenshi* (*Fifty Years of Idemitsu*), Tokyo, Idemitsu, 1970; *idem, Idemitsu 50 nenshi zokuhen* (*Fifty Years of Idemitsu*, vol. 2), Tokyo, Idemitsu, 1981; Sazo Idemitsu, *Ningen soncho 50 nen* (*Fifty Years of Respect for the People*), Tokyo, Shinjusha, 1962.
4 Free competition in the banking sector has also been regulated, by the Ministry of Finance. Nevertheless, the Japanese banks were able to obtain an international competitive edge. The regulation policies in these two sectors had opposite results.
5 Among the oil companies, Toa Nenryo Kogyo Co. (now Tonen Corp.) ranked 115th in the list of profit-making legal entities and was the top-ranked oil company; Nippon Oil was ranked 153rd overall and in third place among the oil companies; and Esso Oil was 177th overall and in fourth place among the oil companies.
6 He was a member of Japan's Upper Chamber for ten years from 1937, by

virtue of the fact that he was the person who paid the largest amount of tax in Fukuoka Prefecture.

7 Idemitsu's total employment amounted to 1,095, and also included 110 women clerks, 289 workers and ninety-two sailors.

8 As Stanvac and the Asiatic Petroleum Co. (a subsidiary of Shell) controlled the Chinese market, Texaco only obtained a small market share, though it had large facilities for oil storage.

9 In 1948, the policy of refining in the local market emerged among the majors. Caltex selected Nippon Oil rather than Idemitsu because the former had a refinery while the latter did not.

10 *Idemitsu 50 nenshi*, vol. 2, p. 169.

11 In 1962 Idemitsu's share in refining capacity was 11.8 per cent and its sales share was 14.5 per cent.

12 *Idemitsu 50 nenshi*, vol. 2, p. 176.

13 Idemitsu could obtain more of a sales margin than Nippon Oil. Because the special agencies used by Nippon Oil were large and strong, they requested Nippon Oil to grant them a larger margin than Idemitsu had to do. If Idemitsu's sales margin in petrol was one yen higher than Nippon Oil's, Idemitsu's operating profit would be ¥5,600 million more than Nippon Oil's.

9 Post-war growth of agricultural machine production: the case of Kubota Ironworks

Toshikatsu Nakajima

INTRODUCTION

Kubota Ironworks[1], with 15,400 employees, working in five divisions, produces more than 2,000 different products. In 1990, the firm's total sales (708,922 million yen) comprised pipes (29 per cent), machines (49 per cent), anti-pollution equipment (7 per cent), housing materials (10 per cent), and semi-finished goods (6 per cent). Kubota has a 60 per cent share of the Japanese market for cast steel pipes, but at the same time the firm is known to the public as the top manufacturer of agricultural machinery. These two activities remain the principal source of Kubota's profits, in spite of the recent prosperity of its two subsidiaries, one in housing and the other in the computer business.[2]

In this chapter, attention is focused on Kubota's growth as an agricultural machinery manufacturer, mainly in the post-war period from 1945 up to 1973. The success of Kubota's small power tillers in the mid-1950s mirrored the explosive development of the Japanese economy at that time. What enabled Kubota, which formerly had been known as a large and prudent manufacturer of water mains, to gain the lead in this new business? The difficulties the firm encountered are worth examining. But before proceeding with a detailed analysis of Kubota's management, it is necessary first to survey briefly the recent history of Japanese agriculture.

POST-WAR MECHANIZATION OF JAPANESE AGRICULTURE

Japanese agriculture was widely mechanized even before the Second World War. As early as 1925, there were 25,000 oil-fired engines, used mainly for irrigation. There were 140,000 threshing machines in 1937, 230,000 in 1939 and 360,000 in 1942.[3] But wartime damage and post-war economic disruption prevented farmers from pursuing further mechanization. It was not until the second half of the 1950s that power tillers, cultivators and garden tractors began to replace cattle for ploughing and conveying. The following decade was characterized by the overwhelming diffusion of medium-sized tractors, reapers and rice-planting machines (see Figure 9.1).

This process was concurrent with the acceleration in Japan's economic and industrial growth. Mechanization of agriculture made possible the supply of sufficient food to the growing population. Between 1953 and 1968, the production of rice and potatoes increased by 75 per cent and 68 per cent respectively.[4] Machines improved land productivity, especially in north-eastern Japan (Tohoku and Hokkaido).

More importantly, labour-saving innovations encouraged the transfer of the agricultural workforce into heavy industry. In 1960, there were 13.1 million farmers, representing 30 per cent of Japan's active population. This number gradually decreased to 10.9 million in 1965, 9.3 million in 1970, and 6.8 million in 1972. Farmers' younger sons and daughters moved into the new industries mushrooming around Tokyo, Osaka and Nagoya. Consequently, the average active population per household engaged in agriculture declined from 2.2 in 1960 to 1.3 in 1972.[5] Without mechanization, agricultural production would have been severely affected by this loss of farmers.

In this sense, the diffusion of agricultural machines formed the basis of Japan's post-war growth. Ownership of tillers and tractors jumped from 89,000 in 1955 to 2,500,000 in 1965.[6] This expansion entailed a fundamental change in the way agricultural machines were produced.

In the early stages, agricultural machines were manufactured almost everywhere. The 1937 Factory Statistics enumerated 559 agricultural machine shops employing more than five workers.[7] Country craftsmen could make and repair simple threshers, grain mills and even small engines. However, from the 1950s on, as the assembly line system made possible the mass production of power tillers, the unit price declined to a level acceptable to ordinary farmers.[8] The growth of the market, accelerated by the aggressive sales strategy on the part of the manufacturers, encouraged the introduction of interchangeable parts, reducing assembly costs and facilitating maintenance and repair.

These innovations resulted in a rapid concentration of production. The big five manufacturers (Kubota, Yanmar, Mitsubishi, Iseki and Sato), with their low prices and widespread advertisements, overwhelmed the small machine shops (see Table 9.1). In 1956, a third of agricultural machine factories employed fewer than twenty-nine workers; by 1964, this proportion had declined to a sixth. Manufacturers

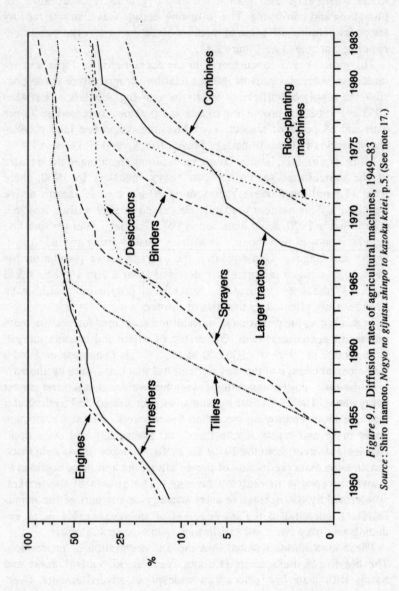

Figure 9.1 Diffusion rates of agricultural machines, 1949–83. (See note 17.)
Source: Shiro Inamoto, *Nogyo no gijutsu shinpo to kazoku keiei*, p.5.

Table 9.1 Principal makers of agricultural machines in 1969 (¥m)

Name	Capital	Total Sales	Sales of agri. machines	Market shares(%)
1 Kubota	30,172	149,107	53,636	24.9
2 Yanmar	1,700	45,293	40,144	18.7
3 Mitsubishi Heavy	80,166	627,235	27,757	12.9
4 Iseki	3,547	23,897	23,897	10.6
5 Sato	2,400	14,870	14,870	6.9
6 Fuji-Komatsu-Robin	500	8,801	8,390	3.9
7 Kyoritsu	1,200	8,012	7,895	3.7
8 Ishikawajima-Shibaura	720	6,209	5,709	2.7

Source: Yosaku Matsuo 'Wagakuni noki sangyo hatten no atozuke', (Development of Japanese agricultural machine industry), *Norin Kin'yu*, 1970 vol. 23, no. 2, p.31.

employing more than 300 workers in 1960 occupied only 35 per cent of the market; ten years later, their market share amounted to 76 per cent.[9]

Given the role of large machine manufacturers in the modernization of Japanese agriculture, it is worth examining their competence – in terms of both technology and management. Without doubt, the Kubota Ironworks is the most spectacular example of the manufacturers.

HISTORICAL BACKGROUND OF THE KUBOTA IRONWORKS

In 1890, Gonshiro Kubota (1869–1959) set up a small foundry in south-west Osaka.[10] At first the shop produced balances, then cotton gins and lathe parts. In 1900, Kubota invented a new system of casting pipes, the vertical circular process. The construction of mains water systems in the large cities encouraged the growth of his business. In 1912, Kubota's 500 workers produced 40,000 tons of pipes – 60 per cent of the Japanese water-main market. During the three decades up to 1945, his company established seven new factories, four in and around Osaka, one in Tokyo and two in China. The efficiency of some of these factories, adopting the centrifugal process, was the equal of the world's principal pipe foundries.

The instability of the water-main market forced Kubota Ironworks to diversify its products. In 1914 its machinery division started producing small lathes; in 1919 the company moved into automobile manu-facturing. After many trials, including the creation of the Datsun (forerunner of Nissan) in 1931, Kubota transferred this business to Tobata Foundry in 1933.[11] In exchange, Kubota acquired Tobata's agricultural engine manufacturing business. As a result, Kubota, which had produced its own oil engines since 1922, became the foremost of small engine manufacture, surpassing Yanmar. But the machinery division, producing 7,000 to 12,000 engines a year, was never profitable.

In 1937, Kubota established a large new factory for machine manufacture in Sakai, the south-western suburb of Osaka. Equipped with the latest machine tools imported from Europe and the USA, the Sakai plant adopted the conveyor system and introduced Taylor's time-and-motion ideas. Within two years, the annual production of oil engines amounted to 15,000. As the war progressed, Kubota's machinery division made engines for landing boats and artillery tractors.

After 1945, the urgency of the urban reconstruction and food supply situation helped Kubota's water main and agricultural engine production to recover from its wartime paralysis. By April 1946, Kubota was already manufacturing 100 engines a month; by October 1952, monthly production had risen to over 5,000. However, in the latter year, mould-making and foundry engines represented only 25 per cent of Kubota's sales, while pipe casting represented 64 per cent. The production of garden tractors and cultivators was still in its infancy: Kubota had manufactured a prototype in 1947, and had sold twenty-two units in the first quarter of 1949, but in 1952 cultivators only accounted for 3 per cent of annual sales.

AGRICULTURAL ENGINE PRODUCTION IN THE EARLY 1950s

The impact of the power tiller boom in the late 1950s and 1960s cannot be properly understood without first examining the primitive state of agricultural machine production in post-war Japan. In February–April 1953, the Institute of Industry and Commerce of the Osaka Prefecture investigated ninety establishments engaged in agricultural oil-engine manufacture. The results of this investigation include precious information on the situation of small machine shops in the Osaka region.[12]

Formerly, agricultural machine production was undertaken for the most part by small ironworks, and machine shops proliferated in the countryside in the 1920s and 1930s. Some of them even made and sold low-speed oil engines; although the market share of Kubota and other large firms was on the increase, they were never able to satisfy the entire demand.

In spite of the shortage of materials, the post-war explosion of pent-up demand ensured some years of success for these small shops. However, the depression of 1949 brought this to an end and resulted in their closure. As medium-speed engines (800 to 1,500 rpm) came into wide use in 1951, technically incompetent manufacturers dropped away.

An exception to this was in the Okayama Prefecture, where thirty-nine small engine makers still dominated the local market in 1953.[13] But none of these firms built more than 500 engines in a month, and the production of twenty-one of them was less than fifty engines a month. Moreover, they came to rely on the Osaka region for special parts.

Osaka was the most vigorous centre of agricultural engine manufacture; the Kinki district (comprising eight prefectures, including Osaka) produced 60 per cent of national output. Kubota, Yanmar and other big firms, had their assembly plants in and around Osaka. Among others, Kubota's Sakai Factory, with its 388 workers and 750 machine-tools, produced 7,000 engines every month.

But even Kubota depended on outside suppliers for more than 25 per cent of its machine components. In Osaka and Sakai, small shops were organizing networks to supply assemblers with engine parts – cylinders, piston rings, crankshafts, connecting rods, valves and so forth. Traditionally, the eastern outskirts of Osaka, near the Arsenal, was the principal centre of Japan's hardware business. The Sakai region also had its original cutlery trade, some of which went over to the manufacture of bicycle parts in the twentieth century. Ambitious, skilled workers could purchase cheap second-hand machine tools there, and establish, relatively easily, their own machine shops. Dealers in hardware and machine parts provided them with an assured basic market. In spite of intense competition in both techniques and business, those who took up such an opportunity could expand their business quite rapidly.

Mass production, first of military equipment and then of agricultural engines, encouraged the specialization of these small workshops. Large manufacturers ordered from them many parts which were unsuited to large-scale production. In some cases, technical and financial aid was given to enthusiastic subcontractors. The 1953 investigation examined the careers of many small shop-owners engaged in this business and found that they were formerly makers of iron gates, bicycle locks, spinning-machine parts, etc. Steady orders of small engine parts enabled them to realize long-term investments and to accumulate special know-how.

In the case of Kubota, the investigators were able to find seventy closely related subcontractors, a quarter of whom surrounded the Sakai Factory. Of these seventy firms, forty-nine were examined in detail. Most of them were small shops: thirty-three firms had fewer than twenty-nine workers, though four firms employed more than a hundred. Twenty-seven firms depended absolutely on Kubota, which absorbed more than

70 per cent of their output. Furthermore, many of these firms had their own relationships with even smaller machine shops. Kubota's early development in agricultural engine production would not have been possible without this extended network of subcontractors.

However, it is important not to over estimate the competence of these subcontractors. Some of them, with their scanty equipment and poor technological knowledge, won orders simply by relying on a cheap labour force. It should also be noted that the 1953 investigation enumerated, besides Kubota and Yanmar, many small and medium-sized firms (with fifteen to fifty workers) assembling oil engines independently. They had maintained their own channels of distribution, and persistent personal credit from customers, since the 1920s and 1930s. As small engines were still used for various purposes, the production system retained some heterogeneity. This situation was to change with the introduction and spread of power tillers and small garden tractors; agricultural machinery manufacture was profoundly rationalized.

THE TILLER BOOM

In the pre-war period, the land-tenure system and heavy rents obstructed the diffusion of agricultural machines in Japanese villages. The land reform of 1947, which created millions of small landowners, provided the basis for rural innovation. Agricultural co-operatives (1947) and the Public Fund for Agriculture, Forestry and Fishery (1953) facilitated small farmers' efforts to increase productivity.

In 1953 the Agricultural Mechanization Encouragement Act was promulgated, and the Mechanization Council was created under the auspices of government. Policy measures included the importation of technology, regulations on the quality of machinery, the creation of propagation systems, financial aid to farmers, and so on.[14]

Both central and local government gave farmers long-term, low-interest loans in order to encourage the common usage of large machinery, especially in the Tohoku and Hokuriku districts. As a result, from 1954 to 1957 common usage tended to become general practice. But after 1958, as farmers became more inclined to buy machines for their private use, the common usage organizations dwindled. In this respect, the policy ended in failure.[15] Public money was spent more efficiently on the Land Improvement Schemes. Thanks to this investment, Japanese rice fields were adapted to forms that met the requirements of mechanized agriculture.[16]

The contribution of government was much greater in technological fields. With the assistance of machine manufacturers, agricultural laboratories successfully undertook experiments to develop machines suited to Japanese agriculture. A very small walk-behind type of garden tiller, equipped with a 2.5 hp air-cooled engine and a European plough, was imported from the United States in 1952. Engineers immediately attached to it a Japanese plough, two rubber tyres, gearings and a side clutch.[17] This tiller-tractor, sometimes referred to as a 'hand tractor', was a dramatic success, selling more than 100,000 units yearly during the 1960s (see Figure 9.2).

With this cheap garden tiller-tractor, which was particularly welcomed by small farmers, Japanese agriculture entered a period of full-scale mechanization. From the end of the 1960s, there were successive booms in various machines: reapers, medium-sized tractors, rice-planting machines, combines and so forth. Mechanization enabled farmers to cope with the labour shortage and to reduce production costs. Their profits were reinvested in the acquisition of larger and more efficient machines. It was in these circumstances that Japanese agricultural machine manufacturers enjoyed their golden age.

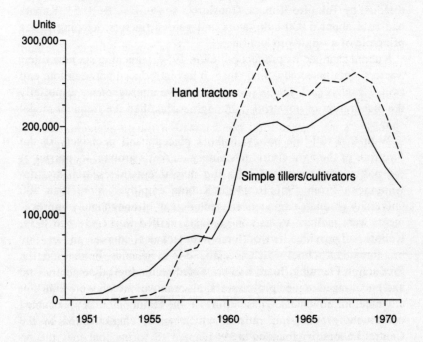

Figure 9.2 Annual production of power tillers, 1951–71
Source: Inamoto. *op. cit.*, p. 45.

KUBOTA'S STRATEGY

Kubota and the other manufacturers not only seized the opportunity of growth, but also took an active part in accelerating the mechanization of Japanese agriculture. Without such efforts, both in production and distribution, conservative small Japanese farmers would not have been persuaded to purchase expensive machines. In this respect, Kubota's daring strategy merits attention.[18] As already indicated, most of Kubota's activity, until the beginning of the 1950s, consisted of iron- and steel-pipe production. But in 1962, 56 per cent of Kubota's total sales consisted of machines, and agricultural machines alone amounted to 40 per cent of total sales. It is important to examine the elements of this very rapid expansion.

Research and development

In 1947, Kubota's first cultivator was produced by the Sakai Factory. The main contributors to the creation of this prototype were a group of motor engineers who had formerly belonged to a subsidiary of Nissan, directed by Tokujiro Kubota, Gonshiro's son-in-law. By 1953, Kubota had sold about 6,000 cultivators and garden tractors, keeping to the principle of a single product line.

Kubota changed its product policy in 1954, launching six new tiller-tractors simultaneously. Since then, it has introduced between four and twelve models each year. Various, successive improvements, especially the elaboration of powerful light engines, justified the frequent model changes.

With this full-line policy, Kubota placed itself decisively in the forefront of the agricultural machinery market's growth. Its pursuit of the policy was supported by a big investment in research and development. From 1956 to 1965, Kubota employed more than 500 university graduate engineers and technicians, although many improvements were realized by its non-graduate, skilled workers. Since 1935, Kubota had provided its workforce with technical courses, and in 1940 had founded a school which specialized in mechanics. From 1956, the Production Planning Board had promoted technological seminars, and had encouraged any employee work-place moves which were aimed at technical improvement. These efforts at the factory-floor level enabled continuous product innovations, which were complemented by the Central Laboratory founded in 1961.

Kubota also participated in government projects. In particular, from 1958 on, Kubota's engineers were engaged in research in Hokkaido and

Niigata in order to develop a medium-sized tractor suitable for use in Japan. Their fruitful results ensured Kubota's position in agricultural machine manufacture in the 1970s.

Marketing

The growth of agricultural machine production did not result from a passive reaction to the expansion of demand; it was the rational consequence of coherent marketing strategies. So far as Kubota was concerned, the damage to its pipe-casting section caused by the depression of 1952–3 motivated the expansion of its machine business.

Kobota's marketing system for tillers and tractors succeeded that for oil engines. Originally, Kubota had consigned its engines to two general agencies – Mitsubishi Trading Company and Sugiyama Shoten. In 1947, Kubota discontinued these agencies, and integrated the networks of its two former traders so as to create a single sales system composed of 198 direct agents. Subsequently, Kubota extended this system and applied it to the marketing of various new agricultural machines.

Most of these agents must have been small, even in 1960. Of the 8,068 retailers of agricultural machinery and implements in Japan, 5,107 (63.8 per cent) had fewer than two employees; the average number of their employees was only 3.1.[19] But some of them, eager to expand their business, were on the way to introducing elements of modern management. Kubota gave financial, commercial and technical aid to its direct agents. Since 1948, all agents' meetings, held periodically, have been under Kubota's leadership. This network has enabled Kubota not only to sell its products efficiently, but also to anticipate consumers' needs.

Kubota's local offices and service stations multiplied to support this network. Besides Tokyo, local offices were created in Nagoya (1957), Sendai (1960), Hiroshima (1966), Oita (1969) and Takamatsu (1965–70). Service stations were located in Asahikawa (1955), Kumamoto (1957), Kanazawa (1959), Okayama (1960), Niigata (1963), Urawa (1966), Nagano (1966), Fukuoka (1967), Mito (1969), Natori (1969) and Yonago (1969). The Management Planning Board, created in 1956, controlled these local outlets from the Osaka head office. It initiated management courses, both for Kubota's own office staff and for outside dealers, in order to facilitate distribution and to elaborate marketing techniques.

Since 1952, Kubota has sponsored radio programmes, published periodicals and produced advertising films. A special advertising department was created in 1956. Newspapers, and radio and television commercials, helped consumers to obtain information on Kubota's new models. Kubota's talented advertising staff, through the contrivance of a series of attractive catchwords, integrated the image of a very varied product range.

Production system

The increase of production capacity enabled the expansion of agricultural machinery sales. After many improvements and extensions, Sakai Factory had become highly specialized in agricultural machine production, particularly of tillers and tractors, the rest of its original activities having been transferred to the other factories. Rationalization was pursued to its logical conclusion; to the extent that, in 1956, the Sakai Factory was awarded the Technology Institute Prize for achieving job standardization.

But these measures hardly kept pace with the growth of the market. In 1964, therefore, Kubota opened a machine assembly plant, covering 33 hectacres, in Hirakata, a north-eastern suburb of Osaka. In 1969, another new factory, devoted solely to the assembly of reapers and rice planters, began operations in Utsunomiya, 100 kilometres north of Tokyo.

The proliforation of machine plants was all the more noteworthy because Kubota simultaneously accomplished some important innovations in its manufacture of pipe section – plastic pipe (1954), spiral sheet steel pipe (1959) and so on. The introduction of these new products required huge investment. Without an adequate financial policy, this expenditure would have discouraged machine production.

Fortunately, Kubota's pipe and agricultural machinery sections both yielded considerable returns. Profits were poured into investment in expansion and research and development activity. Kubota increased its capital stock almost yearly. Capital, already 280 million yen in 1950, reached 13,500 million yen in 1960 and 31,600 million yen in 1970. While Kubota sometimes introduced outside money, unlike the ex-*zaibatsu* firms, it borrowed from various banks and institutions, including foreigners,[20] and was careful never to depend too heavily on outside finance.

Heavy investments, therefore, ensured the extended production capacity of agricultural machinery. But the simple multiplication of assembly plants alone would not have sufficed to fulfil the demand, because of the full-line principle and frequent model changes that had characterized Kubota's product policy on agricultural machinery since 1954. Improvements in the way jobs were administered saved Kubota from lapsing into chaos: undoubtedly, the efficient use of computers introduced in 1960, was important in this context.

In particular, however, continuous job training and prompt job reorganization kept production lines adaptable. Over an eight-year period, the Technical Formation Centre, created in 1958, took on more than 1,100 junior high school graduates and gave them three years of the latest technical education. For ordinary workers, on-the-job training was systematized in a three-stage programme. And, as indicated above, the Production Planning Board organized seminars on a variety of topics, including job administration; first-rate participants were awarded special certificates which would facilitate rapid promotion.

The system worked well, because turnover in the workforce was relatively low. This was the fruit of Kubota's long-term labour policy. In 1923, the firm had been damaged by a fierce strike in its Amagasaki Factory. Since then, Gonshiro Kubota, and his executive Daizo Odawara (1892–1971), had paid close attention to the problems of labour relations and workers' welfare. For example, in the period 1955–65, Kubota constructed for its workers ferro-concrete apartments in forty-three different areas of Japan. It financed workers' housing plans and subsidized room rents. It also provided workers with numerous recreation facilities – villas, gymnasiums, halls and so forth. Various measures were taken to inspire workers with loyalty and affection towards the firm.

When meeting the evolving demands of the market, however, the disadvantages of mass production plants must have been compensated for by the advantages of having networks of small suppliers. Recognizing their value, Kubota tried to support its subcontractors – including Asahi Industries, an agricultural machine parts supplier which became a wholly-owned subsidiary in 1961 – by transferring to them numerous resources. This had not always been the case. In 1953, Kubota was still quiescent over organizing its suppliers, afraid of possible conspiracy.[21] But soon afterwards, it formed associations of its 'co-operating factories', for the purpose of reinforcing relations with them. Efforts on the part of suppliers also merit attention. In the 1950s and 1960s, as giant assembly plants for home electronics multiplied, small machine shops mushroomed proportionately in the eastern outskirts of Osaka. These machine shops, numbering 1,000 or more in Higashi-Osaka City alone, demonstrated their dynamism by combining to create their own technical centres, financial institutions and social security organizations.[22] The extension of this network, and the advanced specializations of its members, helped Kubota and the other assembly firms to respond promptly to changing demand.

Organization

Kubota became a joint-stock company in 1930 and then a public company in 1939, but was not listed until 1949. Gonshiro Kubota always retained absolute power within the firm. In 1949, he retired. The following year, Daizo Odawara, who directed Sakai Factory during the war and who had been managing director since 1945, succeeded him as president.

On the advice of Konosuke Matsushita, Daizo Odawara immediately reorganized the firm by introducing a multi-divisional system. Under the supervision of two executive directors (for production and management), and two chief engineers (casting and machine-manufacturing), the heads of the five divisions – pipes, foundry, engines, machines and balances – were able to exercise significant power and make rapid decisions. This reform contributed greatly to the dramatic expansion in the production of agricultural machinery.

By 1970, the five divisions had been sub-divided into eleven. All the supervision and co-ordination functions were concentrated in the general head office created in 1960. Project management, introduced gradually in order to meet market changes, preserved the firm from sclerosis.

SATURATION OF THE AGRICULTURAL MACHINE MARKET

The production of power tillers reached its peak in 1963. In 1965, the ownership level reached its 50 per cent ceiling.[23] Fierce competition between tiller and tractor manufacturers accelerated the spread of the long-term and low-interest credits to customers, together with expensive trade-ins, reducing the profits of each firm.[24] Kubota confronted these difficulties by adopting three different measures.

In the first place, Kubota sold its tillers and tractors abroad, especially in South-East Asia. The firm had been exporting its oil engines since the 1930s. In 1961, however, it created a knock-down factory in Taiwan, which had taken more than 1,500 Kubota tillers and tractors before 1960. At 308 million yen in 1959, Kubota's exports of agricultural machinery represented only 33.7 per cent of the firm's total exports; ten years later, at over 2,000 million yen, they were more than half. In the second place, Kubota shifted its machine-making activities to the top end of the national market; it encouraged the sales of large and medium-sized tractors and combines, whose unit profit was much higher than that of power tillers. These tactics, employed by Kubota and other machinery manufacturers, together with the inflationary national economic policy of Kakuei Tanaka, engendered the emergence of another mechanization boom, albeit a fragile one, in the early 1970s.

Evidently these measures had their limits, however. So, in the third place, Kubota made, and continues to make, desperate efforts to diversify. In 1969, it launched itself into the house construction business. Housing materials were among the habitual products of its foundry, and the requisite civil engineering knowledge had been accumulated in the course of undertaking its water supply business. House construction was therefore a natural extension of its original activities. Entry into the computer business also had its origins in Kubota's own technology to regulate pumps and valves. In any event, what is abundantly clear is that, for Kubota, the golden age of agricultural machinery manufacture is over.

CONCLUSION

The tiller boom of the late 1950s and 1960s, which increased agricultural productivity and created a rising income-output spiral, laid the foundation of Japan's post-war economic growth. Moreover, the mass production of power tillers, along with that of motorbikes and auto-tricycles, prepared the ground for the full blossoming of the motor industry in the late 1960s.

Kubota Ironworks, which had already gained a good reputation as a pipe manufacturer and was experienced in oil engine production, contributed largely to the innovations in both production and marketing. With its bold strategy, it took the lead in the modernization of the agricultural machinery industry in Japan. In this connection, it is important to point out that Kubota's managerial elasticity originated in its drastic organizational reforms and careful manpower policies.

NOTES

1 Before the adoption of its new name, Kubota Inc., in 1969, Kubota's official name was Kubota Iron and Machinery Works. In this article, for convenience, it has been called Kubota Ironworks, or simply Kubota.
2 *Kaisha shiki ho* (Quarterly Directory of Listed Firms), Summer 1991.
3 Hiroshi Shimizu, *Nihon ni okeru nogyo kikaika no tenkai* (*Development of Agricultural Mechanization in Japan*), Tokyo, Chuo Koronsha, 1953, pp. 8, 44.
4 FAO, *Yearbook of Food and Agricultural Statistics*.
5 Ministry of Agriculture and Forestry, *Agricultural Whitebook 1973*, 1974.
6 Shin norin sha, *Nogyo kikai nenkan* (*Yearbook of agricultural machines*).
7 Ministry of Commerce and Industry, *Kojoo Tokei Hyo* (*Tables of Factory Statistics*), 1937.

8 Between 1960 and 1968, the nominal price of agricultural machines stayed at the same level. This stability meant a sensible decrease in real price, because the CPI almost doubled in this decade. See Akira Takei, *Nihon nogyo no kikaika* (*Mechanization of Japanese Agriculture*), Tokyo, Taimeido, 1971, pp. 45–7.

9 Ibid., pp. 81–3.

10 The history of Kubota Ironworks is described in detail in *Kubota Tekko 80 nen no ayumi* (*The Eighty year history of Kubota Ironworks*), Osaka, Kubota Inc., 1970. For the early development of this firm, see the following articles: Takamasa Ichikawa, 'Nihon no kogyoka to sono ninaite' ('Japanese industrialization and its leaders'), *Shakai Keizai Shigaku*, 1984, vol. 50, no. 1; Konosuke Odaka, 'Kinzoku kakogyo ni okeru syokunin no yakuwari' ('Role of craftsmen in the metal industry'), *Keizai Kenkyu*, 1986, vol. 37, no. 3.

11 In December 1933, the automobile division of Tobata Foundry became the Japan Motor Manufacturing Co. The following year, the latter changed its name to Nissan Motors and started to make 5,000 Datsuns a year in Yokohama.

12 *Kikai kogyo ni okeru gaichu shitauke no jittai* (*The State of Outside Orders and Subcontracts in the Machine Building Industry*), Osaka, Osaka Furitsu Shoko Keizai Kenkyujo, 1954.

13 In Okayama, where the ground for growing wheat was exceptionally hard, farmers had been using oil-engine cultivators since the 1920s. The prototype was a Swiss-made walk-behind type of cultivator imported in 1919, which was gradually improved by rural blacksmiths. Some hundreds of these Okayama-type cultivators were in use by the late 1930s. See Shimizu, *Nihon ni okeru nogyo kikaika no tenkai*, pp. 48–52.

14 Tokio Mitsuhashi (ed.), *Sengo nihon nogyo no shiteki tenkai* (*The Historical Development of Post-war Japanese Agriculture*), Kyoto, Minerva Shobo, 1975.

15 Takei, *Nihon nogyo no kikaika*, pp. 189 ff.

16 Keizo Tsuchiya, 'Nihon nogyo ni okeru kikaika no igi to yakuwari' ('The significance and role of mechanization in Japanese agriculture'), in Keiji Kamiya (ed.), *Gijutsu kakushin to nihon nogyo* (*Innovations and Japanese Agriculture*), Tokyo, Taimeido, 1969, pp. 142–3.

17 Shiro Inamoto, *Nogyo no gijutsu shinpo to kazoku keiei* (*Technical Progress and Family Business in Agriculture*), Tokyo, Taimeido, 1987, p. 43.

18 The facts and figures cited in this section were found, for the most part, in Kubota's annual reports and in its eightieth anniversary pamphlet (see note 10).

19 MITI, *Commercial Census*, 1960.

20 There were, for instance, issues of debenture bonds in the United States (4.9 million dollars in 1963) and in Luxembourg (15 million dollars in 1969).

21 *Kikai kogyo ni okeru*, p. 198, *et passim*.

22 *Higashi-Osaka Shoko Kaigisho 50 nenshi* (*50 years of the Higashi-Osaka Chamber of Commerce*), Higashi-Osaka, Higashi-Osaka Shoko Kaigisho, 1988, pp. 293 ff.

23 Inamoto, *Nogyo no gijutsu*, pp. 5, 45.

24 Takei, *Nihon nogyo no kikaika*, pp. 85–6.

Part III

Service industry, accounting systems and education

10 The industrial organization of Japanese life insurance: historical aspects

Takau Yoneyama

INTRODUCTION

The amount of life insurance taken up per capita in Japan was 9,791,000 yen in 1988 – more than twice what it was in the United States (ranked second) and Canada (ranked third). Japan is the most insurance-conscious country in the world,[1] and the larger Japanese life insurance companies – Nippon Life Insurance, Dai-ichi Life Insurance and Sumitomo Life Insurance – are all top-ranked world companies. The business results of these three companies are summarized in Table 10.1.

The beginnings of Western-style life insurance in Japan, however, came later than in the West.[2] Although some foreign life insurance companies conducted business in Japan in the late nineteenth century, the life insurance market was small and not worth serious attention.[3] Even in 1930, the life insurance take-up per capita was only about 21 yen, less than a half of the starting salary of a university graduate. In the same year, too, Nippon Life's business was much less than that of Prudential Life of New York, the largest company in the world.

Although the business made a late start, however, life insurance rapidly became widespread in Japan.[4] Figure 10.1 illustrates the rate of expansion, and also the effects of the war. At the end of 1988, the proportion of life insurance take-up in Japan's National Income was 411 per cent, more than double that of the USA (202 per cent).[5] Some of the world's largest insurance companies are Japanese[6] and recently, the large overseas investments of Japan's life insurance companies have become the focus of world attention. The abbreviation 'Seiho', which stands for *Seimei-Hoken Kaisha* (life insurance company), is well known in international financial circles.

Why did Japan's life insurance market expand so rapidly? How did the Seiho grow to world-class levels? There seem to be two general

168   *Takau Yoneyama*

Table 10.1(a) Business results of the top three companies in 1989 (¥m.)

Co.	Policies held	Premium income	Total assets
NLI	297,205,779	5,051,322	24,881,436
DLI	207,378,257	3,638,934	17,360,831
SLI	192,666,999	3,357,688	14,861,661
All cos.	1,372,734,402	28,040,284	116,159,725

(b) Business results of the top three companies in 1989 ($m.)

Co.	Policies held	Premium income	Total assets
NLI	2,248,153	38,210	188,211
DLI	1,568,671	27,526	131,322
SLI	1,457,390	25,399	112,418
All cos.	10,383,770	212,105	878,667

(c) Business results of the top three companies in 1989 (%)

Co.	Policies held	Premium income	Total assets
NLI	21.65	18.01	21.42
DLI	15.11	12.98	14.95
SLI	14.04	11.97	12.79
All cos.	100.00	100.00	100.00

Sources: Insurance: Annual Statistics of Life Insurance in Japan; Annual Report of the DLI, 1989; Annual Reports of the NLI, 1989 and 1990
Notes: 1. Amounts less than ¥1 million omitted.
2. $1 = ¥123.20 on 31 March 1989.

explanations for these questions. One concerns the drastic changes in Japanese social and cultural structures; the other relates to the rapid growth of the Japanese economy after the Second World War.

At the end of the war, the GHQ (General Headquarters of the occupying forces) ordered Japan to reform its economy and make it more democratic. The result was the immediate institution of a series of reforms. There were four main measures: dissolution of the *zaibatsu* and a purge of the top management of big business, abolition of the system of absentee landlords (agrarian reform), educational reform, and approval of the basic legal rights of labour. These reforms radically altered Japanese social and cultural structures: the Japanese people abandoned much of their traditional way of thinking, including their public antipathy towards life insurance. As a result of the rapid growth

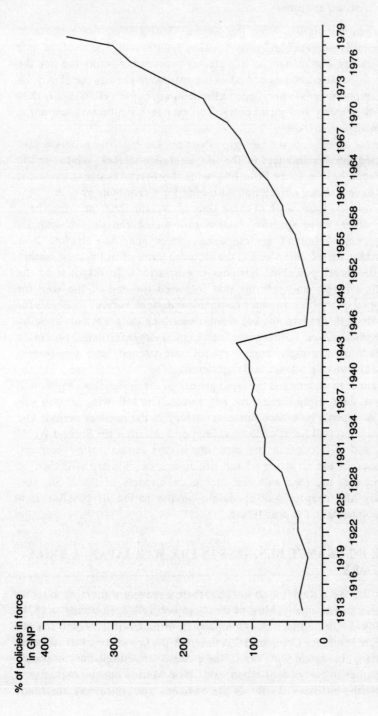

Figure 10.1 The growth of the life insurance business in Japan, 1913–1980

Sources: *Hoken nenkan* (Japanese Insurance Almanac), annual; *Insurance: Statistics of Life Insurance Business in Japan*, annual, *et al.*

of urban population after the Second World War, the number of households increased and small families proliferated. The heads of such families came to recognize, to a greater degree than before the war, the necessity of life insurance. And as life insurance grew in popularity, its most important customers became the ordinary city-dwellers, rather than men of property and social élites. This is a very important facet of the life insurance market.

On the other hand, the high growth rate of the Japanese economy also affected the development of the life insurance market. While the life insurance business has little link with short-term business cycles, it does have a strong correlation with long-term economic growth.

Within the framework of these general explanations, there may have been other, more specific, factors influencing the growth and development of Japan's insurance companies and their market. It is important, therefore, to look at the sector in terms of its business history and the development of business organizations. In response to the drastic changes and reforms that followed the end of the war, for example, every life insurance company undertook various strategies for growth. In this regard, the key words describing the growth of the Seiho are *mutualization* (conversion into mutual organizations), non-price *competition* (through large corps of saleswomen) and *government* (administrative guidance and regulation).

In order to understand the rapid growth of the Seiho, this chapter will analyse them using these three key words. The following section will look at Japan's insurance business history in the pre-war period. The next section will focus on the turning point just after the Second World War, and will confirm the meaning of the *mutualization* concept. Changes in the structure of the life insurance industry will then be considered, together with the theoretical aspects of these changes. Finally, the chapter will speculate on the nature of possible new developments in the near future.[7]

LIFE INSURANCE BUSINESS IN PRE-WAR JAPAN: A BRIEF HISTORY

After the Meiji Restoration in 1868, there were many attempts to set up an insurance company. Most of these projects failed. However, in 1879, the Tokio Marine Insurance Company (forerunner of the Tokio Marine and Fire Insurance Company) was founded, the first successful insurance company in Japan.[8] At first, there were no composite insurance companies in early Meiji Japan, and Tokio Marine opened exclusively for marine business. As far as life business was concerned, the Meiji

Life Insurance Company (MLI) was established in July 1881, starting operations soon after.[9] MLI was the first company in the life business, and its founders were pupils of Yukichi Fukuzawa, a famous teacher and founder of the *Keio Gijuku* (forerunner of Keio University).[10] He actively promoted Western culture, and his pupils learned much from his approach. The Teikoku Life Insurance Company (TLI, founded in 1888) and the Nippon Life Insurance Company (NLI, founded in 1889) followed the MLI.[11] The TLI was established in Tokyo by a person with naval connections. The NLI started life in Osaka, its founders consisting of a number of wealthy men who lived in the Kansai district (the area around Osaka and Kyoto). The character of these companies was very different, but they had one thing in common – all three were joint-stock companies.[12] Moreover, they were not organized according to the pre-modern mutual system but according to modern Western insurance principles.[13]

The MLI, TLI and NLI were all successful insurance companies, but other projects were not always so fortunate. After the first Sino-Japanese War (1894–5), in particular, many insurance projects followed in the footsteps of the successful companies.[14] But most of them were fragile enterprises, having either a weak constitution or a pre-modern insurance business organization. Because some failed immediately, the government realized that it would have to step in and regulate the industry officially.

The first insurance law to come into force was introduced in 1900.[15] This required insurance companies to report on their financial status. Its importance lies in the fact that, on the one hand it marked the start of government supervision of the insurance business, and on the other it was the prototype of the law currently in operation. It prescribed that insurance business should be undertaken exclusively by joint-stock and mutual companies, and prohibited the simultaneous running of life and non-life business.[16] These provisions continue to this day.

In part, the insurance law had the effect of restraining competition, by regulating small and thrusting companies. But it also resulted in a new form of competition in the long term. Based on the law, a new form of life insurance company came into being, operating on the basis of the mutual system. The Chiyoda Life Insurance Company (CLI, established in 1904) and the Dai-Ichi Life Insurance Company (DLI, established in 1902) were just such mutual companies. These companies sold their product with the inducement of a high bonus, and adopted a sales policy that concentrated on the big cities. As a result, the CLI and DLI had contrived to catch up with the 'big three' by the early 1920s.[17]

In 1927 Japan suffered a major financial panic, and the economy was in a state of crisis up until 1931 because of the effects of the Great Depression. During the Depression, sales competition among the life insurance companies became more severe. What was worse, the finances of some of the smaller companies were adversely affected, many companies becoming virtually bankrupt. In order to restrict excessive competition and unfair sales, a law to regulate the practice of illegal canvassing was enacted in 1931.

Owing to a short wartime boom following the Manchurian Incident of 1931, and the depreciation of the yen, the Japanese economy was quick to recover in 1932, before the Western nations managed to reconstruct their economies. It was at this time that Japan's heavy and chemical industries grew. Then, in 1937, the second Sino-Japanese War began, and the heavy and chemical industries devoted themselves to the manufacture of munitions instead of their normal products. In the early stages of this war economy Japanese business prospered, at least superficially. In reality, however, every aspect of business and the economy came to be regulated by government.

None the less, in spite of severe sales competition and the long depression of the early 1930s, Japanese life insurance business increased in importance in the national economy. In particular, as its total gross reserve grew, so the industry's prominence amongst financial institutions increased rapidly.[18] This is the reason why government tried to control the life insurance companies. In the early years of the war economy, the authorities requested that the life companies should hold a greater proportion of national debt. When the state of the war demanded more than this indirect approach, government took direct control of the life insurance companies. It was at this time that supervision of the insurance industry was transferred from the Ministry of Commerce and Industry (forerunner of the Ministry of International Trade and Industry) to the Ministry of Finance (MOF).

The MOF's supervision was somehow different from that of its predecessor. Although the effects of the war have to be discounted, industrial policy became markedly more regulated than it had been. The MOF preferred to control asset management and looked for uniformity in insurance products. And, in order to restrain excessive competition in sales, the MOF introduced for the first time a limit to the amount of money that could be spent in order to win new business. The essence of this policy continued after the Second World War.[19]

THE PERIOD OF SCRAMBLE FOR POLE POSITION, 1945–57

With the end of the Second World War, the life insurance companies lost their large overseas assets and were holding large national debts which were practically valueless. The position was made worse still by the fact that the government's wartime compensation payments ended, so that the value of the assets of the life insurance companies was badly depreciated and their loans of 350 million yen were uncollectable. In addition, the life insurance companies were unable fully to meet their liabilities to policyholders.

In order to find a way out of the difficulty, the life insurance managers divided their business into two accounts. The so-called 'Old Accounts' comprised those assets that had suffered heavy damage, and the portion of the reserve that was related to large contracts (i.e. policies of over 10,000 yen and/or policies which had total premiums of over 1,200 yen). In contrast, assets that had not suffered damage, and the portion of the reserve that related to smaller contracts, were known as the 'New Accounts'. The former were put into liquidation, and new business was built on the basis of the latter.

Simultaneously, nearly all the life insurance companies tried to form new companies based principally on the 'New Accounts'. At this time, just after the war, the life insurance companies were given the opportunity to transform themselves into mutual companies – an option which the majority of life insurance companies in Japan took up.[20]

In pre-war Japan, life companies with joint-stock structure were mostly mixed companies, i.e. proprietary companies distributing bonuses to policyholders as well as dividends to shareholders.[21] The mutualization movement did not entail a drastic change in their products. As far as management was concerned, however, the absence of large stockholders was crucial.

There were never the problems with mutual companies in pre-war Japan that Keller describes.[22] On the contrary, it was the joint-stock companies which experienced difficulties. Life managers were frequently pestered by their shareholders, and some companies were weakened by their shareholders' offensive and defensive battles. Generally speaking, therefore, most life managers considered mutualization to be an advantage. Of course, circumstances differed for each company. However, the top joint-stock companies recognized that the payment of shareholder dividends was a disadvantage for sales in the severe sales competition they faced against tough mutual rivals. Some life managers also thought it wise to convert to mutualization in order to disguise any connection with the previous 'Old Accounts' company, hoping that it would seem that a completely new company had been established, not merely a 'New Accounts' one. In addition, with the strengthening of labour power under the labour reforms introduced in the early stages of the administration of GHQ – some companies being troubled by severe trade disputes – life managers may have recognized the importance of cutting down their shareholders and changing the structure of their management.

Whatever the motive, fourteen of the twenty life insurance companies converted to a mutual structure in 1947. Only three joint-stock companies did not adopt this strategy, and they were small or specialist firms. In short, all the top-ranked joint-stock life companies were transformed into mutual organizations, so that they could compete with each other on equal terms. Furthermore, since the growth of such mutual companies was rapid, they came to dominate joint-stock companies still more.

From a slightly different viewpoint, between 1945 and 1956 life insurance companies followed a variety of policies and strategies. The ranking of firms changed quite frequently. This is one reason why the power of the authorities was weak and government could not establish a clear framework for industrial policy.

In conclusion, it is interesting to note that those companies which had achieved a good ranking by the end of this period were able to maintain their position thereafter. The years 1945 to 1956 can therefore be characterized, in motor-racing parlance, as the scramble for pole position. But did this mean that competition all but disappeared in the Japanese life insurance industry after 1956? This question will be examined in the next section.

CHANGES IN THE STRUCTURE OF THE LIFE INSURANCE INDUSTRY AFTER THE WAR

Table 10.2 shows the number of current policies held by each of Japan's life insurance companies at the end of each fiscal year from 1958 to 1988. The companies are listed according to their ranking order in 1988. The graphs in Figure 10.2 are derived from this table. The following conclusions emerge from the table and accompanying graphs.

Firstly, the increasing stability of the industrial organization of the life insurance sector is revealed. In particular, stabilization was strengthened after 1958. The ranking for 1988, for instance, is very different from that of 1948, but has changed relatively little since 1958. The latter year can be said to have been a turning point. Secondly, it may be possible to cluster some companies after 1968. Thirdly, it is evident that stabilization among the top-ranked companies was greater than among those of a lower rank; the relative position of the top three companies did not change after the early 1960s, for example.

The concentration of business towards the higher-ranked companies increased gradually. This trend is clarified in Table 10.3 and Figure 10.3. The top six or seven companies traditionally have accounted for about a third of the business, but recently their share has risen to nearly four-fifths.

For almost thirty years after the end of the Second World War, foreign-affiliated life insurance companies were not permitted to establish themselves, although within the last ten years these newcomers have received such authorization. Also, with one special exception, there were no mergers in this industry. These are important factors in

Table 10.2 Policies in force of all Japan's life insurance companies 1948–88, (¥ m.)

			Policies in force		
	1948	1958	1968	1978	1988
1 Nippon	83,143	872,355	10,321,575	100,429,675	258,336,498
2 Dai-ich	43,377	595,203	6,379,669	64,132,340	181,040,246
3 Sumitomo	14,584	386,211	5,143,646	59,226,018	168,698,985
4 Meiji	30,466	512,580	4,427,378	45,531,420	118,145,231
5 Yasuda	16,704	212,155	3,156,966	35,809,099	87,510,411
6 Asahi	34,603	440,238	4,692,111	32,483,724	82,101,317
7 Mitsui	19,071	288,804	2,902,096	29,906,600	73,192,223
8 Kyoei	1,298	145,398	1,190,340	13,655,031	40,425,067
9 Chiyoda	25,092	268,746	2,220,670	14,531,277	38,174,471
10 Daido	7,037	69,611	640,388	12,916,965	31,632,090
11 Toho	16,626	149,218	1,648,158	10,563,402	24,704,869
12 Nippon-Dantai	8,720	117,189	966,307	12,688,012	24,356,128
13 Fukoku	18,102	110,043	770,271	8,501,320	23,821,193
14 Dai-hyaku	5,288	53,654	547,052	5,505,132	14,841,625
15 Taiyo	1,219	66,930	591,350	5,150,536	12,241,802
16 Tokyo	13,410	82,360	536,657	3,938,790	10,344,567
17 Nissan	6,115	45,310	880,731	5,580,918	9,396,549
18 Heiwa	15,715	43,779	337,387	1,723,336	2,826,440
19 Seibu Allstate				304,954	2,391,116
20 Yamato	4,715	19,675	121,384	634,925	1,655,333
21 Sony Pruco					1,055,484
22 Taisho	335	8,019	65,803	344,646	959,773
23 INA					531,447
24 Equitable					229,494
25 Prudential					97,641
Total	365,285	4,479,459	47,514,137	463,253,166	1,208,710,000

Notes:
1 Kyoei's policies include reinsurance business in 1948, 1958 and 1968.
2 Kyoei's reinsurance business is not included in the total in 1958 or 1968.
3 Reinsurance policies are not included in 1978 and 1988.
4 The newly established companies are not listed in 1978, but are included in that year's total.

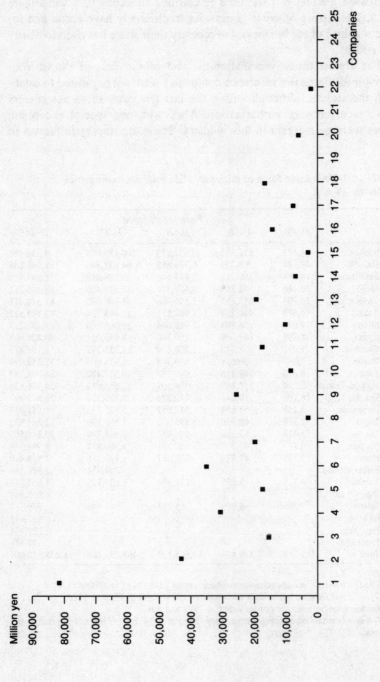

Figure 10.2(a) Policies held by Japan's life insurance companies in 1948

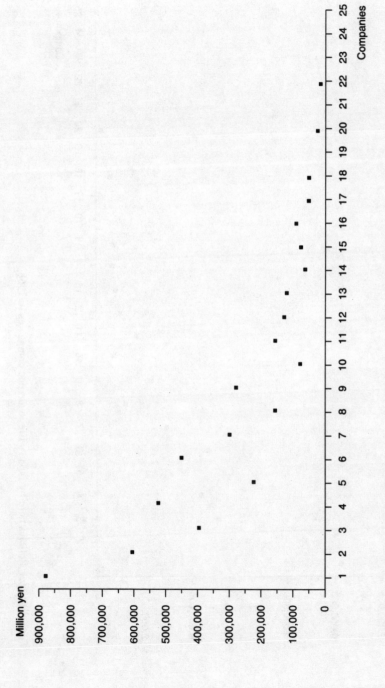

Figure 10.2(b) Policies held by Japan's life insurance companies in 1958

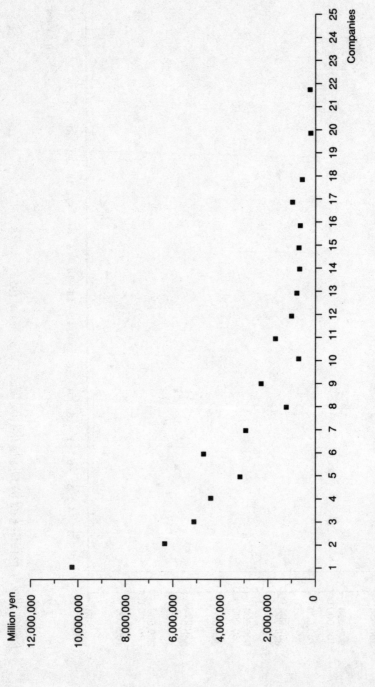

Figure 10.2(c) Policies held by Japan's life insurance companies in 1968

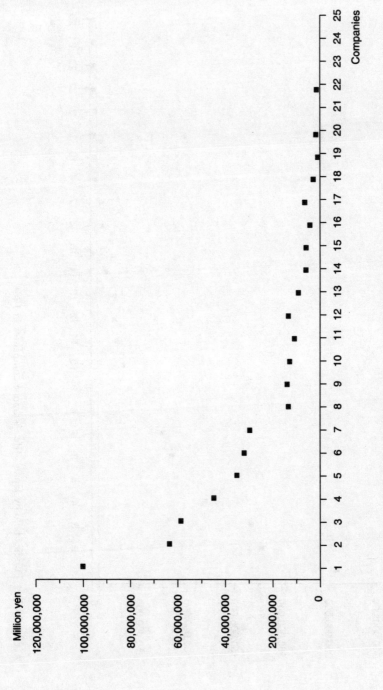

Figure 10.2(d) Policies held by Japan's life insurance companies in 1978

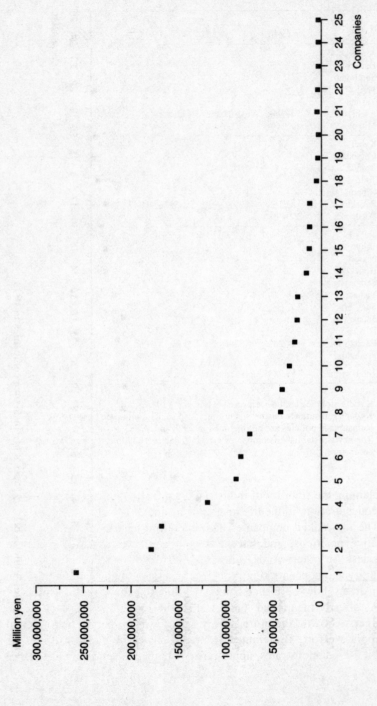

Figure 10.2(e) Policies held by Japan's life insurance companies in 1988

Table 10.3 Concentration of business in Japan, 1948–88

		1948	1958	(¥ m.) 1968	1978	1988
1	Nippon					
2	Dai-ich					
3	Sumitomo					
4	Meiji					
5	Yasuda					
6	Asahi	241,948	3,307,546	37,023,441	367,518,876	969,024,911
7	Mitsui	66.24%	73.84%	77.92%	79.92%	80.17%
8	Kyoei					
9	Chiyoda					
10	Daido					
11	Toho					
12	Nippon-Dantai					
13	Fukoku	82,163	913,858	7,983,186	78,361,139	197,955,443
14	Dai-hyaku	22.49%	20.40%	16.80%	16.92%	16.38%
15	Taiyo					
16	Tokyo					
17	Nissan					
18	Heiwa					
19	Seibu Allstate					
20	Yamato					
21	Sony Pruco					
22	Taisho					
23	INA					
24	Equitable	41,509	266,074	2,573,312	17,678,105	41,729,646
25	Prudential	11.36%	5.94%	5.42%	3.82%	3.45%
	Total	365,285	4,479,459	47,514,137	463,253,166	1,208,710,000

Notes
1 Kyoei's policies include reinsurance business (1948, 1958, 1968).
2 Kyoei's reinsurance business is not included in the total (1958, 1968).
3 Reinsurance policies are not included in 1978 and 1988.
4 The newly established companies are not listed in 1978, but the total includes such companies.

explaining the stability of industrial organization, as well as the extent of concentration, in the life insurance business.

The top-ranked companies have therefore tended to maintain their relative positions, and have attracted a greater share of available business. In other words, since the early 1960s there has been both stability and concentration in the life insurance industry. The question then arises, how were such companies able to expand their business?

As already mentioned, there were, with one notable exception, no mergers. Growth, therefore, was not the result of merger but of actual corporate effort. It stemmed from the power of the salesforce. As Table 10.4 demonstrates, upper-ranked companies tended to have large

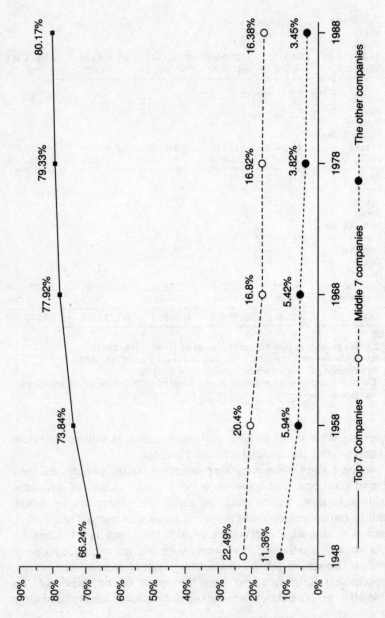

Figure 10.3 Concentrations of Japan's life insurance companies, 1948–88

Table 10.4 Numbers of clerks and salespersons, 1960–88

	1960		1969		1979		1988	
	Clerks	Salespersons	Clerks	Salespersons	Clerks	Salespersons	Clerks	Salespersons
1 Nippon	6,672	22,686	14,749	52,141	16,197	54,650	13,477	68,326
2 Dai-ich	4,407	38,690	11,825	44,778	13,001	42,219	11,262	59,292
3 Sumitomo	3,807	19,135	7,686	52,827	10,641	41,731	11,595	60,600
4 Meiji	3,785	11,116	7,344	26,376	9,826	32,334	8,730	37,562
5 Yasuda	1,449	7,668	4,989	16,037	5,906	13,179	6,866	16,636
6 Asahi	3,992	14,433	8,083	33,029	8,957	25,026	8,397	30,155
7 Mitsui	1,736	9,743	3,304	27,749	6,480	19,231	6,010	22,146
8 Kyoei	800	2,075	1,200	4,977	3,353	5,381	3,315	13,312
9 Chiyoda	2,294	4,845	4,451	15,422	4,532	8,570	3,445	13,211
10 Daido	942	5,795	1,474	5,391	2,007	3,177	2,396	4,325
11 Toho	1,193	6,552	3,193	15,181	3,404	7,387	4,129	9,081
12 Nippon-Dantai	309	585	833	986	1,493	1,041	2,406	3,972
13 Fukoku	822	3,068	2,077	8,661	2,952	6,509	3,048	9,027
14 Dai-hyaku	636	2,679	1,500	7,545	2,440	8,833	2,421	11,005
15 Taiyo	816	2,821	2,116	5,896	3,454	10,712	4,093	11,992
16 Tokyo	785	5,450	1,605	4,353	1,388	2,758	1,365	3,292
17 Nissan	464	1,692	1,079	4,156	1,178	2,095	1,366	3,681
18 Heiwa	328	4,116	1,088	4,343	964	2,520	949	2,219
19 Seibu Allstate					203	267	503	840
20 Yamato	319	841	470	1,197	473	621	513	1,260
21 Sony Pruco							257	365
22 Taisho	181	578	322	574	324	741	375	988
23 INA							180	50
24 Equitable							169	344
25 Prudential							64	148
Total	35,737	164,568	79,388	331,619	99,173	288,982	97,331	383,829

salesforces – in general well over 10,000 people. Almost all were women, and the large numbers of saleswomen provided the second major key factor (characterized above as competition) in the growth of the upper-ranked companies.

It seems clear that there are both social and cultural explanations for such large numbers of women in the salesforces of the life insurance companies. For instance, one social explanation which has been suggested is that these companies gave employment to war-widows. At the same time, the cultural argument has been put forward that women have the qualities needed in canvassing for insurance. This is because most Japanese people dislike speaking directly about either money or death, and there is a perception that women have a more gentle approach than men in dealing with such subjects. There is some truth in both of these explanations, but there are counter arguments also. It was, for example, only after 1955 that there was a rapid increase in the numbers of saleswomen; there was thus a time-lag between the end of the war and the increase in numbers.

The third key factor to be examined is the administrative guidance and regulation of the life insurance business (represented earlier above by the word government). The characteristics of Japan's life insurance companies, as already described, could have been the result of such government industry policy. Until 1942, the MOF was the authority in charge of the industry. And although this control was weakened when Japan was under the army of occupation, the foundations of the MOF's policy towards the insurance industry were strengthened again from 1956.

In simple terms, the policy consisted of two basic tenets – standardization of the price of life insurance products and protection of small life companies. The first of these is so important that it will receive most attention in this chapter. As far as this author is aware, there is no published source clarifying the subject. But although the price mechanism of Japan's life insurance business is not well-known, it is not very complicated.

To begin with, under the MOF's guidance, the most efficient life insurance company proposed a cut in the rate for life insurance. Strangely, the MOF did not immediately approve this cut. It did not consent to the proposal until it was clear that nearly all of the life companies could run their businesses at the cheaper rate. Temporarily shelving the proposal, therefore, the MOF pressed the other companies to be more efficient. And then, when the new cheaper rate was introduced, it came into effect on the same day across the board. Thus all Japan's life insurance companies found themselves acting together over pricing. This happened five times after 1952.[23] The MOF also regulated dividend policy, so that the price of life insurance products was not only the same across the board in the short term but also in the long term.[24]

Under the administrative guidance and regulation of the MOF, an efficient life company could build up a surplus until approval was given for the adoption of a new, cheaper insurance rate. If, as was usual in the pre-war period, such a company had been a joint-stock institution, this surplus would probably have been distributed to the shareholders. However, as described above and indicated by the first key word 'mutualization', almost all life companies were converted into mutual organizations in 1946–7. Then was the surplus turned over to policy-holders by way of a policy dividend? The answer is no: as stated above, the authorities forced the life companies to limit policy dividends.

In the event, unable to distribute their surplus or to use it to cut the price of insurance, the more efficient companies invested it in other areas – for instance, in meeting the costs of expanding their business, in financing their academic and cultural activities, and in providing for the rewards of officers and salaries of clerks.[25] For the purposes of this study, the most important area of investment was in building up powerful sales organizations.[26]

Upper-ranked companies which had the surplus competed fiercely for business. As price competition was prohibited, they tried to achieve their ends by intensifying sales. The main way of doing this was by forming sales corps, consisting largely of women.

As the interrelation between the size of business and the number of saleswomen has already been noted, it is appropriate here to explore the reason for this phenomenon. Most saleswomen engaged in door-to-door canvassing. Customers could therefore insure their lives anywhere by making an appointment, instead of visiting an agency or life insurance company. Since almost all saleswomen worked flexible hours, though few were actually part-time, and their salaries were strongly dependent on the number of sales made, they were willing to offer prospective customers a specialized service. A meeting with a saleswoman could be arranged at a time and place convenient to the client; for example, at the client's office, during a break, or at his own home, out of working hours. And, although a bad practice, sometimes saleswomen were so eager to make a sale that they would present customers with gifts at their own expense. It is no exaggeration to say, therefore, that the saleswomen provided a very high level of service. In Japan, a consumer pays the same price to insure his life whether he gets this level of service from saleswomen or visits an insurance office which does not provide it.

To sum up, standardization of the price of life insurance forced the upper-ranked companies to intensify service competition instead of price competition in Japan's life insurance market. This is the reason why the bigger companies, except those not having any surplus to invest, have larger corps of saleswomen than the smaller ones. The unique sales channel results both from the MOF's guidance and regulation and from the intensification of sales competition rather than from social and cultural factors mentioned above.

CONCLUSION: TRENDS IN THE LAST FIVE YEARS AND THE FUTURE

The industrial policy of the MOF is now gradually changing. Step by step, the authorities are going to deregulate the standardization of the price of insurance. The first step is likely to be the variable life insurance, that started being sold in 1986.[27] This is an insurance policy in which the sum insured reflects the investment returns on the life funds.[28] Each company can therefore sell the policy at a different rate in the long term.

The authorities approved the different prices of these policies in view of the recent introduction by the companies of the special dividend system. The latter allows the distribution of money accruing on the use of the insurance companies' funds. In spite of different levels of performance, the same eleven companies have retained their positions in the ranking order. In 1990, the authorities apparently decided to permit different special dividends.[29]

The rate for an initial life insurance policy has, up until the present time, been at the same level for all companies. However, as efficiency may be promoted by increased use of the market mechanism, it is not unexpected that the authorities should be prepared to progress such a deregulation.[30]

So far as the corps of saleswomen is concerned, although this exists as an explicit policy tactic, it is possible that gradual change will take place. In the opinion of this author, it seems natural that the price of life insurance should differ according to different sales channels. If prices which reflected exact costs were to be permitted, companies might be forced to cut back on personnel, reducing their large female salesforces. The early 1990s have indeed seen a gradual change in the organization of Japan's life insurance industry.[31]

In conclusion, the rapid growth of Japan's life insurance companies was due mainly to the high rate of economic growth in the country, which brought about the expansion of the life insurance market.

However, the sales policies of the life companies and the industrial policy of the MOF also have some bearing on the issue. The three key words, *mutualization*, non-price *competition*, and *government*, are clues to the reasons why the top-ranked life companies grew so rapidly. These factors are specific to Japanese life insurance companies, but they came about artificially in the post-war period and were not indigenous to Japan. Finally, although not radical, some changes in policy can now be seen, especially in the industrial policy of the MOF.

NOTES

1 *Seimeihoken Fact Book* (*Fact Book of Life Insurance*), Tokyo, Seimeihoken Bunka Centre (Japan Institute of Life Insurance), 1990, p. 19.

2 In the years 1868–70, just before Japan had a life insurance company of its own, there seem to have been some 294 companies worldwide. Of this number, 113 were in the UK, sixty-nine in the USA, thirty in Germany and sixteen in France. See *Assurance Magazine* (*The Journal of the Institute of Actuaries*), 1887, p. 459.

3 Although the market was small, a few British and American life companies nevertheless found new business in Japan.

4 The transfer of actuarial techniques was accomplished smoothly. Japan's Institute of Actuaries started life in 1899. At first it was a private organization, but it soon became a public body. See *The Eighty-five Year History of the Japanese Institute of Actuaries*, Tokyo, 1984. The UK apart, similar Institutes were established in the West from the late 1880s, e.g. in the Netherlands in 1888, in Belgium in 1895, in Austria and Italy in 1898. Germany established a society of insurance science, with considerable difficulty, in 1899. See H. Braun, *Geschichte der Lebensversicherung und der Lebensversicherungstechnik*, 2nd edn., Berlin, 1963, pp. 390–3.

5 *Seimeihoken Jigyo no Aramasi* (*A Summary of the Life Insurance Business*), Tokyo, Seimeihoken Kyokai (Life Assurance Association of Japan), 1990, p. 40. The percentage for Japan does not include foreign-affiliated companies; if they are included, the figure rises to 422 per cent.

6 J.C. Abegglen and G. Stalk, *Kaisha. The Japanese Corporation*, New York, Basic Books, 1985, p. 4.

7 For the organization of the life insurance industry, see Kouichi Hiroumi, *Hoken Gyokai* (*The Insurance Industries*), Tokyo, 1982; and Kazuya Mizushima, 'Seimeihoken' ('Life Insurance'), in Hisao Kumagai (ed.), *Nihon no sangyo-soshiki* (*The Industrial Organization in Japan*), Tokyo, Chuo Koron Publ., 1976.

8 See *The Tokio Marine & Fire Insurance Company: The First Century 1879–1979*, Tokyo, the firm, 1980.

9 Tsunehiko Yui, 'The Development of the Organizational Structure of Top Management in Meiji Japan', *Japanese Yearbook on Business History: 1984*, vol. 1, pp. 5–6.

10 Kesaji Kobayashi, 'Introduction', in K. Kobayashi and Hidemasa Morikawa (eds), *Development of Managerial Enterprise*, Tokyo, University of Tokyo Press, 1986, p. xii.

11 The TLI was renamed the Asahi Life Insurance Company (ALI) in 1947. This company published its history in 1990. It is an interesting book, but unfortunately there is no English edition. The NLI published an English edition of its history in 1991, see M. Tatsuki, T. Shiba and T. Yoneyama, *The 100-Year History of Nippon Life; Its Growth and Socioeconomic Setting 1889–1989*, Tokyo, Nippon Life Insurance Co., 1991. A Japanese limited edition of the centenary history was published in 1992. The present author also took part in the research programme for the centenary history of Nippon Life.

12 Regarding joint stock companies, and top management in Meiji Japan, see Yui, 'Development'.

13 There was an assessment assurance on mutualism in Japan as well as in the West. It is true that Sukesaburo Hirose, one of NLI's founders, was familiar with a society of this sort, called Banzai-Kou (Forever Society), which was attached to a well-known Shinto shrine, Taga-Taisha, in the Kansai district. In his time, however, the role of assessment assurance dwindled and the societies became friendship groups. See Tatsuki *et al.*, *100-Year History*, pp. 22–5.

14 These projects included many societies which resembled the UK's amicable and friendly societies. Regarding the former, see C. Walford, *The Insurance Cyclopaedia*, vol. 1, London, 1781, pp. 74–87; and regarding the latter, see *idem.*, *Insurance Cyclopaedia*, vol. IV, 1876, pp. 379–616.

15 The law was influenced by German laws governing the insurance industry. Dr Keijiro Okano, chief architect of the bill, and his assistant Tsuneta Yano, a government official, had both studied in Germany. Moreover, before studying abroad, Yano was in the insurance business as 'der Revisionsarzt' of the NLI. After working on the law, he returned to the insurance business, founding the DLI, Japan's first mutual life insurance company. Regarding Yano, see, despite some errors, *Who Is Who in Insurance 1908: An International Biographical Dictionary and Year Book*, New York, Singer Company, 1908, p. 350.

16 Before the enacting of the law, there were some 'composite' companies, though compared with their British counterparts they were not influential. See Harold E. Raynes, *A History of British Insurance*, London, 1948 (revised and reprinted, 1950), pp. 372–91.

17 For the simple history of life insurance up to 1907, see *Who Is Who in Insurance 1908*, pp. 433–7.

18 Wartime inflation needs to be discounted in assessing the growth of the industry's total gross reserve. In addition, the war gave rise to several problems in the sphere of business activity. For example, whereas British life offices could charge 'war risk' to new business, Japanese life offices were unable to do so. A comparative study of the relationship between the war economy and life insurance is of considerable interest. For the UK's experience, see John Butt, 'Life Assurance in War and Depression: The Standard Life Assurance Company and its Environment, 1914–39', in O.M. Westall (ed.), *The Historian and the Business of Insurance*, Manchester, Manchester University Press, 1984.

19 The fundamental sources for the study of the business history of the Japanese insurance industry are the collected historical documents, published in two series: *Meiji Taisho Seimeihoken Shiryo* (*Collected Historical*

Documents of the Meiji and Taisho Eras), Tokyo, 1934–1942; and *Showa Seimeihoken Shiryo* (*Collected Historical Documents of the Early Showa Era*), Tokyo, 1970–75. The basic records of financial statements, compiled from the compulsory reports to the authorities, can be found in the annual publication, *Hoken Nenkan* (*Japanese Insurance Almanac*).

20 Fourteen out of the twenty companies in existence got the opportunity to mutualize at almost the same time. Only three companies continued as joint-stock companies. Now, all foreign affiliates are joint-stock companies.

21 Barry Supple, *The Royal Exchange Assurance: A History of British Insurance 1720–1970*, Cambridge, Cambridge University Press, 1970, p. 133.

22 Morton Keller, *The Life Insurance Enterprise, 1885–1910: A Study in the Limits of Corporate Power*, Cambridge, Mass., Harvard University Press, 1963. See, also, J.O. Stalson, *Marketing Life Insurance: Its History in America*, Cambridge, Mass., Harvard University Press, 1942 (reprinted by the McCahan Foundation, 1969).

23 Regarding the series of price-cutting approvals, see Kenji Usami, *Seimeihokengyo 100 Nen Shiron* (*One Hundred Years of the Life Insurance Business*), Tokyo, Yuhikaku, 1984 (in Japanese).

24 This regulation is now beginning to change, as will be explained in the concluding section. It is not possible here to examine the protection of small life companies. However, it may be enough to stress that there have been no mergers or bankruptcies since the war, save in one special case.

25 I owe this point to Ryutaro Komiya, 'Seiho as a business firm', in R. Komiya and Kenichi Imai (eds), *Nihon No Kigyou* (*Japanese Business Firms*), Tokyo, University of Tokyo Press, 1989 (in Japanese).

26 It is important to refer to other factors, but to examine them in detail would be beyond the scope of this chapter. It will be sufficient to cite the following examples of investment in academic and cultural activities. The *Seimeihoken Bunka Center* (Japan's Institute of Life Insurance) in Tokyo endeavours to propagate the idea of insurance to the general public; the *Seimeihoken Bunka Kenkyujo* (Research Institute of Life Insurance Welfare) in Osaka contributes much information to both the business and academic world. Both of these institutions were established by Japan's life insurance companies, and subsidize many activities concerning and diffusing life insurance.

27 Japan was not the first country to sell such insurance. A previous example is provided by France, which started to sell 'assurances revalorisables' in the 1950s. On this topic, see P.J. Richard, *Histoire des Institutions d'Assurance en France*, Paris, Editions de L'Argus, 1956, p. 295.

28 'The insurance industry was developed against the background of the rise of interest consciousness of the public and of the increasing need for securing retired life following prolonged life expectancy, and was sold by 13 companies from October 1986': *Insurance: Statistics of Life Insurance Business in Japan*, Tokyo, 1978, p. 5. Only the business review of the year section of this annual publication is in English.

29 The fact that one company had decided to pay a smaller special bonus than the others was heralded in a newspaper, *Nihon Keizai Shinbun* (*The Economic Newspaper of Japan*), 7 June 1990.

30 Some changes have been examined in Takau Yoneyama, 'Life Insurance Companies and the Government's Control of the Industry in Japan,

1974–1988', *Ikkyo Ronso* (*Hitotsubashi Review*), vol. 103, no. 5, May 1990 (in Japanese).

31 Basically the core of the MOF's policy has not changed, in my opinion. In classical economics, regulation is usually out of harmony with efficiency; but the MOF has sought efficiency under regulation. The frequent rate cuts may well be evidence of efficiency. Consumers did not obtain the benefits of efficiency through the market mechanism but through cuts in their future premiums.

11 The accounting inheritance of the Tokugawa period

Noboru Nisikawa

INTRODUCTION

Studies of economic and business history have revealed, as a matter of common knowledge, that the economic development achieved during the Tokugawa period (1600-1867) was a fundamental condition underlying the process of modernization or industrialization after the Meiji Restoration of 1868. In the field of accounting, however, there have been few historical studies. Most accounting scholars have taken the view, rightly or wrongly, that there was no double-entry book-keeping during the Tokugawa period, and that Japan's double-entry accounting began with the Meiji Restoration. But some accounting historians, as well as business and economic historians, have proved that double measurement of net income by revenue-expenditure and asset-equity (liability) calculations, or double measurement of net worth or equity, was undertaken in large merchant houses from the late seventeenth century. The indigenous accounting experience of the Tokugawa period probably had some effect on the acceptance and development of the Western system of double-entry accounting during the process of Japanese industrial modernization. In the accounting practices of Japanese companies today, there seem still to be some characteristics that are similar to those of the Tokugawa period, or whose roots lie in that period.

ACCOUNTING METHODS AND PRACTICES IN THE TOKUGAWA PERIOD

Many documents of Japanese merchant houses in the Tokugawa period have survived and can be found in various archival institutes in Japan. Study of these documents, most of which are accounting reports, reveals that merchant houses in the mid-Tokugawa period measured net profit or net worth (equity) by double calculation; that is, there were two methods by which accounts were settled.[1] One method was 'double profit measurement' or double-profit calculation: 'property calculation' as assets – [liabilities + opening equity] = net profit (or [assets – liabilities] – opening equity = net profit); and 'income calculation' as revenue – expenditure = net profit. The other method was 'double net property calculation' or double-equity calculation: opening equity or 'capital' + revenue – expenditure = net worth (closing equity); and assets – liabilities = net worth.

Some Japanese accounting historians, though recognizing the existence of double calculation, have still argued that there was no double-entry book-keeping.[2] They say that, because some of the characteristics of Western (or, rather, Italian) double-entry book-keeping methods are lacking – such as perfect double-entry in all records, balance or equilibrium of the debit and credit sides, and debit-credit journalizing – the indigenous Japanese accounting method is not double-entry book-keeping. Other scholars (the present author included) hold the view that these characteristics are trivial matters. For example, in the view of Kemeny *et al.*, 'A little reflection shows that the important point about double-entry book-keeping is not that each transaction is *recorded* twice but rather that each transaction is *classified* twice.'[3] Chatfield has written: 'Yet equilibrium alone does not make double entry and its absence – for instance, in modern computer systems – does not prevent complete, coordinated record keeping.'[4] And Littleton's prophecy about the journal entry, that it might at some time drop off the structure again – like a 'polliwog's tail' – is coming true as a result of electronic data processing systems.[5]

The oldest surviving accounting record preserved in Japan is the book, *Tashiri-cho* (*tasu* or *tashi* meaning 'add' or 'adding', *ri* meaning 'profit' or 'interest', and *cho* meaning 'book'), which recorded the increase and decrease of the net worth of the Tomiyama House, located in the Ise (now, Mie) Prefecture, from 1615 to 1640. The Tomiyama House's oldest surviving balance sheet, dated 1638, is the *Sanyo-cho* (*sanyo* meaning 'calculation' or 'economic calculation'). The *Tashiri-cho* may well be a successive record, derived from the results of the *Sanyo-cho*. No income statements or profit and loss accounts of the Tomiyama House in that period have survived.[6]

The oldest existing record with double-equity calculation is the *Sanyo-cho* of the Konoike House in Osaka, and dates from 1670.[7] At almost the same time, double-profit calculation was carried out by the Nishikawa House in the Omi (now, Shiga) Prefecture,[8] and the Kawakita House in the Ise Prefecture. Kawakita's Edo (now, Tokyo) branch-shop sent a set of financial statements to the head office in Ise every year. Duplicates of the balance sheets, known as *Sosanyo-mokuroku oboe* (*so* meaning 'total', *mokuroku* meaning 'statement' or 'report', *oboe* meaning 'record'), and of the income statements, known as *Rikintsukai-sashihiki-oboe* (*kintsukai* meaning 'money expenditure' or 'expenditure and loss' and *sashihiki* meaning 'subtraction'), are available from 1670.[9]

Between the late seventeenth and early eighteenth centuries, double-profit or equity calculations seem to have been widespread among large merchant banking houses with head offices located in the Kansai districts (Kyoto, Osaka, and the Omi and Ise Prefectures included) and with branch-shops in the three metropolises of Edo, Osaka and Kyoto. After the *sankin kotai* system of alternate attendance was made compulsory during the 1630s, Edo rapidly expanded and its population reached one million in the early eighteenth century. Osaka, whose commercial role had been important since ancient times, emerged as the central market city for the whole country. It was closely linked to Kyoto, where the technological level of handicrafts manufacturing was unsurpassed. Systems of commodity distribution, therefore, and of banking or financing, with the bill of exchange in draft form, developed among these three metropolises, and between Osaka and castle towns all over the country.[10] The merchant bankers recognized the house itself as a distinct entity, distinguished from a family head and other family members, in the belief that it had to be a going concern.[11] All the merchant banking houses that have been found to have had double-profit or equity calculation accounting before the end of the eighteenth century, had their head offices in Kansai, with nationwide activities. Double calculation has not been found in the accounting records of rural merchants at that time.[12]

The economic structure mentioned above, which served to support and maintain the feudal rule of the *shogun* and *daimyo* (feudal lords), began to collapse in the mid-eighteenth century. During that century, according to Nakamura, 'the Osaka market was transformed from an institution serving the lords into one that served the common people'.[13] Nakamura goes on: 'from the late eighteenth century to the early nineteenth . . . Japan entered the stage of early capitalism or proto-industrialisation'.[14] In the nineteenth century, double-profit or equity calculation appeared in the accounting records of the rural merchants and brewers.[15]

A relatively high level of accounting expertise can be seen in the accounting practices of the Tokugawa period. Accruals and deferrals of revenue and expenditure began, naturally, with the emergence of double-calculation. For example, accrued interest revenues were recorded in the above-mentioned Konoike's *Sanyo-cho* of 1670. Various reserves or allowances – such as fire-loss reserves, shipwreck reserves, bad debt reserves, reserves for retirement allowances, etc. – were enumerated so that the necessary provision could be made or in order to calculate whether or not the income of a certain period would be adequate.[16] In the hierarchical administrative structures of the large merchant houses (see below), head office costs were charged to operating units and transfer pricing was used.[17]

There was little cost accounting until the end of the Tokugawa period, and almost no depreciation accounting throughout the period. However, it should not be considered that their absence was the result of underdeveloped accounting expertise, but rather that it reflected the underdevelopment of industrialization in the Tokugawa period. Merchant bankers had little in the way of machinery or equipment that needed renewal or replacement. Property was regarded as a permanent, non-wasting asset. But although there was no depreciation of tangible fixed assets in the Tokugawa period, amortization of deferred charges did exist.

THE PROMINENCE OF INTERNAL REPORTING AND ABSENCE OF EXTERNAL REPORTING IN THE TOKUGAWA PERIOD

Nowadays, accounting textbooks, especially in the United States, are mostly divided into the two areas of 'financial accounting' and 'management accounting'. The 'external' reporting of accounting information, useful to investors, creditors, governmental agencies and others outside an organization, is referred to as financial accounting, and the 'internal' reporting of accounting information, useful to those who are charged with the responsibility of making operating decisions in an organization, is referred to as management or managerial accounting. It may be said that management accounting, or internal reporting, made remarkable progress, but that financial accounting, or external reporting, was practically non-existent in Tokugawa Japan. Chandler has written that 'managers of large American railroads during the 1850s and 1860s invented nearly all of the basic techniques of modern accounting'.[18] Similarly, it may be said that Japanese merchant bankers during the period 1670–1730 invented the basic techniques of modern management accounting, including responsibility accounting, with the exception of cost accounting.

In order to administer and control several branch-shops in the three

metropolises and other castle towns, the large merchant banking
houses developed a hierarchical, decentralized structure, and a reporting system of responsibility accounting to support it. They formed
a central body known as a *motokata* (the original meaning of which was
'proprietor' or 'controller'), whose equity was held by a family head or
by the heads of kindred families called *domyo* (*do* meaning 'the same',
myo meaning 'family name'). Legally, a *motokata* was a proprietorship,
or partnership, which held investments in operating shops in much the
same way that a holding company does nowadays.[19]

Administratively, a *motokata* resembled the 'general office' of a
multi-divisional organisation, which 'plans, coordinates, and appraises
the work of a number of operating divisions and allocates to them the
necessary personnel, facilities, funds, and other resources.'[20] The top
management of a *motokata* often consisted of employee- or salaried-
managers, the so-called '*banto-keiei*' (*banto* meaning 'head-' or 'upper-
employees', and *keiei* meaning 'management').

Looking specifically at the House of Mitsui, Takatoshi Mitsui
(1622–94) established dry goods stores in Kyoto and Edo by 1673,
'and established a bank – still operating in the same location – in
1683, a decade before the Bank of England was founded'.[21] In 1710, the
omotokata was formed in Kyoto with nine equity-holders, the heads of
nine families of Takatoshi's descendants. Mitsui's structure gradually
changed under the *omotokata*. By 1729, it had come to consist of two
major operating divisions – the dry goods division and the banking
division – and one original shop in Matsusaka, Ise, the birthplace of
Takatoshi. The *omotokata* invested in and gave loans to the Kyoto
Banking House and the Kyoto Dry Goods Store, and each of these had
its own affiliated or branch-shops in Edo, Kyoto, and Osaka. Since
almost all the premises of the House of Mitsui in effect belonged to the
omotokata (though the nominal holders were different individuals), the
operating shops leased their premises from it and paid their rent to it.

Each shop in the banking division sent its accounting report, known
as a *kanjo-mokuroku* (*kanjo* meaning 'accounting' or 'settlement of
accounts') and consisting of a balance sheet and an income statement, to
the Kyoto Banking House semi-annually. And each shop in the dry
goods division sent its accounting report, consisting of a trade account,
a fund account, an income statement, and a balance sheet, to the Kyoto
Dry Goods Store. The two main Kyoto shops audited the accounting
reports of their respective affiliated or branch-shops and sent them,
together with their own *kanjo-mokuroku*, to the *omotokata*. The latter
audited the accounting reports of the two Kyoto shops, then made up its
own *kanjo-mokuroku* and sent this to the family heads, to be approved.

The residual profit generated by the operating shops, over and above the cost of capital, was employed as a measure of shop performance. From this, reserves for bad debts and for employees' retirement allowances were set aside. Then, every three years, 10 per cent of the residual profit was set aside as bonuses to managers and other employees, and 90 per cent was transferred to the *omotokata*'s profit account. Similar practices as those of Mitsui, with variations of detail, were carried on in the houses of Nakai[22] and Shimomura[23], and seem also to have been carried on in the houses of Nishikawa, Kawakita, Hasegawa and Sumitomo.

Thus Japanese internal accounting made remarkable progress in the Tokugawa period. But there was no external accounting. All accounting may be said to be financial, in the sense that all accounting systems are in monetary terms. Equally, all accounting may be said to be management accounting, because of its usefulness to management. The emergence of the present distinction between financial and management accounting is relatively modern, and European and American accounting systems were also oriented towards management in their early years. External reporting, or financial accounting, however, did not appear as a sudden change but evolved gradually throughout Western history.

In the commercial world of medieval Italy, the 'tendency to standardize and codify the better practices was an important factor in the development of double entry bookkeeping'.[24] Moreover, in the Middle Ages, property taxes of Italian city-states and German municipal cities required the preparation of financial statements.[25] English 'joint-stock companies' of the seventeenth century 'found it necessary to produce financial statements' in order to benefit shareholders who could not directly access the companies' books.[26] The East India Company, the first limited liability company, had 'triennial appraisements' and 'periodical statements of assets' from 1664. A French ordinance of 1673 required merchants to make 'a statement (*Inventaire*) of all their fixed and movable properties and of their debts receivable and payable' every two years, in order to aid possible bankruptcy proceedings by preserving an overview of a firm.[27] These antecedents resulted in European commercial codes by the nineteenth century that were intended to protect investors and creditors by way of the distribution of audited financial statements. In the United States, although the tendency towards secrecy had been common in the nineteenth century, reporting by way of financial statements certificated by independent auditors had become the rule rather than the exception by 1930.[28]

In contrast, in the Tokugawa period the Japanese took it for granted that accounting properly belonged in the secrecy category of a firm's operations. They never intended to standardize nor codify their practices, and there were no textbooks on book-keeping or accounting in the period. Their ledger books were never allowed to be taken out of the house, and accounting reporting was only undertaken within the house. There was no obligation to pay property or income taxes, which might have required the presentation of financial statements to government agencies. Because of the absence of a capital stock market, there was no reason to develop financial reporting. Since Tokugawa *shogun* and feudal lords had no notion of protecting creditors, merchant-bankers needed to lend money on ample security and to accumulate reserves for bad debts and retained earnings.

IMPACT OF THE INTRODUCTION OF WESTERN ACCOUNTING IN THE MEIJI PERIOD

Just before the end of the Tokugawa Shogunate, the technique of Western book-keeping was introduced. For example, in the Yokosuka Steel Works, founded in 1865, it was laid down that all books of accounts should be kept in both the Japanese and French languages by the Japanese and French chief officers.[29] After the Meiji Restoration (1868), modern Japanese corporate financial accounting practices were formed, under the strong influence of British accounting practices, in the areas of both renewed financial business and newly introduced industries.[30] And many introductory book-keeping textbooks were published, translated from or based on American works,[31] though these are said scarcely to have influenced practices.[32] On the other hand, native Japanese accounting methods were still used in the traditional industries.

To illustrate the progressive nature of accounting practices in pioneering corporations in the early Meiji era, Hisano has mentioned (i) the amortization of deferred charges, (ii) the depreciation of fixed assets, (iii) the provision of reserves or allowances and (iv) accruals and deferrals.[33] Except for depreciation, these practices were, as already indicated, available in the Tokugawa period. Because of the high standard of indigenous Japanese book-keeping methods, Takatera has observed, 'For this reason, after introducing the Western book-keeping method in 1870's, the old Japanese bookkeeping method was easily convertible into the Western bookkeeping method'.[34] However, the conversion from indigenous Japanese to Western practices in native firms was not so smooth. For example, Daimaru, which is one of the largest department stores in Japan, converted its book-keeping system to a Western system in 1915 only after business failure had forced it to reorganize.[35] In many cases, conversion to the Western system came with, or resulted from, a change of structure such as incorporation.

British accounting practices were introduced into Japan in the Meiji era and Westernization of accounting gradually took root in the big companies, with delays in some of the native firms. But 'aspects of autonomy or self-regulation of the British accounting system were apt to be ignored'.[36] British financial accounting had developed in the public sphere of its civil society, where accountability had previously been based on the principles of trusteeship. These British principles were not familiar to the Japanese, whose civil society had not reached maturity. Such experiences of accounting in the Meiji era had an important influence upon subsequent Japanese accounting practice, even after the Second World War. So 'the Japanese financial accounting system is a very peculiar system, and quite different from European and American accounting systems'.[37]

The closed capital composition of the family holding in merchant houses in the Tokugawa period was succeeded by the *zaibatsu*, some of which were descendants of Tokugawa merchants, such as Mitsui. It is said that the development of Japan's capital market was impeded by the fact that affiliated corporations of the *zaibatsu*, which were the leading companies in Japan before the Second World War, kept on with their closed financing systems.[38] After the war, the democratization of securities was carried out, but it has only been since the beginning of 1950s that progress has been made with *kabushiki-sogo-mochiai* (meaning 'mutual stockholding in a group of companies'), and now individual shareholders may hold only one-fifth of all issued shares or stocks.

CONCLUSION

The change from 'stewardship-oriented financial reporting to investor-oriented financial reporting' just after the Second World War was, according to Someya, one of the 'two revolutions in accounting' in Japan.[39] (The other was the 'introduction of the Western-style double-entry notation' in the latter half of the 1800s.[40]) However, it seems to this author that the Japanese companies of today have some characteristics that may have their origin with the merchants of the Tokugawa period: a passive attitude to the distribution of profits to stockholders; indifference towards investor relations (i.e. to developing good relations between shareholders or investors and a company, through the dissemination of information); negligence towards disclosure, which leads to the crowding of the shareholders' meetings of the vast majority of listed companies into one specific day; negativity towards segment disclosure and quarter disclosure; profusion of insider transactions; window-dressing by teaming up with certified public accountants, and so forth.

It may be said that the Tokyo Stock Exchange nowadays resembles the New York Stock Exchange of some sixty years ago. This is by no means to imply that everything about it is outdated. But it may well be the case that, in terms of accounting practice as well as of many social phenomena since the Meiji Restoration, the Japanese have been trying to put not only new but also old wine into new bottles. Japanese managements have been able to invest most of their profits in production, concentrating on long-term strategy and paying little regard to their capricious stockholders. Although they have contributed to Japan's economic progress, there remains plenty of room for improvement in Japanese accounting practices.

NOTES

1 Sadao Takatera, 'Comparative Analysis of the Old Japanese Bookkeeping Method with the Western Bookkeeping Method', *Kyoto University Economic Review*, Apr.-Oct. 1980, Vol. 1, No. 1–2, pp. 35, 36.
2 For example, Kojiro Nishikawa, 'The Early History of Double-entry Book-keeping in Japan' in A.C. Littleton and B.S. Yamey (eds), *Studies in the History of Accounting*, London, Sweet & Maxwell, 1956, p. 381.
3 John G. Kemeny, Arthur Schleifer Jr, J. Laurie Snell, and Gerald L. Thompson, *Finite Mathematics with Business Applications*, New Jersey, Prentice-Hall, 1962, p. 347.
4 Michael Chatfield, *A History of Accounting Thought*, revised edn., Huntington, N.Y., Robert E. Krieger Publishing Company, 1977, p. 35.
5 A.C. Littleton, *Accounting Evolution to 1900*, American Institute Publishing Company, 1933, (reissued: New York, Russell & Russell, 1966), p. 107.
6 Kazuo Kawahara, *Edo Jidai no Choai-ho* (*Book-keeping Methods in the Tokugawa Period*), Tokyo, Gyosei, 1977, pp. 8–12, 22–8.
7 Yotaro Sakudo, *Kinsei Hoken Shakai no Kahei-kinyu Kozo* (*The Money-Finance System in Pre-Modern Society*), Tokyo, Hanawa Shobo, 1971, pp. 147–9.
8 *Nishikawa 400 nenshi kohon* (*The Original Draft of the 400 Year History of Nishikawa*), Nishikawa Sangyo Corporation, 1966, pp. 50, 51, 72 (appendix).
9 Reiko Hayashi, 'Momen-tonya Kawakita-ke Siryo (1)' ('Materials Relating to the Kawakita's, Cotton Wholesaler, 1671–1692'), *Ryutsu-keizai Daigaku Ronshu*, July 1976, Vol. 11, No. 1, p. 75.
10 See Satoru Nakamura, 'The Development of Rural Industry', and Yotaro Sakudo, 'The Management Practices of Family Business', in Nakane Chie and Oishi Shinzaburo (eds) and Conrad Totman (translation ed.), *Tokugawa*

Japan: The Social and Economic Antecedents of Modern Japan, Tokyo, University of Tokyo Press, 1990.

11 Johannes Hirschmeier and Tsunehiko Yui, *The Development of Japanese Business, 1600–1980*, 2nd edn, London, George Allen & Unwin, 1981, pp. 38–9.

12 Noboru Nisikawa, 'Edo Jidai no Boki-kaikei' ('Japanese Bookkeeping and Accounting from the late Seventeenth through the first half of the Nineteenth Centuries'), *Yearbook of the Accounting History Association*, 1991, no. 9, p. 24.

13 Nakamura, 'Development of Rural Industry', op. cit., p. 86.

14 Ibid., p. 92.

15 Nisikawa, 'Edo Jidai no Boki-kaikei', p. 25.

16 Ibid., pp. 29–30; Kawahara, *Edo Jidai no Choai-ho*, p. 355.

17 Eiichro Ogura, *Goshu Nakai-ke Choai no Ho* (*The Book-keeping Method of the Nakai House in Omi Province*), Kyoto, Minerva Shobo, 1962, ch. 6.

18 Alfred D. Chandler Jr, *The Visible Hand: The Managerial Revolution in American Business*, Cambridge, Mass., Harvard University Press, 1977, p. 109.

19 Sakudo says that it seems 'more appropriate' for the relationship between the *omotokata* (*o* meaning 'great') and the operating shops in the Mitsui House to be likened to 'that between the main and branch stores of a single enterprise' than to a holding company system because of 'unlimited liability'; see Sakudo, 'Management Practices', pp. 158, 159. However, and not only in Mitsui's case, each shop generally had its own company name, and the *motokata* did not owe unlimited liability for investment in the shops but rather semi-limited liability, known as *shintai-kagiri* (*shintai* meaning 'net worth', and *kagiri* or *kagiru* meaning 'limit'). Takatera and I once wrote that the 'Mitsui's investment-holding general family partnership was rather unique'; see Sadao Takatera and Noboru Nisikawa, 'Genesis of Divisional Management and Accounting Systems in the House of Mitsui 1710–1730', *Accounting Historians Journal*, Spring 1984, vol. 11, no. 1, p. 142. However, I now think that it was not unique but in fact rather common in *large* merchant houses.

20 Alfred D. Chandler Jr, *Strategy and Structure: Chapters in the History of the American Industrial Enterprise*, Cambridge, Mass., The MIT Press, 1962, p. 2.

21 John G. Roberts, *Mitsui: Three Centuries of Japanese Business*, New York, Weatherhill, 1973, p. 3. The Mitsui Bank merged with the Taiyo-Kobe Bank to form the Taiyo-Kobe-Mitsui Bank in April 1990; its name changed to the Sakura Bank in April 1992.

22 Ogura, *Goshu Nakai-ke Choai no Ho*, ch. 7.

23 *Daimaru 250 nenshi* (*The 250 Year History of Daimaru*), Tokyo, Daimaru Incorporated, 1967, p. 99.

24 Chatfield, *A History of Accounting Thought*, p. 33.

25 Ibid., p. 68.

26 Vahé Baladouni, 'Financial Reporting in the Early Years of the East India Company', *Accounting Historians Journal*, Spring 1986, vol. 13, no. 1, p. 29.

27 Littleton, *Accounting Evolution to 1900*, p. 136.

28 Chatfield, *A History of Accounting Thought*, pp. 272–3.

29 Shinshichiro Shimme, 'Introduction of Double-Entry Bookkeeping into Japan', *The Accounting Review*, September 1937, vol. XII, no. 3, p. 291.
30 Junichi Chiba, 'British Company Accounting 1844–1885 and Its Influence on the Modernization of Japanese Financial Accounting', *Keizai to Keizaigaku*, October 1987, no. 60, pp. 1–27.
31 Nishikawa, 'Early History of Double-entry Book-keeping', pp. 383–4.
32 Hideo Hisano, 'Senkuteki Kabushiki-kaisha no Senshinsei to sono Taiko Gensho (The Progression and Retrogression of Accounting in a Pioneering Corporation in Japan)', *Gakushuin University Keizai Ronshu*, June 1989, vol. 26, no. 1, p. 32; *Kaikei Seido-shi Hikaku Kenkyu* (*Comparative Study of the History of Accounting Systems*), Tokyo, Gakushuin University, 1992, pp. 312–13.
33 Ibid., p. 313.
34 Takatera, 'Comparative Analysis', p. 36.
35 *Daimaru 250 nenshi*, appendix, p. 9.
36 Chiba, 'British Company Accounting 1844–1885', p. 1.
37 Ibid., p. 12.
38 Hisashi Masaki, *Nihonteki Keiei-zaimu-ron (Japanese Financial Management)*, Tokyo, Zeimu-keiri Kyokai, 1985, p. 53.
39 Kyojiro Someya, 'Accounting "Revolutions" in Japan', *Accounting Historians Journal*, Spring 1989, vol. 16, no. 1, p. 75.
40 Ibid., p. 83.

12 The making of Japan's business élites: Tokyo University of Commerce in its historical perspective

Tamotsu Nishizawa

INTRODUCTION

'If England afforded the best example of nineteenth century industrialism', wrote G.C. Allen in his first book on Japan in 1927, 'Japan may be considered . . . a typical country of modern industrialism'.[1] It was about then that the Lancashire cotton industry, having seen 'seven terrible years' from 1920, was exposed to the menace of the 'Manchester in the Orient'. *Lancashire under the Hammer*, by B. Bowker, which was published in 1928,[2] was followed in the 1930s by the Anglo-Japanese cotton war. The rise of Japan and decline of Britain in the trade in cotton textiles in the interwar period has been regarded by a current business historian as representing 'the competitive realities of the Japanese version of collective capitalism'.[3] Much earlier, in 1904, a well-known foreigner, Henry Dyer, who had been principal of Japan's Imperial College of Engineering (*Kobu Dai-Gakko*), wrote of *Dai-Nippon* as 'the Britain of the East', foretelling 'the victories of the Britain of the East in the twentieth century'. Referring to the Russo-Japanese War in her Diary on 22 December 1904, Beatrice Webb also praised highly 'the innovating collectivism of the Japanese'.[4]

Japan entered its take-off stage at a period when the economic philosophy of *laissez-faire* was gradually giving way to collective regulation, co-operation and organised control. To this new state of affairs, Allen noted, 'she was singularly well suited, whose people had been trained hard in the spirit of Bushido and the Samurai'. The prestige of individual enterprise was declining with the rise of the corporate economy in the developed capitalist countries. It was the dawning of 'a second cycle of industrial growth', which perhaps meant 'the end of the practical man'. Japan learned quickly from the most progressive ideas and institutions of the time. Compared to the early industrialized countries, organized education played a much more important role in Japan's industrialization. Japan's jump from its past, said *Nature* in its review of Dyer's book, was 'achieved by occidental education fostered by and implanted on a system of oriental ethics'. Japan thus became one of the first nations to use its national education system as a strategic factor in its industrialization process.[5]

The purpose of this chapter is to explain how Japan's higher education system was developed, concentrating on collegiate education in business and economics, in close relation to the stages of economic development. Hitherto, the written history of Japan's higher education system has centred on the Imperial University, which was institutionalized by the Imperial University Order early in 1886. Its graduates, as a privileged élite in Japan's modernization process, were largely absorbed into government service, playing the leading part in *Gakureki-ism* (educational credentialism). Graduates of Imperial University's Law College were actually exempted from the higher civil service examination.[6] Recently, a lot of attention has been paid to the role of technical education and of engineers in Japan's industrialization process.[7] However, business or commercial education for the human resources employed in mercantile and financial activity has been rather neglected. Using largely case-study methods, the evolutionary development of Tokyo Higher Commercial School – later Tokyo University of Commerce (and now Hitotsubashi University) – will be examined because it seems to exemplify a typical development of Japanese business education; to be the model for other higher commercial education institutions; and to achieve, to some extent, a unique 'balanced excellence' of what might be called the academic and the vocational models.

After forty-five tumultuous years, Tokyo Higher Commercial School finally became a University under the terms of a University Order in 1920. Around 1900, 73 per cent of its graduates were employed in private business, and only 8.6 per cent in government. At the same time, 64 per cent of the graduates of the Law College (later Law Faculty) of Tokyo Imperial University entered government service.[8] The chequered history of Tokyo Higher Commercial School presents a quite unique case in business and economics education, in striking contrast with Tokyo Imperial University, which developed under the aegis of government.

THE AGE OF BUSINESS

On 27 August 1897, a few years after the Sino-Japanese War of 1894–5, a substantial article appeared in *The Times*, entitled 'Commercial

Education in Japan'. 'The marvellous transformation' that had taken place in Japan since the Meiji Restoration seemed to *The Times*'s correspondent to be as inexplicable as it was unexpected. Surveying commercial education in Japan, he concluded that 'Japan's whole system of commercial education is one to which, in its completeness, even Anglo-Saxon countries have not yet attained'. A similar opinion was expressed by R. Beigel of Germany in 1898: in his booklet *Der Kampf um die Handelshochschule*, he praised highly the Higher Commercial School (*Koto Shogyo Gakko*) in Tokyo, whose origins dated back to 1875, and which developed into Tokyo University of Commerce. After reading the English edition of the *Calendar of the Higher Commercial School*, Beigel observed that the Higher Commercial School was 'most nearly allied to what the German people tried to establish as Handelshochschule or Fakultät für Handels-wissenschaft'. Indeed, since the *Handelshochschule* at Leipzig had not yet been established, Beigel thought that Japan was more advanced than Germany, even saying that the German intelligentsia should follow the Japanese example.[9]

From 1887, Tokyo Higher Commercial School was the only higher commercial school in Japan, following the model of Antwerp's *Institut Supérieur de Commerce* (founded in 1852) or Paris's *École Supérieur de Commerce* (founded in 1820), which, before the advent of the *Handelshochschule* model, were the prototype of the higher commercial education institution. As will be seen below, Tokyo Higher Commercial School set up its Professional Department or Post-graduate Course (*Senkou-bu*) in 1897, and awarded the degree of Bachelor of Commerce to its graduates from 1901. In that year, the Osaka Commercial School, which had originated in 1880, was promoted by its municipal authority into the Osaka Higher Commercial School. Then, in 1902, a second government Higher Commercial School was established, in Kobe. It was in this latter year that the first Faculty of Commerce in England was inaugurated, at the University of Birmingham which dated from the mid-1870s as did many other English civic universities. Japan, though a latecomer, seemed never to have been far behind in organizing business education.

The Japanese economy entered into a period of self-sustained accelerated growth after the two successful wars with China (1894–5) and Russia (1904–5). The growing social demands for the collegiate training of future businessmen and entrepreneurs reflected the rapid development of Japanese business firms after these wars. In order to meet these needs, and institutionalize vocational higher education separately from the High School–Imperial University system, the

College Order (*Senmon-Gakko Rei*) was issued in 1903. The various industrial colleges were to be under its control. The Higher Commercial Schools were thus authorized as Colleges (*Senmon-Gakko*), together with a number of national professional schools (such as the Higher Technical Schools in Tokyo and Osaka, and Sapporo Agricultural College) and various private colleges (for example, Keio, Waseda, Meiji, Hosei and Nihon). The numerous *Senmon-Gakkos*, which had developed spontaneously in response to social demands 'from below', would present an alternative way through the higher education system to that of the Higher School–Imperial University path created 'from above'. While the graduates of the latter were to become 'the driving forces of Shokusan-Kougyo (the promotion or development of industry policy) from above', the former played a 'central part in training and supplying its driving forces from below', despite their 'subordinate role of Gakureki-ism'. It was these colleges, in fact, which met the changes of the times and rapidly increased their numbers; they trained and supplied the human resources for the Japanese capitalism which began its full-scale development after the two wars.[10] The commerce and economics graduates of these colleges thus contributed greatly to the moulding of the modern business community of Japan before the First World War; the graduates of the Imperial Universities did the same for Japan's modern bureaucracy.

As is common knowledge, there was a movement for higher commercial education, or for a collegiate school of commerce, in all the leading industrial countries around the turn of the century. In the United States, the Wharton School was established in 1881; then, in 1898, Colleges of Commerce were set up in Chicago and California. These were followed by one commercial college after another, the movement culminating in the inauguration of the Harvard Graduate School of Business Administration in 1908. In Germany, the first *Handelshochschule* was founded in Leipzig in 1898; then came Cologne in 1901 and Berlin in 1906. In England, the creation of Birmingham University's Faculty of Commerce in 1902 was followed by Manchester's the next year.

As economic and commercial affairs became ever more complicated, both internally and externally, so the level of knowledge and degree of training required of those involved in these affairs rose higher than ever before. It came to be realized that the training of businessmen in colleges or universities was just as important for the community as the training of lawyers, doctors and engineers. Celebrating the foundation of the Birmingham Faculty of Commerce, W.J. Ashley observed that the creation of a 'Faculty of Commerce' was 'one of the most striking manifestations of a new and most significant movement in university circles by no means confined to Great Britain'. Although much celebrated, however, the experiment of university education for businessmen in England did not go smoothly. The work in Birmingham, according to Ashley, first head of the Faculty of Commerce, 'has been of an uphill character', and 'the conservatism of the English business world' occasionally discouraged him.[11]

The numbers of students in the early years of Birmingham's Faculty of Commerce were astonishingly low, and, what was worse, many of them were foreigners. (One of five in the second group of graduates was Shinji Tazaki from Tokyo Higher Commercial School, who later became the first president of Kobe University of Commerce.) Hannah has pointed out that at a time when the Faculty was attracting an average of eight regular students a year, six of these would be Japanese.[12] G.C. Allen, who graduated from Birmingham and was appointed to the Higher Commercial School in Nagoya in 1922, observed:

> It is symptomatic of national attitudes towards innovation that, while British firms regarded the venture with coolness, if not suspicion, the Mitsui family of Japan . . . should send one of its members to become an early pupil.[13]

Receiving warm hospitality from the Ashleys, Takakiyo Mitsui attended Ashley's commerce seminar in October 1903. His presence was due to the foresight and efforts of Sankichi Komuro, branch manager of Mitsui Bussan in London, who wrote to Kaoru Inoue, adviser to the Mitsui, in March 1903, enclosing *The Faculty of Commerce in the University of Birmingham: Its Purpose and Programme*, written by Ashley in 1902, and other similar material.[14]

Allen, living in Japan in the early 1920s, was surprised to discover that 'the banks and business firms recruit themselves very largely from the graduates of the commercial and higher commercial schools', and that he rarely met a bank manager or an important officer in a joint-stock company who had not been trained at these institutions. In Britain, on the other hand, the majority of managerial and administrative posts were filled by people with a general education, or by self-made men who had worked their way up. Allen noted 'very clearly the contrast in intellectual quality between the typical Japanese executive or manager and his British counterpart'. By the 1930s, Japanese universities offering economics and commercial studies, and the higher commercial schools, produced at least 3,000 graduates a year, while only a few hundred students graduated annually in these subjects at British universities.[15] This Anglo-Japanese contrast has persisted until the present day. In 1990 it was estimated that less than 25 per cent of managers in Britain had a university degree or a professional qualification, compared with about 85 per cent in Japan.[16]

EMERGENCE OF COMMERCIAL SCHOOLS IN JAPAN

In order to meet the urgent need for men capable of managing modern banking and accounting affairs, the Meiji government set up the Department for Banking Studies in the Ministry of Finance in 1874, following the advice of Allan Shand, who had been hired by the Ministry and wrote the first text on bank book-keeping in 1873. But the first commercial school in Japan was the Business Training School (*Shoho Koshujo*), founded by Arinori Mori, Japan's first Minister of Education. A small private school in Tokyo, it began teaching and training under the direction of William C. Whitney in September 1875, with some fifteen students. Before then, Whitney had been running a business college in Newark, New Jersey – one of the 'Chain of Commercial Colleges' started by Bryant and Stratton in the 1850s. The Business Training School, which was eventually to develop into the present Hitotsubashi University, was thus set up as a model, fashioned in the American style, to offer a very rudimentary and practical business training. Since then, schools of this kind have grown apace in such places as Kobe, Osaka, and Okayama.

These local commercial schools were directed by the pupils of Yukichi Fukuzawa, 'the champion of the Japanese enlightenment' and founder of Keio Gijuku College in 1867, who translated Bryant and Stratton's *Common School Book-keeping* in 1873 and spread Western book-keeping methods throughout Japan. Fukuzawa also wrote the 'Prospectus' for Mori's Business Training School, in terms which vividly revealed their intentions:

> In fighting one another by means of the sword, one cannot go to the battlefield without learning the art of fencing. In the case of fighting by means of commerce, one cannot confront foreigners without learning the art of commerce. There should be a place to study for everyone who wants to join the commercial wars in the world as businessman.

The main subjects in the early commercial schools were English, book-keeping, commercial correspondence, foreign exchange and so forth. The purpose of the schools was to produce basic commercial clerks who were immediately employable by banks, insurance companies and trading companies. They were, to all intents and purposes, places for the technology transfer of practical business matters.

In contrast with Tokyo (Imperial) University, which was founded from the first as a governmental institution, Hitotsubashi came into being as merely a small business school with a weak financial base. In its early years, therefore, it had to fight its way through many difficulties, not the least of which was the contemptuous disregard for business education. The attitude that 'the best commercial school was business itself' was as widespread in Japan as elsewhere, and dry commercial subjects had been singularly absent from the curricula of the Imperial Universities. Only a few months after its launch, the new School was transferred to the Tokyo Council. Then, in 1876, it was placed under the Tokyo Prefectural Government, with its director Jiro Yano. It is to the fortitude of Yano that the School is indebted in weathering the successive storms of its formative years and in finally having its foundations securely laid in the course of the first two decades of the Meiji era. In 1884, the School was transferred to government control, under the Ministry of Agriculture and Commerce, and renamed Tokyo Commercial School (*Tokyo Shogyo Gakko*). The same year, Eiichi Shibusawa (of the First National Bank), Tetsunosuke Tomita (of the Bank of Japan) and Takashi Masuda (of Mitsui Bussan, brother-in-law of Yano) were appointed to its Advisory Council, which acted, in effect, as the connecting link between the School and the business community. From its very beginning, Shibusawa exerted himself for the welfare of Hitotsubashi with singular continuity of purpose. In so doing, he stood always for the dignity of commerce, and never tired of preaching self-respect to the rising generation about to go into business.[17]

Tokyo Commercial School was finally settled under the Ministry of Education in May 1885. Two years later, it was renamed the Higher Commercial School (*Koto Shogyo Gakko*), to reflect the fact that it was to be the place where business managers and commercial school teachers were trained. It remained the only government higher commercial school until 1902.

The Higher Commercial School at Hitotsubashi was thus to become one of the two main sources of supply of commerce teachers and business leaders, the other being Keio Gijuku. Keio had been the most notable supplier of modern businessmen, (bankers in particular) before the turn of the century. There were 266 Keio graduates in the period 1876–85, as compared with sixty-one from the Commercial School; though if the drop-outs from the latter were counted, its number would have been nearly doubled. Of the seventy-three graduates from the School in the period 1877–86, twenty-four became commercial school teachers; in the field of business, thirteen went to Mitsui Bussan, and thirty-one were absorbed into trading companies, insurance, banking and transport; only four went into government employment, and one into manufacture. Later, in 1899, the Training House of Commerce Teachers was inaugurated as part of the School, so as to secure teacher training.[18]

Meanwhile, by the twentieth year of the Meiji era (1887), there were already in Japan some ten commercial schools of a practical nature run by local governments, whereas in England, as E. Lautey reported in 1886, 'there was no commercial school properly called'. The *Report of the Royal Commission on the Depression in Trade and Industry* (1886), and the Consular Reports, were full of the incompetence of British businessmen and exporters. It was at this time that the pressing need for commercial education was widely recognized in England. Various articles and reports on commercial education in Europe and America appeared, many of them read and quoted in Japan. Sir Philip Magnus's paper on 'Commercial Education', which came out in December 1887, was translated and printed in Japan's official government gazette in less than six months.[19]

At first, it was intended that the Higher Commercial School in Japan should follow the Belgian model. Julian van Stappen, a graduate of the highly successful *Institut Supérieur de Commerce*, was invited to teach at the School in 1885. He was followed by E.J. Blockhuys, who came in 1892 to teach subjects such as the practice of foreign trade. Blockhuys remained at the School, and subsequently at Tokyo University of Commerce, until March 1930. No other foreign teachers of specialized subjects came to the School until 1897, when Ernest Foxwell, a Cambridge graduate and brother of H.S. Foxwell, was appointed as a lecturer in commercial economics. Clearly, in its early days, it was commercial science, not political economy, which characterized the curriculum of the School. This was in striking contrast with Keio Gijuku and the Imperial University, where, under the strong influence of the German historical school, subjects were centred on political economy.

A number of the students and staff of the School went to Antwerp to study at the *Institut* during the third decade of the Meiji era. Sometimes called the 'Consular School', the *Institut* attracted students from all over the world. William Layton, its professor of English, deplored the decline of English commerce and the backwardness of English commercial education, writing that 'not only France, Germany, Switzerland, and Italy, but also Japan in the Far East, followed the Belgian example in founding higher commercial schools'. Referring to commercial education in Japan, he also wrote a letter to *The Times* on 10 September

1897 saying that 'today . . . England is the only country which does not possess any such higher commercial schools'.[20]

During the first two or three decades of the Meiji era, the 'recovery of commercial independence' had been a sort of ideology in the business world. Since the opening up of Japan, most foreign trade had been monopolized by foreign merchants from the settlements in Yokohama, Kobe and other cities, and before the turn of century there were very few firms, with the exception of Mitsui Bussan, which did not rely on those foreign merchants. The urgent need for the training of modern businessmen, so that external business affairs could be undertaken on an equal footing, was felt strongly. The curriculum of the Higher Commercial School was deeply affected by the requirements of the business community. Indeed, the School appeared to be a 'foreign trade school'; it was even nicknamed the 'Mitsui Bussan School', because it looked like a 'training institute of human resources for Mitsui Bussan'. Moreover, its graduates were inclined to be employed by a few specific firms, such as Nihon Yusen, Osaka Shosen and Yokohama Specie Bank (now Bank of Tokyo). These were firms that were wholly concerned with external business, which needed knowledge and skills not accessible to traditional domestic merchants. Many of the graduates also went into the insurance business, marine insurance in particular. One such was Kenkichi Kagami who entered Tokio Marine Insurance in 1888 and became a world-famous businessman.[21]

In its early years, two schools of thought prevailed among the students of the Higher Commercial School, categorized by the enlightened reformist group, and the conservative group (who tended to be the young masters of old merchant families). Members of the latter group were inclined to learn business techniques, only for immediate employment as common clerks. Students in the reformist group, on the other hand, were eager to pursue the new and advanced arts of commerce, and came to think that the School should be a place for training the leaders of business and industry. The tension between these two streams of thought on commercial education – i.e. vocational education for the acquisition of techniques as against a more advanced, scientific education – underlay the evolution of the Higher Commercial School up until its transformation into Tokyo University of Commerce in 1920. Throughout its history, this conflict of two differing ideals seems to have contributed to the dynamics of the School's development.[22]

It is said that 'the reorganizations of the Higher Commercial School in 1896 and 1897 were epoch-making in its history and laid the foundation for the future Tokyo University of Commerce'.[23] Thinking it essential to nurture trustworthiness, headmaster Kenzo Koyama established commercial morality as a subject. In addition, the disciplines of political economy and law were enlarged, so that these, along with commercial subjects, became part of the core curriculum. It was at this stage that the term 'commercial science' (*shogyo-gaku*) or '*Handels-wissenschaft*' was coined to distinguish the discipline as an independent and dignified science, the basis for the later development of business studies. Furthermore, in 1897, Koyama, who was very well informed about commercial education in Europe, instituted a post-graduate course for those who desired to pursue further studies in particular fields or to enter the consular service. This was to be the first stage of the evolution of the Higher Commercial School into the University of Commerce. The term of study was extended from one to two years in 1899, resulting, from 1901, in the degree of *Shogaku-shi* (Bachelor of Commerce). In 1902, there were seven study courses, comprising foreign trade, banking, exchange, transport, insurance, business accounting and consular service. These seemed to reflect the practical requirements of the economic and commercial world, and could be adapted to meet the needs of the times.[24] The post-graduate course could thus be termed the Professional Department; it still aimed at a professional or vocational education, rather than an academic one.

The graduates of the School were largely absorbed into trading or shipping companies and banks. Up to 1902, the main business firms to employ graduates were Mitsui Bussan (eighty-two), Nihon Yusen (forty-two), Japan Railway (thirty-four), Osaka Shosen (twenty), Yokohama Specie Bank (seventeen), Mitsubishi (ten), Daiichi Bank (nine), Bank of Japan (eight), 119 National Bank (seven), and Takada Shokai, Sumitomo Bank and Mitsui Bank. These twelve firms absorbed about 32 per cent of all the graduates in 1902, Mitsui Bussan taking nearly 16 per cent. Meanwhile, the Foreign Office employed thirteen graduates between 1894 and 1900, probably for consular service. From 1903 onwards, the numbers of graduates increased suddenly, and exceeded 100 in every year. In the last decade of the Meiji era (1903–12), the ten largest employers of graduates, and the numbers they employed, were as follows: Mitsui Bussan (189), Nihon Yusen (sixty-three), Yokohama Specie Bank (fifty-three), Mitsubishi (fifty-one), Manchurian Railway (forty-three), Osaka Shosen (forty), Bank of Japan (twenty-eight), Takada Shokai (seventeen), Furukawa Mining (seventeen) and Sumitomo Goushi (eleven).[25]

Towards the end of the Meiji era, the rapid development of Japanese capitalism demanded the massive collegiate training of future businessmen. The issue of the College Order in 1903 was followed by the foundation of numerous colleges, both government and private. Many private colleges had originally been established as law schools in 1880s, when it seemed essential, because of the need for amendment of unequal treaties, for Japan to be recognized as a nation governed by modern law. Now, however, the emphasis of these colleges shifted from the teaching of law to economics and business education. The years following the Russo-Japanese War have sometimes been called 'the age of business'; it was claimed that the age of law and politics was over and that a new age of commerce and economics had arrived. Between 1905 and 1915, the numbers of graduates from the private colleges increased by 2.4 times. By far the greatest increases were graduates from commerce (from 235 to 1,317) and economics (from seventy-seven to 331). During this boom in commerce and economics studies, there was a perceptible shift in emphasis in the training of human resources at the private colleges, away from those who were bound for the traditional sector of family business and self-employment and towards those who were bound for modern business firms. Meanwhile, competition to take the entrance examination was beginning to pose something of a social problem; in 1905, for example, there were three times as many applications for entry to the government colleges as there were places, but there were more than four and a half times as many applications for entry to the higher commercial schools. Furthermore, it was the higher commercial schools, and the commerce and economics departments of the private colleges, which had become the training ground of the modern salaried businessmen who were to comprise the salaried managerial classes. Even the graduates from the Imperial Universities began to look to private business instead of government service for employment.[26] Against this background, a Higher Commercial School, which had grown up spontaneously, was to make its own way in advancing towards university status.

OVERSEAS INFLUENCE

Around the turn of century, a number of promising young staff at Hitotsubashi were sent abroad to study. It was they who, on their return, raised their voices in favour of a university of commerce. Tokuzo Fukuda, the greatest pioneer of modern economic thinking in Japan, went first to Leipzig, then moved to Munich under Lujo Brentano in 1897 (the thirtieth year of the Meiji era). Many others followed him to Germany; Seki and Ishikawa moved from the Antwerp *Institut*, where the curriculum and teaching were felt to be neither sufficient nor competent any more, to Berlin and Göttingen. Fukuda and Seki, above all, were deeply involved in the contemporary international movement for higher commercial education, initiated now by Germany and the United States instead of Belgium and France, and followed by England. They were drawn into the maelstrom of the *Handelshochschule* movement, driven by R. Ehrenberg and the German Association for Commercial Education (founded in 1895). Fukuda became a special collaborator of this Association. He sent back to Japan his own translation of Ehrenberg's *Handelshochschulen*, soon after its publication in 1897. It was the dawn of 'the age of Handelshochschulen', which started in 1898 with Leipzig and ended in 1919 with Nuremberg.

By attending conferences and sending back numerous reports on the position of European and American commercial education, Fukuda and Seki made great efforts to ensure that Japan never slipped behind worldwide development. The *Journal of the Alumni Association*, founded in 1890, and *Shogyo Sekai (Commercial World)*, founded in 1898, were full of these reports and translations. The *Report of the Special Sub-Committee on Commercial Education*, produced in 1899 by the Technical Education Board of London County Council, was also translated in an abridged form by Seki, and published by the Education Ministry in the same year. At the 1899 International Congress on Commercial Education in Venice, Fukuda received courteous treatment as a guest of honour, and Tokyo Higher Commercial School was highly praised, as reported in the *Gazzetta di Venezia* of 7 May 1899. In 1900, the Paris International Exhibition was chosen as the occasion on which to hold the first International Congress of the Alumni Associations of Higher Commercial Schools, to which Seki, as a delegate of the Tokyo Association, presented a paper. Meanwhile, Zensaku Sano, later to become the first president of Tokyo University of Commerce, moved from Columbia to the London School of Economics in 1899, giving there a lecture on 'Commercial Education in Japan', part of which was printed in the *Special Reports on Educational Subjects* by the Board of Education in 1902.

In addition, an event of particular importance was a meeting of the staff of Hitotsubashi in Berlin in January 1901. On this occasion, eight professors who were studying abroad gathered in Berlin. After five days of discussion, a draft statement on the 'Urgent Necessity of Establishing a University of Commerce', along with a detailed 'Curriculum', was signed by the two Ishikawas, Kanda, Takimoto, Tsumura, Shida, Fukuda and Seki, and sent back to Japan. Just before this meeting, Seki had written in his Diaries that, because of 'the advancement of entrepreneurship of Japanese people ... the science of business administration and the necessity of training its skills has never been so urgent as for today's Japan'. The statement was to become widely known as the 'Berlin Declaration': a response to Shibusawa's call in 1900 for Tokyo Higher Commercial School to be promoted to the status of University.[27] It was just about the time of Joseph Chamberlain's struggle for the independent University of Birmingham and its Faculty of Commerce, which was institutionalized on 31 May 1901.

With the turn of the century, promising young scholars returned home to Japan one after another. They taught the new disciplines of political economy and commercial science, and spoke enthusiastically to the students about commercial education in Europe and the necessity of securing Japan's commercial predominance by means of producing educated businessmen. Considering that 'so much importance [had been made] of the position and duties of entrepreneur in the modern industrial society, compared with commercial workers', Fukuda encouraged the study of business firms and of entrepreneurs. One of his students published *Kigyo-ron* (*Theory of Business Enterprise*) in the same year as Veblen's book appeared (1904). Thus the need for the creation of a 'Captain of Industry', 'not business technologist but business man' as Fukuda argued, was proclaimed far and wide by Tokyo Higher Commercial School, principally through the newly founded *Ikkyo-kai Zasshi* (*Journal for the Hitotsubashi Association*).[28]

With the end of the Russo-Japanese War in 1905, the voices insisting on the need for a commercial university surfaced and grew louder. It was 'the age of business', and the rapid growth of Japanese business firms after the war required not only a mass of commercial workers but also the 'captains of industry' or 'entrepreneurial classes'. This need could only be satisfied by the creation of an independent commercial university. These voices increased in volume until they represented public opinion. In 1907, against the background of worldwide commercial competition, government decided to establish a commercial university. At Hitotsubashi, it was argued that Tokyo Higher Commercial School should be reorganized and its graduate course elevated as an independent commercial university. However, the Education Ministry, believing that only the Imperial University deserved to be called a university, decided that the proposed commercial university should be set up as a department of the Law College at Tokyo Imperial University. Thus, first the Economics Department in 1908, then the Commerce Department the next year, were instituted at Tokyo Imperial University, in addition to the existing Law and Politics Departments. This marked the start of an epoch in the institutionalization of economics and commerce education in Japanese universities.[29]

In 1905, Teijiro Ueda, one of the new generation of scholars at

Hitotsubashi, left for England, to study 'Business Policy' under W.J. Ashley, who was directing the recently opened Faculty of Commerce at Birmingham. Before he left, Ueda wrote a 'Note on Business Economics', describing Ashley as one of the earliest advocates of business economics – the very subject that was emerging and taking shape just after the turn of century. On his return in January 1909, Ueda published *What is Business Economics?*, following Ashley's *The Enlargement of Economics* (1908), and he taught a newly created course in Business Policy. It may well be that he was an international pioneer in this field; he was certainly the founder of business economics in Japan, a subject promoted by him and his disciples at the growing number of higher commercial schools.[30] Subsequently, the Japanese Society of Business Economics was formed in 1926, a development which did not occur in England.

The teaching staff of Tokyo Higher Commercial School had thus grown numerous enough to constitute an independent university for economics and business studies. Moreover, the 'economic mind' at the School was naturally orientated towards business economics. Staff were inclined to treat economic affairs from the viewpoint of the private sector rather than the national economy. The curriculum was largely drawn up 'from a businessman's viewpoint', again in contrast to the Economics Department at Tokyo Imperial University, which came under the strong influence of *Staatswissenschaft*.[31] The arguments in favour of an independent commercial university at Hitotsubashi grew increasingly heated and stirred up considerable public sentiment.

Yet the Ministry of Education turned a deaf ear to the request of Hitotsubashi. In its opinion, Hitotsubashi was merely a college that came within the jurisdiction of the Ministry's College Office, not the University Office. To make matters worse, the Ministry decided to abolish the graduate course at Tokyo Higher Commercial School, absorbing it instead into the newly founded Commerce Department at Imperial University. This drastic measure by the Ministry provoked a fierce movement against it at the Higher Commercial School, which culminated in all the students leaving the school on 8 May 1909. The commercial university question thus became a social problem, which filled the columns of the newspapers. The great struggle over the commercial university, which extended over two years, was widely known as the '*Sin'yu* Affair'. It is said that the *Sin'yu* Affair was in fact Hitotsubashi's tough stand against government, or rather its brave fight against the Education Ministry's firm 'Imperial University First Policy'. With this affair supplying momentum, the movement for the consolidation of academic, or *gründlich*, studies at the Higher Commercial

School deepened and strengthened. The contrasting ideals of commercial education of the late 1880s reappeared. From now on, they were to create an undercurrent as alternative proposals: practical and technical studies or academic and *gründlich* studies.

In 1912, Ueda, in collaboration with Shinshichi Miura, initiated the reorganization of the curriculum. They aimed at increasing the number of general subjects and decreasing the number of technical subjects. The extensive revision of the curriculum between 1914 and 1916 is said to have laid a substantial foundation for Hitotsubashi's future development as a University. However, the need for vocational or technical education had continued in parallel with that for a more academic curriculum. Takashi Masuda of Mitsui Bussan had held a different opinion from that of Shibusawa. Opposing Shibusawa's advocacy of a Commercial University, Masuda believed that the existing Higher Commercial School was itself most in accord with the needs of a commercial society. He wished, therefore, to see the continuation of the Higher Commercial School, whether or not the University was established.[32]

THE ESTABLISHMENT OF THE UNIVERSITY OF COMMERCE

The First World War brought about a great economic boom and generated a rapid increase in employment opportunities for university and college graduates. Japanese industry was in a position to take full advantage of the fabulous trade opportunities which presented themselves. The well-known boom in textiles accelerated the emergence of Osaka as the 'Manchester in the Orient', which was to supplant Lancashire as the leader of the world's cotton goods trade by the early 1930s. The dramatic foreign demand for Japanese goods and services brought about the rapid growth of trading and shipping companies, something totally new in Japanese experience. A large number of companies, even those of medium size, now began to recruit university and college graduates on a regular basis. Non-*zaibatsu* companies, like the Kobe-based Suzuki Shoten, advanced by leaps and bounds, and the so-called 'textile trading companies' grew in clusters, which provided an extensive market for the graduates of the Higher Commercial Schools – in particular, those in Kobe and Osaka. In this context, a vigorous movement arose for the promotion of these two schools to university status.

There was a great increase in the numbers of jobs offered to the graduates of Tokyo Higher Commercial School: in 1918, there were

125 job offers from Mitsubishi, 100 from Mitsui Bussan, and many others from a number of shipping companies. The number of jobs offered that year was much greater than the number of graduates (i.e. 267). With regard to the graduates of Tokyo Imperial University, it was at about this time that the numbers of graduates employed in industry and business increased rapidly, greatly surpassing the numbers employed by the government. Since the beginning of the twentieth century, graduates of the Imperial Universities had been seeking jobs in private companies.[33]

In an important study, Yonekawa has shown that Japanese companies employed a conspicuously larger number of university graduates than did their Western counterparts. He gave an indication of the numbers of university graduates employed by 100 large companies in 1914. The total figure was 8,262, of which the following seven sectors employed 70 per cent: banking (sixteen firms, 1,315 persons), trading (nine firms, 1,228 persons) mining (eight firms, 948 persons), textiles (ten firms, 764 persons) shipbuilding (five firms, 603 persons), shipping (five firms, 557 persons), and insurance (nine firms, 319 persons). The foremost firm was Mitsui Bussan, with 731 university graduates out of a total workforce of 1,676 – in other words, over 40 per cent of the employees were graduates, and nearly two-thirds of these were from Tokyo Higher Commercial School.[34] Some ten years later, however, Mitsui Bussan was recruiting about the same numbers from Tokyo Imperial University, Keio and Hitotsubashi.

The number of applicants for universities and colleges also increased remarkably at this time. Applicants for Tokyo Higher Commercial School in 1914 numbered 1,683, of whom only 370 were admitted. In 1915, the respective numbers were 1,650 applicants and 328 admissions; in 1916, 2,048 applicants and 319 admissions; in 1917, 2,579 applicants and 409 admissions; in 1918, 2,714 applicants and 427 admissions; and in 1919, 4,171 applicants and 115 admissions. The rapidly increasing demand for university and college graduates was, moreover, both wide and extensive. Equal educational opportunities, too, were called for by a democratic movement named '*Taisho* Democracy'. It was against this background that a Provisional Conference on Education was convened in 1917, and that, under the new Education Minister, Nakahashi (former chairman of Osaka Shosen, Japan's second largest shipping company), the innovative scheme for the proliferation of higher and university education was implemented. In 1918, the University Order was issued; in addition to the existing Imperial Universities (Tokyo, Kyoto, Tohoku, Kyushu, and Hokkaido), it authorized the founding of not only national but also municipal and private universities.

In 1919, the Imperial University adopted the faculty system as a replacement for the existing college system. The Departments of Economics and Law at Tokyo's Law College were then separated off to become an independent Faculty of Economics. At the same time, the Faculty of Economics at Kyoto Imperial University also came into being. In 1920, the official organization of Tokyo University of Commerce was sanctioned. That year, too, Keio, Waseda, Meiji, Hosei, Chuo, Nihon, Kokugakuin and Doshisha were all authorized as private universities; and, one after another, the faculties of commerce or economics were institutionalized. The number of universities which had faculties of commerce or economics increased from eleven in 1920 to twenty in 1930, and the number of students from 5,434 to 11,378. The total number of universities increased from four in 1914 to forty-six in 1930, and the total number of university students from 9,000 to 70,000. Furthermore, between 1920 and 1924, new government Higher Commercial Schools were founded in eight cities; Nagoya, Yokohama, Fukushima, Wakayama, Hikone, Oita, Takamatsu and Takaoka. There were then eighteen Higher Commercial Schools altogether (including *Senmon-bu*), as well as 243 ordinary level commercial schools.[35]

Unlike British companies, Japanese companies were quick to seek out and hire university graduates, and to offer them promotion and salary increases based on their educational credentials. The results of a nationwide survey in 1930 showed that 72 per cent of the middle and upper-level managers in private companies, and 57 per cent of engineers, were graduates of higher educational institutions. Higher education had, therefore, become a necessary condition for promotion in business and industry. Nor did progress depend on educational levels alone, but also on which university a person had attended. Starting salaries (per month) for graduates entering Nihon Yusen in 1917 were: 40–45 yen for graduates of Tokyo Imperial University, 30–40 yen for graduates of Tokyo Higher Commercial School, 30 yen for graduates of Keio and Waseda, and 25 yen for graduates of the other private colleges. The term *Gakureki-shugi* or *Gakureki-shakai* (educational credential society) only came into common use in the 1960s, but the phenomenon had existed since the early 1920s, and had become one of the most important ways of defining a person's status and prestige within Japanese society. The 'examination hell', as it is known today, existed in Japan as early as the 1920s.[36]

Tokyo University of Commerce thus came into being in March 1920 – twenty years after the 'Berlin Declaration'. The university course was of three years' duration; a preparatory course was also established. The existing Tokyo Higher Commercial School was abolished, but was immediately succeeded by the Professional School (*Fuzoku Shogaku Senmon-bu*), which was attached to the University and was aimed at completing vocational education. This indicated that the requirement for vocational training remained strong among the business community. However, the differences and conflict between the ideals of the University and the Professional School were soon to be revealed. In 1923, there were 816 students enrolled in the University Course, 639 in the Preparatory Course and 641 in the Professional School.

The period before and after the inauguration of Tokyo University of Commerce seems to have been one of great transition in its history. Whereas Fukuda and the leading scholars at Hitotsubashi wanted to create the University as a seat of the highest learning, there were other, substantial demands for the establishment of professional education. The Fukuda group placed greater emphasis on economic studies, intentionally attempting to broaden the curriculum to encompass literary culture, including philosophy, literature and the history of civilization. This widened the gap between the University and the ideals of the Professional School. It was a time when Hitotsubashi moved from being a centre for commercial science and professional education to being a true university of social science and literary culture. There were four towering personalities on the staff who were largely responsible for this transformation – Fukuda in economics, Ueda in business economics, Kiichiro Soda in the economic philosophy of Neukantianer, and Shinshichi Miura in the history of civilization.[37] They were very important in creating the intellectual tradition and in preparing the foundations for the later development of the 'new' Hitotsubashi University, which came into being after the Second World War.

In 1922 the curriculum was largely revised so as to remove the last vestiges of the Professional Department and of vocational education. However, a strong demand for vocational education still existed. *Senmon-bu* was vigorously supported by the Alumni Association led by Teijo Eguchi of Mitsubishi. At one time, the University attempted to separate *Senmon-bu* and *Yosei-jo* and merge them with the Yokohama Higher Commercial School (founded in 1923). Then there was an energetic movement to secure the independence of *Senmon-bu*, supported by the Alumni Association, which, from 1920, was called *Josui-kai*. But, eventually, *Senmon-bu* and *Yosei-jo* were absorbed into the new organization of the renamed Hitotsubashi University and ceased to exist.[38]

In pre-war Japan, there were 606 higher educational institutions: 58 universities, 43 preparatory courses for university, 32 higher schools, 332 professional schools and 141 teacher training schools. Immediately after the Second World War, this complicated mixture of higher educational institutions was reorganized into a simple and uniform system called the 'new' universities, under the strong influence of the American education mission, who thought that the curricula of the pre-war Japanese universities and colleges were too specialized and too vocational to foster cultured citizens. Many 'new' universities had their roots in the professional schools. The 'old' professional schools, which had played 'leading role' in Japan's industrialization, ended their glorious but frustrating history with the inauguration of the 'new' universities in 1949. The 'new' universities comprised 72 national, 34 prefectural or municipal, and 120 private institutions, which had, in 1952, 393,051 students (352,756 male and 40,295 female).

POST-WAR DEVELOPMENT

Tokyo Imperial University became the University of Tokyo under the New Education Law. Thereafter, its Faculty of Economics was to encourage commercial education. In 1962, reflecting the current trend in a field strongly influenced by the United States, the Department of Commerce in the Economics Faculty became known as the Department of Management. It could be said that the change of name symbolized the ending of German influence in business studies. The large numbers of Faculty members who now went to the United States demonstrated the strong influence of American academics. It was significant that the old term 'Business Economics' (*Betriebswirtschaftslehre*) gave way to 'Management', following the American style.

The study of commerce and economics at Hitotsubashi University, which had evolved from Tokyo University of Commerce, now divided into the Faculties of Commerce and Economics. In general, the Commerce Faculty comprised courses which adopted a micro approach to economic phenomena, starting with the analysis of the firm. The Economics Faculty, on the other hand, had a macro viewpoint, starting with the national economy. In the Faculty of Commerce, in particular, courses that in the pre-war period had been directly relevant to business needs and practices were largely retained. The interaction of theory and practice was constantly an issue in this sphere, and the close connections between them were sought.[39]

However, Japanese business education at the universities after the Second World War has had a tendency to stress general and theoretical (or scientific), rather than practical studies. Notwithstanding the strong American influence, practical education has been increasingly neglected, and there has been a widening gap between what universities do for the students and what 'end-users' expect from the universities. Unlike the United States, business schools have not developed successfully in Japan. Intensive efforts to train graduates ('in-house training') have been undertaken primarily by the companies themselves, and also by the private institutions, which have engaged in the systematic and practical training not only of new graduates but also of experienced businessmen.

Since the early 1950s, the Japan Federation of Employers' Association (JFEA) has been energetic in advising education circles of the problems, especially in the sphere of professional and vocational education: the need for co-operation between industry and education, for an increase in the number of students in technology and science faculties, and for enforcement of the drive to foster middle managers. However, in spite of these recommendations from the JFEA and other business institutions, the two aspects of Japanese university education, academic and vocational, have not consolidated their curricula.

As the companies or other end-users accept a variety of graduates who have not been educated in the faculty appropriate to their job, it is essential for the companies to train the new graduates themselves, to fill the gap between their university education and the special requirements of business. On the basis of a 'lifetime employment system', Japanese companies consider human resources as a vital factor in the running of the business, so that employees need constant training by companies and by themselves. In other words, 'firm specific training' has been essential. In 1982, all of the firms employing more than 5,000 undertook in-house training; even in the case of small-size firms, with fewer than 100 employees, 78 per cent practised in-house training.

The mass education and training of businessmen is also undertaken by private institutions. The Japan Productivity Centre (JPC) plays an important role in the education of managers; it established the Academy of Management Development in 1965 and the Institute for International Studies and Training in 1967. Since 1981, the Japan Management Association (JMA) has also run a management school known as 'JMS'. The JMA was founded in 1942 when the Nippon Industrial Management Association and Nippon Scientific Management Federation were merged, and the former, founded in 1937 as one of the first professional organizations, had promoted a production management training course for manufacturing companies. The JMA runs more than 1,400 seminars and courses annually, in which around 60,000 people participate, as well as some 100 conferences and symposia for executives and specialists on a broad range of subjects. Each year, approximately 2,500 training programmes are conducted by the JMA's own instructors on the premises of client companies, covering management development, salesforce development, worker training, motivation, and so on.

The Sanno Management School was established in 1979 as a subsidiary of Sangyo Noritsu College to develop the abilities of managers and executives. This School aims to produce a high-level curriculum, with a mixture of traditional Japanese know-how and modern American production management, and to introduce a new teaching method using simulation for analysis of the management process. Sangyo Noritsu College began as the *Nihon Noritsu Gakko* (Japan Efficiency Vocational School), established in 1942 by Yoichi Ueno who introduced the 'Taylor System' into Japan. At the time, the efficiency movement was thought of as a kind of traditional spiritual movement. This is why it was called '*Noritsu-do*', like *bushi-do* in which *do* not only means physical practice but also spiritual training. In this historical context, Sanno Management School stresses aspects of Japanese traditional business know-how.

Since the Second World War, therefore, the gap between university education and the requirements of business circles has been filled largely by the special efforts of the companies themselves to introduce intensive in-house training and make use of special institutions for the training of their staff.[40]

NOTES

1 G.C. Allen, *Modern Japan and its Problem*, London, George Allen and Unwin, 1928, pp. 106–7.
2 This was translated by T. Taniguchi of the Toyo Cotton Spinning Company in 1956, when symptoms of the decline of Japan's cotton industry revealed themselves.
3 W. Mass and W. Lazonick, 'The British Cotton Industry and International Competitive Advantage', *Business History*, 1990, vol. 32, no. 4, pp. 58–9.
4 H. Dyer, *Dai-Nippon: The Britain of the East*, London, Blackie and Son, 1905; *idem*, *Japan in World Politics*, London, Blackie and Son, 1909, p. vi. N. and J. Mackenzie (eds), *The Diary of Beatrice Webb*, London, Virago Press, 1983, vol. 2, pp. 334–5. See also, G.R. Searle, *The Quest for National Efficiency*, Oxford, Blackwell, 1971, ch. 3.
5 Allen, *Modern Japan*, p. 106. *Nature*, 1 December 1904, p. 97. Japanese National Commission for Unesco (ed.), *The Role of Education in the Social and Economic Development of Japan*, Tokyo, Ministry of Education, 1966, pp. 4–15.
6 I. Amano, *Kyusei Senmon Gakko*, Tokyo, Nihon Keizai Shinbunsha, 1978, p. 9.
7 See, for example, H.F. Gospel (ed.), *Industrial Training and Technological Innovation*, London, Routledge, 1991.

8 For this paper, I have made extensive use of chapters 1 and 2 of the following: S. Yonekawa, T. Yuzawa and T. Nishizawa, 'The Development of Economics and Business Education in Japan', *Hitotsubashi Daigaku Gakuseishi Shiryo Supplement*, Tokyo, Hitotsubashi University, 1990 (quoted below as *Shiryo, Supplement*).

9 R. Beigel, *Der Kampf um die Handelshochschule*, Leipzig, Verlag der Handels-Akademie Leipzig, 1898, pp. 31–4. This was translated in an abridged form by Fukuda – see his *Koyama Kenzo Den*, Osaka, Sanjushi Ginko, 1930, pp. 291–300.

10 Amano, *Kyusei Senmon Gakko*, pp. 127–8, 141–2. *The Role of Education*, pp. 145–56.

11 L.C. Marshall (ed.), *The Collegiate School of Business*, Chicago, Ill., University of Chicago Press, 1928. W.J. Ashley, 'The Universities and Commercial Education', *North American Review*, January 1903, p. 31. University of Birmingham, Dean of the Faculty of Commerce Letter Book, II, pp. 402–3.

12 B.M.D. Smith, *Education for Management: its Conception and Implementation in the Faculty of Commerce at Birmingham mainly in the 1900s*, Birmingham, University of Birmingham, 1974. L. Hannah, 'Entrepreneurs and the Social Sciences', (Inaugural Lecture, London School of Economics, 1983), pp. 18–19. The historical development of management education in Britain is examined in detail in S.P. Keeble, *The Ability to Manage*, Manchester, Manchester University Press, 1992.

13 G.C. Allen, *Appointment in Japan*, London, Athlone Press, 1983, pp. 1–2.

14 Komuro to Count Inoue, 11 March 1903. See also, Komuro to Count Inoue, 6 July 1904; and Ashley to Komuro, 18 April and 29 June 1904, and 26 July 1905. These letters, and the booklets of the Birmingham Faculty of Commerce, are among the Count Inoue Papers, Mitsui Library, Tokyo.

15 Allen, *Modern Japan*, pp. 81–2; *idem, Appointment in Japan*, pp. 73–5.

16 *The Times Higher Education Supplement*, 23 February 1990.

17 Yonekawa *et al.*, 'The Development of Economics', pp. 8–9. C. Sugiyama and T. Nishizawa, 'Captain of Industry: Tokyo Commercial School at Hitotsubashi', in C. Sugiyama and H. Mizuta (eds), *Enlightenment and Beyond*, Tokyo, University of Tokyo Press, 1987, pp. 151–69.

18 S. Hosoya, *Shogyo Kyoiku no Akebono*, Tokyo, Josuikai, 1991, II, pp. 309–14.

19 E. Léautey, *L'Enseignment Commercial et les Ecoles de Commerce*, Paris, Librairie Comptable et Administrative, 1886, p. 539. See also, T. Nishizawa, 'Towards the Organization of Higher Commercial Education in England', *Osaka City University Economic Review*, 1988. *Kanpo*, 30 May and 7, 16, 21 and 23 June 1888.

20 Yonekawa *et al.*, 'The Development of Economics', pp. 10–13. Sugiyama and Nishizawa, 'Captain of Industry', pp. 161–3. And see Layton's letters to *The Times*, 12 March and 23 May 1898; and the letters to *The Times* of K. Samuelson and P. Magnus, 14 March 1898.

21 S. Yonekawa, *Hitotsubashi 100 nen: Captain of Industry no Ayumi*, Tokyo, Josuikai, 1987. An obituary of Kagami appeared in *The Times*, 3 June 1939.

22 *Hitotsubashi 50 nenshi*, Tokyo, Tokyo Shouka Daigaku, 1925, pp. 22–3.

23 *Nihon Kindai Kyoikuloo nenshi*, Tokyo, Kokuritsu Kyoiku Kenkyujo, 1973, vol. 9, pp. 403–5. Léautey, *L'Enseignment Commercial*, p.539.

24 Sugiyama and Nishizawa, 'Captain of Industry', pp. 164–5.

25 Yonekawa's article in *Shiryo, Supplement*, pp. 212–13, 224–5.
26 Amano, *Kyusei Senmon Gakko*, pp. 133–55. *Shiryo*, 1983, vol. 3 (1902–9).
27 Sugiyama and Nishizawa, 'Captain of Industry', pp. 167–9. *Shiryo*, 1982, vol. 2 (1886–1901). 'Seki Hajime Nikki', Seki Hajime Papers, Central Library, Osaka City, 11 June 1900–30 January 1901.
28 *Shiryo*, vol. 3. Fukuda's Introduction to *Kigyo-ron*, pp. 1–10. T. Fukuda, 'Jitsugyokai no Zokuryo-seiji', *Nihonkeizaishinshi*, 3 October 1909, pp. 10–13.
29 Yonekawa *et al.*, 'The Development of Economics', pp. 20–1.
30 *Ueda Teijiro Nikki* (1905–18), Tokyo, Keio Tsushin, 1975. *Ueda Teijiro Zenshu*, Tokyo, Dai San Shuppan, 1975, vol. 1.
31 The Alumni Association of Tokyo Higher Commercial School, *Shogyo Daigaku ni kansuru Iken*, Tokyo, 1909.
32 *Shiryo*, Tokyo, 1983, vols 3 and 4 (1910–14).
33 *Shiryo*, Tokyo, 1982, vol. 5 (1915–20).
34 S. Yonekawa, 'University Graduates in Japanese Enterprises before the Second World War', *Business History*, 1984, pp. 193–201.
35 *Hitotsubashi Daigaku 100 nen*, Tokyo, Zaikai Hyoron Shinsha, 1975, pp. 405–43. *Nihon Kindai Kyoiku 100 nenshi*, vol. 10, pp. 479–99.
36 I. Amano, *Education and Examination in Modern Japan* (translated by W.K. and F. Cummings), Tokyo, University of Tokyo Press, 1983, pp. xii–xiv. *The Role of Education in the Social and Economic Development of Japan*, pp. 263, 295. Amano, *Kyusei Senmon Gakko*, p. 154.
37 *Shiryo*, Tokyo, 1983, vol. 7 (1924–45).
38 *Hitotsubashi Senmonbu Kyoin Yoseijoshi*, Tokyo, Hitotsubashi Senmonbu, 1951.
39 Yonekawa *et al.*, 'The Development of Economics', pp. 43–7.
40 Ibid., pp. 57–63.

Index

236 *Index*

Toyota Motor Company Ltd 25, 41
Toyota Motor Corporation 7, 16,
25–35, 71, 77, 134; Corona model
of 31–4; Crown model of 30–1;
mass production facilities of 31,
32; Motomachi plant of 31; *see
also Eiho-kai, kanban* system,
keiretsu, Kyoho-kai
Toyota Motor Sales Company Ltd
25, 31
Toyota Quality Control Prize 34–5
Tsumura 213

Ube Kosan 53
UCC *see* Union Carbide Corporation
Uchida, Saburo 65–6
Ueda, Teijiro 214–15, 216, 219
UK *see* United Kingdom
Umetsu, Matsuro 56
Uneno, Yoichi 222
Union Carbide Corporation (UCC)
89–90
Union of Japanese Scientists and
Engineers (UJSE) 9–10
United Kingdom 3, 18, 105, 106; *see
also* England, Great Britain
United States 2, 3, 9, 10–11, 18, 25,
31, 33, 39–40, 42, 46, 63, 71,
73–5, 78, 97, 99–101, 105, 106,
111–12, 113, 115, 121, 127, 131,
139, 140, 142–3, 157, 167, 194,
196, 205, 209, 213, 220–1;
Department of Justice of 113
Univac Corporation of America 51
Universe Ireland 124, 125
University of Tokyo (formerly
Tokyo Imperial University) 50–1,
66, 220; *see also* Tokyo Imperial
University
Urabe, K. 11
USA *see* United States
US Army Procurement Agency 32
USSR (Soviet Union) 4, 98, 100,
104, 106
US Steel Company 113; merger with
Kobe Seiko 115

van Stappen, Julian 209

Versailles, Peace Treaty of 42, 43
vinylon 82; *see also* synthetic fibre

Waseda University 218
Webb, Beatrice 202
Wharton School 205
Whitney, William C. 207
Willys Overland 26
World War: First 2, 7, 12, 39, 42,
98, 205, 216; Second 1, 2, 8, 17,
25, 47–8, 61, 65–6, 81–2, 97–9,
102–3, 107, 109, 114, 119, 134,
150, 168, 170, 172, 175, 198, 219,
220, 222; in the Pacific 67, 98

Xerox 69
X-ray cameras 67

Yamaguchi, Akinori 51
Yamaguchi Prefecture 53
Yamaichi Security Company 66
Yamaji, Keizo 70
Yamamoto, Takuma 51, 54
Yamashita, Hideo 50–1
Yamazaki, Hiroaki 8
Yanmar 151, 153–4, 155, 156
Yano, Jiro 208
Yasuda Zaibatsu 98; and life
insurance company 175, 181
Yawata Iron and Steel Works 97–8,
102, 103; building of its Sakai and
Tobata Works 104; merger with
Fuji as Japan Steel 115
yen: appreciation of 19, 71; decline
of 44, 66, 172; high value of 75;
revaluation of 89
Yokohama 45, 112, 124, 210;
Higher Commercial School
in 218–19
Yokohama Specie Bank (now Bank
of Tokyo) 210–11
Yokosuka Steel Works 197
Yonekawa, Shin'ichi 217
Yoshida, Goro 65–6
Yoshihara, H. 77

zaibatsu 2, 8, 17, 19 n.2, 40–1, 46,
65, 98, 160, 168, 198, 216